PRA

YOU DON'T HAVE TO CRUSH YOUR EX

"*You Don't Have to Crush Your Ex* is that rare gem—a relatable cautionary tale and guidebook all in one. The results for the children when their parents choose the wrong outcome (winning at all costs) are very real and lifelong, mimicking the outcomes we see for other forms of child abuse. This book encourages the reader in a thought experiment where they can do better and witness the outcomes that experts recommend unfold before their eyes in an equally compelling storyline. As soon as I read the manuscript, I began recommending that professional colleagues look for it as a resource; and once it is published, I will be sharing it with my own clients."

Wendy Bourg, Ph.D., Custody Evaluator, Parent Coordinator, High-Conflict Family Therapist Author of *A Child Interviewer's Guidebook*

"Sometimes divorce is inevitable. Too often in my practice, I see parents who are otherwise well-intentioned drag their children into their war with their former spouse. The damage can last for years. *You Don't Have to Crush Your Ex* provides valuable insight and wisdom into how to best protect your most valuable asset—your children—from irreparable and unintentional harm. This book should be required reading for any parents in my practice going through a divorce or separation!"

RJ Gillespie, MD, MHPE, Pediatrician, The Children's Clinic, Portland, OR

"Lori's book empowers parents to be their best selves and keep the focus on their kids. Her years of experience shine through. She makes it clear to parents, in a creative way, that their decisions will impact their children's lives and futures. *You Don't Have to Crush Your Ex* is encouraging and powerful. A reminder to Choose Wisely!"

Judith Swinney, JD, Parenting Beyond Conflict

"When I was a child welfare worker, it was my responsibility to protect children from the impact of the bad decisions made by the adults in their lives. Even though more children were hurt than not, I knew it *wasn't* because their parents wanted to harm them. Unfortunately, their parents were blinded by hurt and pain, and could not see the consequences of their behaviors. Lori's book offers parents a way to step back and take a close look at themselves, and the impact their choices can have on their children. When individuals know better, they can do better.

"In my role as an Ordained Minister, I often witness the inner turmoil and conflict parents encounter when they are faced with the loss of their family structure. Having a resource such as this book, which helps them tap into their Divinity and inner strength while they build a new family structure, is invaluable. I highly recommend this book as a resource not only to divorcing parents, but to family members, friends, and professionals. Lori has offered a road map to journey down that difficult pathway of divorce."

Dr. Rev. Ahmondra McClendon, Founder of
Circle of Consciousness Ministry

"Lori Bonnevier is one of the most competent and compassionate child custody evaluators with whom I've had the pleasure to work. *You Don't Have to Crush Your Ex* offers a brilliant and one-of-a-kind opportunity for parents to see themselves, their co-parent, and their own child through a whole new lens. Lori offers up her decades of experience, her infectious humor, and her loving spirit in such a way that parents can experience common thinking and behavior that often compromises their child's best interest. She also provides the reader a road map to a healthier future, where generations of families can thrive."

Dr. Paul Stephen Stoltzfus, Psy.D., Pediatric Psychologist, Certified Forensic Psychologist

"In the legal profession, I hear war stories all the time of divorce and child custody cases gone wrong and the chaos it creates for families that lasts for years. This book is a wonderful resource for parents who love their kids and want to make the best choices for their families even as they are going through a challenging separation."

Cynthia Grande, JD, Founding Attorney, The Grande Law Firm

"Lori's book is a practical, hopeful, helpful read which encourages parents to put aside their anger, resentment, and disappointment and focus on the needs of their children. I encourage everyone to read and heed the positive message delivered by Ms. Bonnevier to parents everywhere – compassion, grace, kindness, and respect drive the best choices."

Kathryn Smith Root, Family Law Attorney
Gevurtz Menashe, P.C., recognized in Super Lawyers
and Best Lawyers in America

"As a medical professional, I have the privilege of sharing personal and heartfelt struggles with many of my patients. Exposure to high conflict and emotionally toxic home environments can perpetuate true physical disease and secondary health ramifications. Cleverly and unassumingly written, *You Don't Have to Crush Your Ex* helps parents to navigate complicated custody battles while alleviating unnecessary depression and anxiety derived from these stressful social dynamics. This book speaks to the true nature of my longtime friend and now author, Lori Bonnevier, in its energy and constructiveness. It comes as no surprise that she creatively formed a relatable approach to share her years of clinical experience in order to improve outcomes for families and fill the gap. Lori always speaks from her heart, is genuine in all that she does, and is a true servant to her community. This 'how-to' resource is sure to help enumerable families."

Kristine Schwinof, MD

You Don't Have to
CRUSH
Your Ex

Lori A. Bonnevier, MSW, LCSW

Saved By Story

Saved By Story Publishing, LLC
Prescott, AZ
www.savedbystory.house

You Don't Have to Crush Your Ex/Lori A. Bonnevier—1st ed.

ISBN
Paperback 978-0-9887809-6-5

Cover Design by Alyssa Noelle Coelho and Dan Mulhern Designs
Interior Design by Teagarden Designs

For the millions of young transition warriors—
May your indomitable spirit transcend the chaos.

CONTENTS

EPILOGUE

APPENDIX

FOREWORD

by The Honorable Judge Eve Miller

FOR MORE THAN twenty years on the bench of the Clackamas County Circuit Court, it was my responsibility to decide custody disputes. I earned a reputation as a fair and just adjudicator who focused on children's best interests; and, in 2018, the Clackamas County Bar Association recognized me with its highest award. Having committed my life to keeping children safe and well through one of the toughest transitions they will ever face, it was always with a heavy heart that I listened to parents argue about what they considered to be in the best interests of their children. Most of them failed to understand that the mere act of arguing was detrimental to their child's well-being. While battling for custody, they could not see that they were losing the war for their child's happy future. Despite the heavy heart, I always discharged my duty to make the tough decisions. Fortunately, those decisions were always easier when Ms. Lori Bonnevier was the custody evaluator because her recommendations were invaluable.

My relationship with Ms. Bonnevier is purely professional; she is on a short list of custody evaluators in high demand for the consistent, high quality of her work.

Our first encounter occurred in 2002, when I presided over a family law case where she was the court-appointed evaluator and then called as a witness at trial, in what is now known as a landmark case: Hamilton-Waller vs. Waller. The father had filed a motion for a change of custody of their teenage sons because the custodial parent wanted to move from Oregon to Holland with her fiancé. The case was a difficult one due to the extraordinary distance that would inevitably separate the kids from one parent or the other. As difficult as it was, my decision to award the father sole custody was easy due to the exceptional job Ms. Bonnevier did in evaluating the best interests of the children. Her recommendations rang true.

The mother appealed my decision, and I was reversed, but not before the presiding appellate judge wrote a strong dissenting opinion. In his dissent, Judge Landau wrote that the evidence consisted primarily of the report and testimony of Ms. Bonnevier who, after interviewing the parties, multiple family members, and collateral sources, had concluded that separating the children from their father and extended family "would be devastating for all of them." Judge Landau went on to discuss the findings that led to my decision, including my statement that Ms. Bonnevier's experience as a custody evaluator was not as extensive as others, but she had exhibited a certain maturity and insight that was well beyond the years that she had been doing custody evaluations. Ultimately, I had found her to be a very persuasive witness; and he affirmed that the trial court is in the best position to evaluate a witness's demeanor.

Over the course of twenty years, Ms. Bonnevier has testified before me numerous times, and her polished demeanor has remained on point. Recently, I presided over a very complicated dissolution case involving two young children and many layers of mental health and emotional issues. Through the evidence, I learned that Ms. Bonnevier had spent several months evaluating the parents to make recommendations for legal custody and a parenting plan. Her goal for this family was to minimize the intense conflict between the parents, and she had crafted a detailed protocol for pick-up and drop-off exchanges. Her recommendations were so good that I adopted her custody recommendation and entire parenting plan.

In addition to Ms. Bonnevier's role as an evaluator, she is also well-known in our community for her work with parents who are experiencing high-conflict. She and I share many of the same views in alignment with decades of research affirming that exposure to chronic conflict harms children. First and foremost, the key to creating a healthy space for children is for their parents to communicate safely and without conflict. In order to reduce conflict, both parents must understand and embrace these concepts:

- Children need both parents.
- Badmouthing the other parent backfires.

- Parents need to think beyond the immediate conflict and about the thirty-year plan.

- Siblings are each other's strongest support.

- It takes two to tango.

- "I didn't choose him/her; you did."

- Don't start a new relationship until you end this one.

- Parenting time is the legal right of the child, not of his/her parents.

Over the years, Ms. Bonnevier's professional growth is apparent in how highly sought-after she is for her custody evaluations. She is a staunch advocate for children and genuinely cares about the complete family system. If parents utilize this book to discover likely outcomes of the choices before them, and intentionally make child-focused decisions, the path they are on will lead to better futures for their children.

Every parent navigating a child custody evaluation now has an opportunity to experience, understand, and comprehend the salient insights and lessons offered by this one-of-a-kind resource. The courts throughout Oregon listen to Ms. Bonnevier's ideas about the best interest of children, and it would behoove parents in high-conflict litigation to do the same.

The Honorable Judge Eve Miller

A WORD OF CAUTION

Before You Get Started

~This is Not a Fairytale Adventure~
Ahead is a story-driven book
designed to be experiential.

The stories will provoke emotion,
even in the steadiest individual.

Emotion allows us to dig deeper and learn
more—and fundamentally directs our course.

Valuable tools acquired outside your comfort
zone will help you to come out on top
during your child custody evaluation.

There are multiple levels on which
you can read this book.

A shortlist of Hints, Hacks, and Hell-No's is
in the Appendix for quick reference.

However, genuine understanding and results
require more than a bullet-point list. They
require the intimate knowledge of why.

To discover and understand why you don't have to *Crush Your Ex*, full immersion into the experiential stories is required. Here, you'll meet the parents, Luke and Vanessa, who are shown to make two negative choices and one positive one.

If at any time, you become triggered or emotionally distraught by their negative choices, take a deep breath and move onto Choice 3 to see a healthier approach to navigate the custody concerns about your children.

Crush Your Ex underscores raw feelings that accompany a high-conflict custody dispute. This book is designed to help you *move forward in child-focused ways.*

The title of this book is not intended to encourage or promote violence.

Have another look at the cover and notice the shoe is in motion—*moving past the Ex.*

~ Meet Mateo and Raelyn ~
This brother and sister duo will provide the insight needed to shift your vision from its usual lens, to where change becomes possible.

WHEN IT ALL FALLS APART

THE DAY BEGAN like any other. School first thing in the morning followed by activities, homework, and dinner. Unfortunately, eating a meal together around the kitchen table had become an increasingly unpleasant experience. Tonight, Mateo and Raelyn's parents seemed more on-edge than usual and, despite their best intentions, Vanessa and Luke were unable to keep their arguments away from the children.

Without warning, Luke pushed his chair back with force, stood his muscular frame to its full height, puffed up his chest, and pounded the table with his fist. The anger boiled over as he let his wife of eighteen years have it: "I'm so tired of your constant bitching and complaining, Vanessa. You never stop. Nothing is ever good enough!"

Mateo, who everyone calls Teo, had dismissed himself from the table a bit earlier when the tension had started to build, and Raelyn, known simply as Rae, instinctively ran to her older brother's downstairs bedroom when the yelling began. She was looking for shelter from what had become a familiar routine, in what used to be a far happier home.

Teo waved his little sister in from the hallway, called for their dog, Iggy, and closed the door behind his stumpy cropped tail. Rae reached down, helped Iggy up onto the bed, and pulled him close for comfort. Iggy was Rae's most faithful and very best friend. Rae, Iggy, and Teo all huddled together on his bed and turned the TV volume up to drown out the awful noise their parents were making upstairs.

The children shot each other concerned glances every few minutes, as something was obviously different in their home that night. There was a lot of stomping around and both of their parents screamed louder than usual. The children's worried and wide eyes found each other when they heard the distinct squeak of the upstairs closet door, right above Teo's bedroom, where only suitcases and their dad's travel duffle bag were stored.

The closet door slammed shut and the shouting continued, followed by more stomping.

"Don't take that—it's Rae's favorite blanket!" they heard their mother shriek.

"Do you think he's leaving us?" Rae whispered frantically to Teo, tears starting to pool in her Caribbean blue eyes.

Teo placed a comforting arm around his little sister's shoulder just as his bedroom door burst open, scaring the heck out of them. The children sat up straight, on high-alert. Iggy stood ready on all fours and growled protectively.

"Iggy, come boy!" Luke curtly commanded. Iggy looked at the kids, puzzled, obviously sensing their upset. He gave Rae's face a quick lick before he did as he was told. Teo and Rae noticed their father was holding a full duffle bag. He made eye contact with Rae first and said, "Sorry, baby girl," in an attempt to assure her it would all be okay.

Luke locked eyes with his teenage son. "Teo, take care of your mom and sister. You're the man of the house now." Then he turned on his heel and headed upstairs toward the front door, with Iggy following behind him. Their mother was crying, her eyes red and cheeks fully flushed. She looked to them apologetically and told Teo and Rae to "stay put," then shut the bedroom door behind her. The yelling resumed upstairs until the front door opened and then crashed shut with a weighty feeling of finality.

Complete silence, other than the sound of their mother's quiet sobs upstairs, filled their once-happy home. The children stayed put in Teo's bedroom, as their mother had asked. Teo's long legs were stretched out, and his big feet hung off the edge of the bed. He glanced down at Rae, now curled into a ball next to him, hands covering her face, and a steady rolling cry soothing the ugliness she had witnessed. Eventually, Rae drifted into an exhausted and restless sleep.

Teo was surprised by the intensity of a natural instinct to protect his little sister from their parents' ridiculous behavior. There was a four-year age difference between him and Rae, and they had not always been close, but the more recent chaos at home had strengthened the sibling bond between them. As he watched her sleep, he wondered what actually happened tonight: *What did Dad mean by saying I'm now the "man of the house"? Would Dad be back, or had he left for good this time? Will I ever see him again?* A wave of fear, followed by sharp anger, swept through Teo's body. Ignoring the hot tears that almost fell, he felt a resolve to make sure Rae knew he had her back. After restless hours of contemplating what might happen, Teo also drifted off to sleep.

Upstairs, their mother's sadness had turned to rage.

"I cannot believe that selfish asshole," Vanessa muttered as she finally pulled herself off the couch and wiped the tears from her eyes. She stomped into the kitchen and poured a warm bucket of water, added bleach, put on her rubber gloves, and started to scrub every hard surface in the house. Bleach had always been Vanessa's aromatherapy of choice. She scrubbed for hours while replaying a thousand memories of Luke in her mind's eye. *Eighteen years of one disappointment after another, and he walks out on our family!*

Vanessa seethed through clenched teeth, on her hands and knees, gripping the scrub brush with all of her might. Alone with her racing thoughts, hours passed and Vanessa eventually headed to her bedroom. She, too, cried herself to sleep that awful night.

While Vanessa lay in the comfortable bed, she was used to sharing with him, Luke sat wide-awake on a couch at his best friend's house, and Iggy was curled up on the floor next to him. Luke's one duffle bag of belongings sat out in his truck, which was parked on the street next to an old-school 1965 Mustang convertible with a "for sale" sign in the window. It needed work, but had caught Luke's eye as a bright point in this otherwise hella-crappy day. It was the exact model, make, and year he had always wanted, though never splurged on, because buying something for himself would cause an argument with Vanessa. Adrenaline was still coursing through Luke's body from the intense fight with his wife, but also because he didn't really have a plan. He took several long, deep breaths and a swig of his cold beer, trying to calm his nerves while wondering what would happen to him... *How am I going to fix things for Teo and Rae—the two people that I adore more than life itself?*

Divorce and Choice

If you're reading this book, it's probably safe to assume that upset and tension have boiled over inside your once-happy home the way it did in Vanessa and Luke's. It's also likely that while you tried to keep your kids out of it, they heard or maybe even saw the fighting and probably know more than you think they do. Perhaps feelings of confusion, uncertainty, sadness, anger, and even rage have already had their way with you, or maybe you are experiencing some or all of those powerful emotions right now.

Even if you feel relief that a decision has been made to end it, to walk away and be "free" of that dark cloud hovering over your relationship, you are likely experiencing the feelings associated with being in unfamiliar territory. Maybe it's been years since you've been on your own, and now you have children to care for. What will happen to them?

On the other hand, you may have been divorced for years and are now seeking modification of a custody and/or parenting time plan that no longer works. Old feelings are likely to surface when revisiting a former judgment with your child's other parent, and the same question now looms again: What will happen to our children?

Marriage is a challenging institution that many of us cannot weather, and dissolutions are filed every day.[1] According to the CDC, in the United States, a divorce is finalized every 13 seconds. That means 277 divorces per hour, 6,646 divorces every day, 46,523 divorces every week, and 2,419,196 divorces every year. Half of the people who say, "I do" eventually say, "I don't." The divorce rate for second marriages hovers at 60% and third marriages even higher at 73%. If you and your partner have both had previous marriages, you are 90% more likely to get divorced than if it had been a first marriage for both.[2]

Then there's the money. The average total cost of a divorce in the United States is $15,000. However, if your family has moved into a "high-conflict" situation

[1]   Wilkinson & Finkbeiner Family Law Attorneys, San Diego, California
[2]   https://www.wf-lawyers.com/divorce-statistics-and-facts/Wilkinson & Finkbeiner Family Law Attorneys, San Diego, California

and the court orders a child custody evaluation, it is my personal experience that you can expect to double or easily triple that number for yourself and for the other party. According to the CDC, almost 50% of parents with children who are going through a divorce experience poverty afterwards and 60% of people under poverty guidelines are divorced women with children.[3]

The good news is that 91% of all custody decisions do not require court intervention. That means the vast majority of parents figure things out for their children and their families. Of the10% or less who require court intervention, about 1% of those families participate in a court-ordered child custody evaluation. If you are in this 1%, please keep reading! I authored this book specially for you and your children.

There's an increasing number of parents who are never married or who create domestic partnerships but still end up in the same pool of "divorcing" parents, dividing assets and creating custody and parenting time plans for children. Some dissolutions are amicable, most are tumultuous, and a small population of families end up in "high-conflict" situations that include lawyers, mental health experts, evaluators, and judges. This book is written for those of you involved in high-conflict litigation with children.

While there is an abundance of literature and research that you can sort through to support myriad theories about what's "best," what's lacking is a discussion about *choice*. Specifically, how much choice matters to the outcome of your legal process and, most

[3] https://www.wf-lawyers.com/divorce-statistics-and-facts/Wilkinson & Finkbeiner Family Law Attorneys, San Diego, California

importantly, to the outcome for your children—their long-term health and well-being.

There is something you need to know, that no one is likely telling you: *You hold a lot of power.*

It is important to understand that even if you don't feel like it, you hold very important cards, right now, right where you are at this very minute. You are the only one who has the power to make this experience less messy and less daunting for yourself and for your children. Your attorney, evaluator, or therapist can offer guidance and advice, but only you have the real power to impact the outcome. Absolute power to insulate and protect your children is encapsulated in the many daily choices you make about your own attitude, thinking, words, actions, behaviors, and the people with whom you surround yourself, including friends/family and professionals that will help light a path forward (or alternately incite more conflict, chaos, and discord). The choices you make starting from this very moment in time matter—a lot, regardless of what the other parent is doing!

How do I know?

Well, I've worked with hundreds of divorcing families (about 700 to be precise) and thousands of children affected by their parents' dissolution. For the past twenty years, I have performed child custody and parenting time evaluations for high-conflict families involved in litigation with an agenda to develop best interest plans for children. Before that, the State of Oregon employed me as a child welfare protective services caseworker; and before that, I spent time as an early childhood education teacher and volunteered as a Guardian ad Litem. In other words, I have served children and families my entire adult life. For nearly three decades, I've had the privilege to stand alongside, shelter, teach, guide, and advocate for safe, healthy, and cohesive family systems.

Child advocacy has always been my professional focus and become an area of expertise relied on by families, legal professionals, and circuit courts in the communities where I work. Creating family systems in which children are able to thrive is the goal, and the majority of two-household families get there. But, life veers off course for others, and I have witnessed, time and again, circumstances go terribly wrong and children suffer irreparable harm after absorbing the shrapnel of poor choices made by otherwise loving parents.

Don't despair. There is good news: *It's avoidable.* There is even better news: The book you're holding in your hands was written to help you stay on, or get back on, course. This is a unique chance for you to experience some of the most common mistakes parents make during a child custody evaluation, so you don't accidentally make them yourself.

There is nothing else like *You Don't Have to Crush Your Ex* to help you prepare for, move through, and come out on top during a child custody evaluation. You can find advice and information from other custody litigants on the Internet and opinions from legal professionals. Still, you will not find another book like this, written by an evaluator who does this work, day in and day out. As a seasoned custody evaluator, I have been in the trenches, slogged through the mud, stood in the gap, and advocated relentlessly for thousands of children who want nothing more than to love, and be loved, by their mom and dad and other important people with whom they share a bonded relationship.

I decided to write this book to help you help your children because *conflict hurts children*. The more you protect and insulate your children, the better off everyone will be when this is over. The journey you are embarking upon is an often-overwhelming process. I want to help you move through the custody evaluation with confidence, as your best self, and even during one of the worst times of your life.

After twenty years of witnessing heart-wrenching stories, wiping tears off cheeks of suffering children, and braving the adversarial environment of courtrooms with moms and dads, grandmas and grandpas, well-meaning aunts, uncles, and other third parties, I decided it was time to write this book for you, for them, and for all of us. I had no desire to write a book laden with clinical terminology or one weighted down with research. Instead, I created a safe space where you can experience and feel your own raw emotions and that of the other parties involved, including the children. The relatable stories are crafted to grab your attention, chip away at old patterns, and offer new perspectives and renewed hope for your family to move forward more constructively and peacefully.

What If You Choose Your Way to Resolution?

I've written this book in the style of a choose-your-own-outcome story. You'll read the setup of a character and his/her plot line, after which several choices will be presented to you as the reader. You then get to make a choice and see where that choice leads. When you reach the end of a story, you can go back and make a different choice to experience the whole story and outcome differently. Choices are doors to our next experience.

In this book, you will follow the Smith family that you were introduced to earlier: Vanessa, Luke, Teo, and  Rae. You will witness the choices that Luke and Vanessa encounter as they navigate the new territory of dissolving their marital relationship, while trying to do right by their children, and being ordered by the court to participate in a child custody evaluation. At very crucial moments of choice, *you* will have the opportunity to make a decision for Vanessa and/or Luke and see where it leads. You will see and experience how a small, well-intentioned choice can become a Hell-No mistake, or maybe you'll pick up a Hint or Hack that leads to the outcome everyone wants for your children—thriving in their two homes!

Most importantly, you will have an opportunity to hear what your children may be thinking. (Remember,

I've talked to thousands of children about their parents!) Teo and Rae's dialogues are offered as real to my experience, accurately relating the way children caught in a high-conflict family situations think, feel, act, and speak about what's happening, specifically with regard to their parents. My hope is that you can see a little of your own children, respond, and refocus here, so you can do your best out there.

When you arrive at the end of a choice, it is important to know that the outcomes are overstated— the bad outcomes are *really* bad when, of course, there is likely to be a range on the spectrum of the ways in which things really unfold for children and their parents. The ideal outcomes are purposefully inflated to help you set your sights high for success. While I know extraordinary outcomes are possible, because I've seen them, I also know that it takes families a varied amount of time to recover from some of those initial, reactive, and not-so-great choices they made before they knew better.

We're all human, and each of us make mistakes, especially while we are in emotional pain. Poor choices that parents make before they know better can destroy a child's sense of safety, belonging, and trust. Those don't get restored overnight with a few good choices. It is with consistency and reliability of child focused decisions that children feel secure. Sometimes, there's so much damage done that children lose their way for a while or choose to break off a relationship with their parent. When you read the outcomes, instead of saying,

"Not possible! I've messed it up too much," or "That sounds great but will never happen for my family!" take a breath and make a deeper commitment to aim for the type of happiness and success you and your children deserve. Even if you don't quite reach a lofty goal, the choices you make and the actions you take to get there will land you in a much better place than where you are now and at least create the opportunity for your children to step into that level of well-being and happiness with you.

Let's face it, life is not always what we expect. So rarely is it what we want, how we want it, when and the way we want it to look and to feel and to be. The arduous seasons come unexpectedly and often with a fury to disrupt that which we have worked so diligently to build and preserve. Our journey is between life, and death and no one escapes the adventure, although each of us works at it differently. We have nothing to deal with but our own thoughts, which are best kept to the present moment, ever mindful that the right time is now, and the right place is right here. The most limiting disability in life is a bad attitude, which can be changed with a commitment to positive thinking. We are ever reminded not to look at life and notice all that we don't have, but to look at our life with joy and gratitude for all that surrounds us, for the divinity that is each one of us. Maya Angelo imparted that, "We do the best we can with what we know, and once we know better, we do better." There has been nothing truer for the families I've served.

This book is an opportunity for you to know more, and to do better!

How to Read This Book
(Seriously, a Little Guidance Is Needed)

Choose your character: Vanessa or Luke. There is a set-up for each character that introduces you to their particular challenges, personality, thoughts, feelings, and process that leads up to hiring an attorney and being court-ordered to participate in an evaluation.

Note: It is not necessary to read the same gender character with which you identify; in fact, I highly suggest you read the stories of both characters, start to finish, so you don't miss any of the valuable tools that will help you succeed!

When you arrive at a crossroad where Vanessa or Luke must make a choice, you decide what choice sounds best (or worst, for fun!) and turn to the page indicated. The choices you make are specific to the child custody evaluation. You will not be prompted until arriving at that place. Some of the story content might seem repetitive, with only subtle variations. This is intentional and for your benefit. Duplicate information is a clue to you that reading, rereading, and reading through a third time is likely necessary to grasp the importance of that particular lesson/message/example.

To get your money's worth, keep reading and making choices as you go until you reach "the end" of a choice. Then circle back and make a different choice. Repeat the process until you reach "the end" of that choice.

And then, do it again. You will gain the most knowledge and understanding from this book if you read all six stories. (Vanessa has three different stories and so does Luke.) It is likely that some men will relate better to Vanessa and some women will relate better to Luke or a combination thereof. If you identify as a non-binary individual, please know that I see you and respect you; and for ease of getting this story onto paper, a male and female character simply worked best.

Since some parents involved in domestic relations litigation were never married, the word "divorce" is used as an umbrella term to cover all persons making legal plans for children moving between two homes—married or not and intervenors too (relatives standing in).

When you see the symbol of a *Triskelion* (pictured to the right), this means there is a choice that you are required to make. The Triskelion is a sacred symbol (native to Sicily but found worldwide), which represents journey and the change of life as it unfolds. It represents the tale of forward motion—circular and in-terconnected experiences that lead to understanding. Once familiar with this symbol, you'll start seeing it in everyday places—most notably on the United States Department of Transportation seal and on Marvel's S.H.I.E.L.D. Headquarters. The triskelion is a representation of advancement, wisdom, and choice. When you see it used in this book, it's time to move forward—to choose, to gain knowledge, to deepen understanding, and to discover a new perspective. Time to step outside your comfort zone and look beyond your usual lens, where change is possible.

What to Expect

The stories are written with raw emotion and language that commonly accompanies parents and children involved in a court-ordered custody evaluation. This is an experiential story that is written in a way that is likely to evoke some pretty big feelings. While humor is used as a means to keep you engaged, not everyone will find the same topics to be funny. In fact, it is possible that a subject will trigger you because it hits particularly close to home. If you get triggered, you may need to put the book down, walk away, or skim forward. Take a moment to sit with the "yuck" and see if you can figure out why you're having those feelings: "Am I upset because I've behaved like this on accident? It is because I'm so tired of dealing with my ex's similar behavior? Is it because I am concerned my children are thinking or feeling the same as Teo and Rae?"

Most importantly, while in a triggered state, please:

- Do not call your child's other parent and go on a rant
- Do not send a hasty text or email
- Do not take your anger and upset onto a social media platform

- Do not take it out on your kids, or your mom, your best friend, or your pet
- Do not try and numb the pain with substances

Think through the consequence before you speak and act, and make sure you have people in your life (personal or professional) with whom you can process the many thoughts, feelings, and emotions which are the cause of that whirlwind inside of you. It's important to take steps now, like reading this book and surrounding yourself with the right people, to help create a safe shelter where you can withstand the force of the turbulence that accompanies litigating the best interest of your children. Time to armor up!

You might want to highlight important passages as you move through the stories. It will be good for you to note what is pertinent to your own story and next steps. And, as you read along, check out the valuable resources provided throughout the text and listed in an index at the back of the book. There is also an index of Hints, Hacks, and Hell-No's in the back of the book if you need a quick reference guide. (Yah know, because maybe your custody evaluation starts tomorrow, and you just found this book!)

Finally, and most importantly, please don't do this alone. Get a team. If you don't already have one, find a reputable and responsible family law attorney who understands family systems. Work cooperatively with your evaluator if one is already assigned to your case. And, think about finding a therapist for yourself and your children if you haven't already. The more support you have, the better you and your children will fare in this process.

Quick Disclaimers

* Nothing in this book is diagnostic in nature. While behaviors and circumstances of the characters in this book may look very much like what you are dealing with, only a mental health professional or medically trained individual can provide a diagnosis after they have met directly with and assessed an individual.

* I am not an attorney and nothing in this book is intended as legal advice. You will be introduced to three attorneys in the stories, who advise their fictional clients, Vanessa and Luke. None of the advice the attorneys provide in the book is meant to guide you in your particular situation. Every situation is unique and it is essential you retain a trained legal professional for advice—one who understands your family's circumstances.

* All archetypes are based on conflated characters. Any likeness to real persons or animals is coincidence and there has been no breach of confidentiality.

* Reading this book does not offer a guarantee that you will prevail in an evaluation or your court case, nor that your children will be successful or thrive in their two homes.

* IPV (intimate partner violence) and mental illness are complex issues that require more individual attention and focused guidance than this book offers.

* If you or your child's other parent plan to relocate a long distance away from each other, make sure your assigned evaluator has experience with this particular concern. The "move away" case is not specifically addressed in this book.

* If you are dissolving a same-sex relationship, find a professional who has experience with families like yours. Practical experience of the professionals involved in your case is critical to a positive outcome for you and your family.

Start Your Journey Now!

The best way to get started is to put this book down and go hug your child. Hold them close and really savor the moment with them. Tell your children how much you love them, how you are proud of them, and that you will always be there for them and you'll never leave. Commit to being the superhero they already believe you are. If your children are at their other home right now, take a minute to write them a short note with these same sentiments and put it on their pillow for when they return. Unless a court order says you cannot, send a text message if you have a teenager.

If those words apply to you, or don't apply to you but shocks, scares, or gives you pause, remember: Sometimes things go terribly wrong within families through the process of high-conflict litigation, and this book is designed to help you avoid those pitfalls and recover from them if you have already been thrown into the chasm.

Alright, I think you are well-prepared, as best anyone could be.

- You are not alone.
- You are worth the effort.
- You are the source from which your children thrive.

Down the proverbial rabbit hole...

Come on, I'm going to show you the way!

To Go Down the Rabbit Hole

"To enter into a situation or begin a process or journey that is particularly strange, problematic, difficult, complex, or chaotic, especially one that becomes increasingly so as it develops or unfolds."

(An allusion to Alice's Adventures in Wonderland by Lewis Carroll)

Farlex Dictionary of Idioms

HOW THE HECK DID WE END UP HERE?

UGH, WHAT NOW? I wondered when Luke's name popped up on the face of my phone.

"What do you want?" Contempt was thick in my voice as I answered.

I sat down at the kitchen table and looked out into the backyard at the weathered playset he had built for our kids. The seat of the swing bounced wildly with every gust of wind, and I could smell the humid air of an approaching storm as it blew in through the open window.

Like clockwork, he started in, "You..."

I held the phone away from my ear and felt my blood begin to boil as he reached the end of his verbal assault. And then he stooped to the lowest point possible, calling me the ugliest name in the nasty-name book. My hand started to shake, and I didn't know if it was fear or rage coursing through my veins. Probably both. No one else can infuriate me the way he does.

I can't believe he's talking to me this way. The mother of his children!

Click.

Wait... what... ? He hung up on me!

Instinctively, I slammed the phone down and covered my face with both hands, willing the tears back, not wanting to give him the satisfaction of getting under my skin, even though he wasn't there.

There's no other option but divorce. But, Teo and Rae. How on God's green earth is Mr. Disappointment ever going to take care of the kids without me around to do every single thing? He's never been much of a parent, never changed a diaper, and probably doesn't even know their shoe sizes. I hope the kids don't have to spend much time with him after we are divorced.

I took a deep breath to halt the racing thoughts. The stormy weather outside matched the turbulence of the emotional tsunami that was now stirring inside me. The great unknown was ready to tear through the safety of my home and what used to be our perfect little family, which I'd worked so hard to preserve. I took another deep breath, attempting to reign in the flurry of my negative thoughts, now set to overdrive.

I know the kids love their father and will surely need him for some things in life, but right now, I cannot think of a single thing. And it's my job to protect them from everything, including their father's absolute and utter stupidity. But how? I reached for the laptop resting on the table next to me. *Locating the very best and highly-skilled divorce attorney this town has to offer seems like a good place to start.*

I opened my browser and typed: "Divorce Attorney of the Year."

Wow! Lots to choose from. Hmmm. I scanned the first page of results and opened up a few of their fancy websites. So many qualified Attorneys of the Year, each of them ready to help. Curious and naive, I clicked the tab labeled "Attorney Fee Calculator." *Geez, divorce is expensive! Who can afford to pay this kind of hourly rate? I hope they at least offer some "congratulations on your divorce" welcome gifts—maybe a complimentary spa package with a deep tissue massage, microdermabrasion, foot-rub, and...*

An earsplitting knock, knock on the front door yanked my attention from my spa fantasy, my research, and the panic of inevitable bankruptcy. I cautiously rose from the chair and walked toward the offensive sound that reverberated throughout the entire house.

Who is on my porch this late at night?

It took me a minute to open the door. Deadbolt. Handle lock. Chain lock. Cannot be too careful with Mr. Disappointment. He packed up and left last week, but you never know when he might show up looking for trouble.

It's like I don't even know who he is anymore.

"Vanessa Smith?" questioned the gauche-looking man, with his slight posture and snarky expression. The little twerp sneered like a feral rat, apparently deriving some sort of sadistic pleasure from realizing his immediate impact on my blood pressure.

"Yes," I replied timidly, the rush of anxiety warming my core and turning my ears red.

"You are hereby served, Vanessa Smith."

Gulp. Heat flushed through my body from head to toe, my stomach did a summersault, and my hand shook like a 5.0 earthquake.

As the realization that a process server was standing before me started to set in, an overpowering sensation engulfed me—I wanted to punch this dude square in the face.

All the hours watching the kids' martial arts classes might just pay off tonight!

I ignored the intense urge to jab-jab-right this irritating little fella and then carefully used both of my hands to take the sealed envelope from his. The scrawny dimwit must have felt my impulse to lash out because he turned tail and ran through the pouring rain toward his vehicle.

"Thanks, I guess?" I yelled out to his quickly disappearing backside and then ripped open the envelope that was emitting energy as dark as Voldemort's wand.

You've got to be kidding me! He is divorcing me and wants custody of MY kids??? Oh, I think not, Mr. Disappointment! Game on!

I retreated back into the safety of my home and picked up my phone to call the very expensive attorney from the website I was just perusing.

This distinguished law firm must have a human standing by 24/7 for the price of admission—at least an all-night law student. Gosh, I'd talk to the janitor right about now!

No such luck. I reached an after-hours recorded message and left a bumbling-idiot-sounding voicemail, my unfettered emotions unmanageable.

I really need to speak with a qualified legal profes-sional. Right now!

After pacing around my living room for a while, I turned back toward the kitchen table, stomped over to my computer, and dropped into the kitchen chair.

A couple of clicks later, I found an inquiry tab and submitted my information requesting an emergency meeting the next morning. A message assured me Attorney of the Year would be in touch very soon to schedule a meeting time within twenty-four hours.

Hallelujah! I'll be in expert hands tomorrow.

Completely out of sorts, I gathered my hair into a ponytail, grabbed the super-sized bottle of bleach from under the sink, and started scrubbing. This is what I did when I was stressed. The crispy, clean smell always calms my nerves and was enough to keep me going for hours.

How is it possible that two children can leave so much dirt, grime, stickiness, food, and random messes everywhere?

I found $3.62 in the couch cushions along with gummy bears, watermelon gummies, Sour Patch Kids, a half-licked lollipop, two smashed-up chocolate chip cookies, a pair of dirty underwear, and several balled-up smelly sports socks.

My kids are disgusting, but I sure love them. Those two are my everything—my whole world.

It turned out to be a long, torturous night alone with my thoughts and a now-empty bottle of bleach. The storm continued to rage outside, and inside, as I considered all the ways I wanted to crush my ex—my husband of eighteen years and a Mr. Disappointment of epic proportion.

Eventually, I decided to lie down and somehow managed to fall asleep. None too soon, the sun rose, and it was time for our standard morning routine. I woke the children up for school and went through the usual chaos of getting them ready and out the door, looking reasonably well-put-together and prepared for whatever fourth grade and middle school had in store.

"Turn your shirt right-side-out, Teo. Put on clean underwear, please—both of you! Don't forget to brush your teeth and grab your lunches, guys. Teo, you have basketball practice right after school and need your permission slip for the symphony field trip today. Rae, that amazing paper mâché mask we made last weekend needs to be turned in for your art show on Friday!"

Whoever invented paper mâché should be jailed! Gross—what a mess!

As we buckled our seatbelts, I shook my head at the prospect of Mr. Disappointment trying to do any of this on his own. *He really does not have a clue what it takes to orchestrate Teo's and Rae's lives with all of their food sensitivities and activities and appointments. No way could he get them out the door every morning completely prepared for school. Forget making anything from paper mache, signing permissions slips and daily reading logs, or figuring out middle school math! I cannot let them spend school nights with their loser father after we're divorced. He couldn't handle the responsibility of a pet rock. Man, I sure hope Iggy is okay. I can't believe he took Rae's dog and her favorite blanket when he left the house last week. He is heartless!*

I drove to school through the familiar neighborhood on autopilot, preoccupied with overwhelmingly negative thoughts, and dropped both kids off at the correct times and places.

Those were the correct times and places, right? Since I'd been served the divorce paperwork the night before, it had felt a bit like my brain went on pause and everything had begun moving in slow motion.

When I arrived back home, I promptly checked email and saw the attorney had responded and offered at 10:00 a.m. meeting! I quickly changed out of my pajama bottoms and into the day's outfit. I made an attempt to cover the puffy dark circles under my eyes with concealer, splashed on mascara, added shiny gloss to my lips, and got my hair in order with the help of a clip. I was ready to get this emerging chapter of my life moving in the right direction.

Who could possibly eat at a time like this? I thought, glancing around the kitchen littered with cereal bowls, empty yogurt tubes, and uneaten vitamins. I poured a fresh cup of coffee and headed out the door, ready for my 10:00 a.m. meeting with Attorney of the Year.

Arriving at the attorney's downtown office glossy-eyed, tearful, and sleep-deprived, I noted that the place reeked of Ben Franklin himself. The office displayed artwork of a posh uptown gallery, furniture from a place far more debonair than our Ikea selection at home, and stone floors so shiny that I considered removing my shoes. I proceeded warily and double-checked to be sure I'd remembered all of my credit cards (especially the one in Mr. Disappointment's name).

"Good morning, Ms. Smith," said the young, well-rested, overly-perky, yoga-bodied, insanely-attractive, matcha-tea-drinking assistant behind the front desk.

Obviously, she does not have children of her own to shuffle out the door in the morning, I thought to myself as I forced a smile and greeted her with as much politeness as I could muster.

"Attorney of the Year is ready to see you. Right this way, please." She opened the door to a long hallway, and bile instantly rose in my throat as I ordered my feet to walk toward the door. I knew I was there to get help, but it felt like I was stepping into the temple of doom.

Geez, pull it together, Vanessa. Be strong. You're all the kids have!

At the end of our tandem trek, me following closely behind the gorgeous woman in high heels, I stumbled into a tenth-floor, overly-spacious, window-lined corner office that faced the river.

Attorney of the Year sat behind an elegant cherry wood desk in an oversized, overstuffed leather chair. The office smelled clean, with a hint of cedar and citrus. Decorated with cultured taste, I could even hear the calming trickle of water flowing gently from a desktop fountain. I also noticed family photos on an impressive floor-to-ceiling bookshelf that lined an interior wall of this exquisite space, along with awards that had been bestowed upon Attorney of the Year.

The attorney's quiet expression was righteously assured and sociable, putting me immediately more at ease. The feeling that I had just scored my own personal secret weapon washed over me like cool rain on a hot day. She was about to be the ace up my sleeve who was more than capable of taking down Mr. Disappointment the same way lionesses hunt prey for the pride.

"It's nice to meet you, Vanessa..." She looked to be in her late forties and told me she was a divorced mother of three teenage boys, which immediately increased my confidence in her. Anyone who can keep three adolescent boys in line must be able to tackle just about anything, right? After getting to know each other a little bit, I told her that my priority, all I really wanted to do, was to protect Teo and Rae from the all-consuming evil their father had become and to make absolutely certain he did not win custody of them. "He can have everything else from our pathetic marriage," I told my new best friend, "But those kids are my world, and he is threatening to take them away. Please tell me what to do and I'll do it. Please. Save. My. Kids!"

"We'll need to prepare a response and counterclaim to your husband's petition for legal custody," she started, flashing me a reassuring smile. "You and Mr. Smith will have to complete a court-mandated parenting course and eventually sit together in mediation."

Response and counterclaim. Check.

Parenting Course. Lame, but whatever. Check. Check.

Mediation. Together? If I have to, I guess. Check. Check. Check.

I'm on it. Best client ever. Anything to get this over with as fast as possible!

After our meeting, I walked out of the office feeling a little lighter, having a clear plan and restored hope that this nightmare would be over soon.

No such luck. Day turned to night, night turned to day, turned to weeks, turned to months! We were at a total standstill, just trudging through each day, feeling lost and confused and broke, as if there would never be an end to the torture.

OMG, I'm losing my mind! Why does the legal system move so slowly? This really stinks! I complained to myself late one night at my kitchen table as I checked my email inbox again for an update on the case, hoping there had been some forward progress. The legal system does not regard space and time the same way a frantic, crisis-driven, scared-out-of-their-wits parent does.

Lace up those sneakers, Vanessa, I coached myself. *Looks like it is going to be a long and exhausting marathon to unhitch Mr. Disappointment. It might really be until death do we part at this agonizing pace.*

And so, I waited as patiently as possible, though more like a caged animal, while trying to carry on with daily responsibilities and maintain familiar routines for the kids.

Two months later, having done all I was told to do, there was still no resolution and Mr. Disappointment was acting like a total asshat. There was no resemblance to the person I married, and my life had become a complete shit-show.

The kids were troopers for sure, but this was really taking a toll on all of us. Teo had begun acting out at school and hanging around a whole new crowd of kids. Rae was attached to my side at all times—I could not even leave the room. And I was completely broke. We were forced to sell the family home—the only home the kids had ever known and the one place they felt safe and secure. Mr. Disappointment's entire family now hated me, too, especially his mother. Mediation had failed, the parenting class was obviously designed for him (not me), and my attorney had gotten nothing but crickets in response to our settlement proposals.

There must be a better way. I feel so helpless. There has to be some mechanism to turn things around—something or someone out there who can actually help and do something for my kids.

At our next meeting in the fancy corner office (three months in, and living on borrowed money), Attorney of the Year advised that due to the nature of concerns and ongoing high conflict, it would be best to motion the court for a child custody and parenting time evaluation.

Lord, what is that and how much is it going to cost me? Mr. Disappointment isn't giving me a single dime. I even got myself a job at the coffee shop to pay for all the trouble that he has created by making one bad choice after another.

Attorney of the Year made eye contact with me and explained, "The evaluation will cost a few thousand dollars, and the court often orders both parties to pay half of the professional fee. It will be worth the investment in your family to receive guidance intended to craft the best plan for the children given the total family circumstances and how far apart you and Mr. Smith are when it comes to custody and parenting time. It won't be an easy or fun process. In fact, an evaluator will see everything Mr. Disappointment and you have been up to. There is no confidentiality, and you may feel like your lives have been gutted wide-open, exposed, and maybe even a little bit violated. The evaluator will talk to people who know and love you and your children, and even their teachers and coaches and other professionals."

Sitting forward in her big, comfy, leather chair, hands folded and resting on her desk, Attorney of the Year continued, "If you and Mr. Disappointment cannot agree on the evaluator's suggested recommendations, or a version thereof, the evaluator will then testify as an expert at trial to help inform the judge about your children, their relationship with each parent, and other important people within the family system. She will provide a written assessment of each child's unique needs and draw conclusions about each parents' capacity to meet those needs and best interests. This will include a custody and parenting time plan that she reasons is most suitable for Teo and Rae based on the information collected. She will also recommend services for the whole family with the goal of creating a more tenable dynamic where your children have the best opportunity to thrive in both of their homes. Your children's best interests are the only interests with which an evaluator and the court are concerned."

Am I seriously hearing that all the disappointing things Luke has done do not matter?

Fortunately, my rational voice replied, "An evaluation sounds good, I guess. Kind of scary, but at least it gives the children an opportunity to say what they want, and a professional will hear my parenting concerns about what I think is best. Let's move forward in that direction."

Attorney of the Year smiled a salacious, Cheshire Cat grin. Before I even left the corner office, the ace up my sleeve got to work making things happen for my kids.

As I drove home, I felt pleased we were finally doing something. Walking into my new, cozy and comfortably-decorated apartment, I was mostly relieved, except for the nagging feeling that Pandora's Box might just whoosh open and smack me square in the face.

Wow, all this gives me a massive headache, and I'm going to need a lot more information about that evaluation I just agreed to. Advil® and Google are both on tonight's agenda.

I poured a glass of cold water, popped two Advil®, and opened my laptop that was always sitting on the kitchen table. The kitchen table in our little apartment now doubled as a workspace for me and the kids. They were both super upset about having to leave the big house they'd grown up in, and neither was excited about their father's new studio apartment downtown either. I typed "Amazon" into the search bar, selected "Books" from the dropdown, and then searched for exactly what I wanted to do: "Crush Your Ex."

Six weeks later, after Mr. Disappointment and his stupid lawyer had argued about every professional evaluator Attorney of the Year suggested, a judge finally chose one for us.

That night, after the kids went to bed, I was poking through the refrigerator for a late night, sugary pick-me-up when a thought struck: *What kind of person gets paid to sit in judgment of someone else's parenting? A total stranger cannot possibly understand our family and have any real compassion for my kids in just a few short meetings.*

Anxiety and nausea overwhelmed me, and I quickly put the cupcake back into the fridge.

At least a professional would be calling out all of Mr. Disappointment's problems. The extent of those problems should keep our evaluator focused on him, not me. I should probably do some research on this evaluator before we get started. Yelp seems like a good place to start.

Click, click, click. Enter.

What? This didn't look good at all. I started scrolling through every public forum I could think of—Facebook, Twitter, Pin, Link, Flicker, Tube, Tumble, Digg, Blogs,

Blab, Reddit, Instagram, and those plentiful less-than-five-star Google reviews.

Holy crap! This woman is the antichrist! I cannot believe I agreed to this!

One, two, three, four, exhale, and re-center. I started some calming breaths as instructed by the therapist that Attorney of the Year had sent me to see a month earlier. Apparently, my anxiety about all of this had become visible to her, and she recommended I see a professional.

Vanessa, you've got this. You're going to be okay. I instinctively recited some positive affirmations I had learned in my sessions and reminded myself that Attorney of the Year had said impressive things about this evaluator and her reputation in the legal community.

Sally from the gym also told me she used the same evaluator during her dreadful divorce. *That seemed to turn out well for Sally. I see here the evaluator has a professional license and has never been disciplined by the state regulatory board. Those seem like good things for sure. They say you cannot believe everything on the Internet. Heaven help me, I sure hope so!*

I sat back in my chair, stared at the computer screen, and sipped from the glass of wine I had poured, trying to regain my composure and focus on the task at hand.

How in the world am I going to start preparing for something like this? Where do I even begin to understand the process of an evaluation, how it all works, and what

I should be doing to get ready? There must be some hints and hacks for coming out on top.

Just then, a Universal Studios ad popped up on my computer screen: *"It's our choices that show what we truly are, Harry, far more than our abilities."* The words of that ad for *The Wizarding World of Harry Potter* struck me as somehow deep and significant but didn't fully register.

That's weird! I thought as I closed my computer, took another sip, and sat back in my chair. *Now what? How am I going to win this evaluation?*

Below are three different ways Vanessa can choose to prepare for and navigate through the upcoming child custody evaluation.

Collect the dirt on my ex to show the evaluator why my kids need limited time with their father.
Go to page 59 to follow Vanessa's experience through this choice.

Rediscover myself and recreate a new, improved version of me. If I'm happy, my kids will be happy.
Go to page 117 to follow Vanessa's experience through this choice.

Demonstrate why the kids will be better off with me, since I have always been their primary parent.
Go to page 191 to follow Vanessa's experience through this choice.

"Forgiveness is the fragrance
that the violet sheds on the
heel that has crushed it."

~Mark Twain~

PROVE HE'S AN IDIOT

Dredge up every piece of dirt on Mr. Disappointment and bring him down!

COLLECT THE DIRT on my ex to show the evaluator why my kids need limited time with their father.

Putting my wine glass down on the dining room table a little more forcefully than I meant to, I reached a decision about how to proceed with the child custody evaluation.

I'll start by writing down every terrible thing Mr. Disappointment has ever done, not done, is doing, and will do after we are divorced—so the evaluator gets an accurate idea of how terrible he is and how little time he should be allowed to spend with my kids.

I sat upright in my chair, excited and feeling energized by this brilliant idea. My anger was suddenly front and center. Momma bear is ready to roar for her babies.

I should probably talk with the kids' teachers and their pediatrician about what he is putting us through, so those professionals can be alert and help protect Teo and Rae. Perhaps a quick post on Facebook so our friends and family know what's happening and can watch out for the kids around town and online. We are really going to need all this support—me and my kids. It's time to make Mr. Disappointment pay for the stress and humiliation he has brought on our family!

Palms sweaty with anticipation, I paused, suddenly struck by a hole in my plan.

I suppose narcissists do not have feelings, nor feel anything for anyone at all. I cannot imagine he would give two cents what the kids' teachers or pediatrician think of him. I'm not sure he even knows what schools they attend, what grades they're in this year, or where the doctor's office is. I'll remember to tell the evaluator at our first meeting that he is a narcissist—she needs to know that for sure. I should probably print out a few Internet articles about narcissism for her to read. I'll be sure to tell the kids tomorrow morning about the upcoming evaluation before Mr. Disappointment has time to poison their little minds against me.

I opened Word, titled a new document "Crush My Ex," and began capturing every wrong, disappointing, and self-centered move my soon-to-be ex-husband had made since the day we met. For good measure, I included a few hearsay examples—stories told to me over the years by his mother and his best friend, Mike, about Mr. Disappointment's wayward conduct well before he dragged me into his deceitful web of madness. I took to Google for more stellar ideas about how best to prepare for an evaluation and made a checklist of what I found.

Ready for battle. Armor on. Artillery stocked, locked, and loaded.

Time had passed since that little twerp served the divorce lawsuit on the front stoop of our old house, and the day had finally arrived for me to meet the court-appointed evaluator. In the last few months, I had spent countless hours preparing for this very important day. The truth was ready and stuffed into five plump three-ring-binders of neatly-organized, sticky-note-labeled, and crassly-highlighted volumes of text and email messages between Mr. Disappointment and me. There was one special binder solely dedicated to Narcissism, which included *Psychology Today* articles, WebMD information, and endless real-life examples of his grandiosity and high-need-for-admiration behavior that supported Mr. Disappointment's mental health diagnosis as I saw it. Hopefully, the evaluator would, too.

I'd also saved countless voicemail messages on my cell phone to demonstrate the toxic venom Mr. Disappointment regularly spewed in my direction. Attorney of the Year kept telling me to, "Move those messages into a Dropbox, Vanessa," so my voicemail was no longer full when she called. But whatever— technology is so confusing.

I had also prepared a photo book, showing every scratch, bruise, and grimy fingernail with which the kids have returned from his care since our separation. And I threw in the three-sizes-too-small pair of jeans he made Rae wear, heavily-soiled socks from his gross house, and Teo's right shoe with a huge hole worn all the way through at the big toe—clothing their father had sent my children to school in. Heaping evidence of his blatant incompetence as a so-called parent.

I zipped the giant binders, photo book, and clothing evidence into a wheeled suitcase, as there was no other way to haul all of it into the evaluator's office without throwing out my back. *The evaluator is sure to understand the fraud Mr. Disappointment is after I show her this mass collection of proof. Fingers crossed!*

Motivated to get this show on the road, and feeling thoroughly prepared for our meeting, I opened the door to the evaluator's office. *Nice place, though nothing like Attorney of the Year's corner suite on the tenth floor.* There was a harmless-looking, sensible-shoe-wearing, middle-aged lady with naturally-curly hair sitting at the front desk. She welcomed me and offered a mug of coffee or cup of water. I accepted a glass of water, and she handed me a disclosure form to read over, date, and sign. Almost as soon as I signed the form and paid my portion of the professional fee, the cheerful, middle-aged, sales-rack-dressed evaluator appeared from the back office and introduced herself with a firm handshake. She had kind eyes, a warm smile, and what looked like a faded coffee stain on her shirt.

Is that dried-up paper mâché in her hair?

After releasing my hand, the evaluator led me to our meeting space, which was comfortable and inviting and flooded with soft light. There were two cozy chairs by the window that she walked over to and motioned for us to sit. It smelled like home in there, and I quickly started to feel safe as I noticed the area to my right was set up for kids with toys, art, books, LEGOs, chalk, and even a little table just the right size for Rae.

Maybe a little small for Teo—that kid is growing like a weed. The kids are going to be okay here. Glad I already began preparing them on what and what not to say.

The evaluator smiled at me and apologized for her casual dress, explaining that she had volunteered in her daughter's classroom that morning. "Art class today, helping with paper mâché masks for their art show in a few weeks. They turned out pretty good."

I knew it!

"Vanessa, most parents are a bit nervous meeting me for the first time, although they usually feel much better by the end of our two hours together. I know it has been a long road leading up to today, and you're likely emotionally and financially exhausted. Add to that the constant worry about your children, and a parent can really start to feel like they have been swept down the proverbial rabbit hole. Good news is that this evaluation is an opportunity to step back from the adversarial high conflict that litigation often creates between two parents, as we fully explore and concentrate on the needs of your children. We'll be discussing the strengths of each parent and both parents' concerns, and then put our big brains together to design the best plan for Teo and Rae." She gave me a settling smile, confident in her conviction to do what's right for the kids.

Well, that sounds promising and exceptionally reasonable. My big brain and your big brain, working in tandem, for the benefit of my kids.

But then she kept talking about working *together* as a "team"—her, me, and Mr. Disappointment. "I have never met a parent who didn't love their child. Mothers and fathers come to this process, both wanting what they believe is in their child's best interest. They both want their children to win the game but are working from different playbooks. My hope is to bring you and the children's father 80% of the way towards the middle, and then provide enough guidance and direction that the two of you can finish off the final 20% by infusing the plan for Teo and Rae with details unique to your family structure and needs. When both parents are invested in the final plan, and both parents feel heard and that they had a say in what's best, well, the plan is far more likely to be successful versus a legal and binding judgment imposed on your family by the court. Make sense?" Again, she flashed me that satisfied look, like she really intended the best for our family and had my kids' backs through this nightmare.

I nodded in agreement while thinking, *That is not my plan! Mr. Disappointment is enemy #1 and I'm here to tell all. There is not even a remote chance that we are going to be singing Kumbaya around the campfire anytime soon. You've obviously never worked with a Mr. Disappointment quite like mine before. Boy, oh boy, Pollyanna, you are in for a real shock.*

After fifteen minutes of listening to her prattle on about kids needing both parents and this process being focused on reaching an agreement while avoiding a courtroom trial, I started to question if what I had prepared was going to get the job done.

Too late to change course now. I'm not about to dump the master plan this close to the starting line. Or is this the finish line? This is one confusing marathon.

I really wanted my day in court, and prayed this lady would be on my side by then.

Why does she keep eyeballing my suitcase? Blood, sweat, tears, and leftover shrapnel from my broken marriage is in that case. She must be excited to see all of it!

"So, Vanessa, the goal of our time today is for you to educate me about the story of your family. How you got from point A (meeting the children's father) to point B (a custody litigant). Only a small percentage of divorcing parents ever participate in an evaluation. I'm curious to learn all about why your family is here and begin to understand ways in which I can best assist your children and family moving forward." She paused before giving me further instruction. "It would be helpful if you could go down memory lane..."

At last, my opportunity to share this ugly story with a captive audience—an audience that holds the cards to my children's future. It's exactly what I have wanted from the start!

"Relay information in chronological order—paint a picture of the most significant events in your family's timeline. Throughout the story, please highlight the most important details of your children's lives (residential moves, school/academics, friendships, important relationships, activities/sports/music, health, religion, special needs, services, successes, areas where they struggle and excel, etc.)."

She paused for emphasis.

"In addition to learning as much as possible about your children's lives, it is necessary that we identify and understand patterns of conflict between you and the other parent. Patterns of conflict are important to understand because embedded within them are often your parenting concerns; and unless we make an effort to understand and mitigate the unhealthy patterns of conflict that exist now, those unhealthy patterns will perseverate, harm your children, and continue to cause trouble for your family after the divorce is final. Exposure to conflict is detrimental to Teo and Rae and will inflict irreparable psychological harm over time."

Her body language was relaxed and poised. With raised eyebrows, head tilted slightly to the right, she made eye contact, clearly looking for my buy-in to this process that the court had ordered my family participate in. She repositioned a little straighter in her chair, picked up a notepad and pencil, and gestured to me, as if offering me the floor to start talking.

Ugh, wait. What does she want me to say? I squirmed in my chair since I had mentally checked out after "it would be helpful if you could go down memory lane..." *Right, the story, she just wants to hear the story.*

"Well, it is quite the story..." I started and proceeded to tell her everything. During the next two hours, Mr. Disappointment's deepest, darkest secrets were witnessed by this court-appointed professional. Of course, I supported all the main points with mountains of evidence from the binders of documentation in my suitcase. By the end of our time, I was feeling pretty righteous, but the professional woman across from me looked a bit exhausted and frayed.

She hardly spoke a word after her introductory speech. I hope it wasn't too much. She did seem to lose a little bit of interest while I was reviewing contents of the fourth three-ring binder.

"Vanessa, thank you for sharing your story with me. We will plan to meet again soon, after I have talked with the children's father. During the next meeting, I'll have lots of questions for you about Teo and Rae; and I will also share with you whatever their father's parenting concerns are for the children. I'll send you an email with some possible dates and times." She stood up to walk me out and smiled as she said, "You can take your suitcase home."

What? Home? I put all of this together for you!

Compliantly, I stuffed everything back into the suitcase and zipped it up.

I followed her to the door, thanked her for her time, and left the office.

Gosh, I thought presenting all of this was going to be a cathartic experience. So why am I feeling sick to my stomach now that it's over?

By the time I reached my car in the parking lot, doubt had set in. I phoned Attorney of the Year and told her about the first evaluation meeting. She promptly confirmed this was not the right course of action at all—not how she had advised me to proceed. I must have checked out during one of her speeches, too. Spending the entire session throwing Mr. Disappointment under the bus, while completely neglecting to talk about my own parenting strengths and relationship with the kids, and not talking about Teo and Rae at all—all of these were huge mistakes according to my attorney, confirmed by the churning in my gut that was now making me even more nauseous.

Oh no! What does the evaluator think of me? Have I ruined everything for my kids? I wish I knew what she was thinking.

I started my car and drove straight home. Upon arrival, I went immediately to the kitchen and grabbed the bottle of bleach and started cleaning our little apartment. I had two full hours before the kids needed to be picked up, which was plenty of time to pull our messy home, and myself, together. Everything seemed to function best when it was tidy and smelled good. I grabbed the vacuum and worked my way around every corner of the apartment, sucking up stray earrings, tiny LEGO pieces, hair ties, and lots of crumbs.

When I opened the door to Teo's room, a wave of gym stink almost knocked me over. I quickly picked up the dirty laundry that was scattered all around, opened the window, sprayed the room down with Febreze, changed the plug-in, and called it good.

Now, for Rae's room.

When I opened her bedroom door, a smile stretched across my face. Rae's room was much tidier than her brother's, and it had a pleasing smell. She had lots of stuff, but liked everything to be organized. Her clothes were sorted by color in her closet, and her books were placed on the shelf in alphabetical order. She loved art and had her slime-making supplies stacked on her desk next to pictures of her besties. A picture of our family—all four of us and Iggy—was placed inside the homemade frame she had made at camp and hung above her bed.

Suddenly overwhelmed, I paused and remembered the day the photo was taken.

It wasn't that long ago, but the kids looked so much younger, and happier, and... less burdened than they do now.

My eyes trailed down to the bedside table and Rae's fuzzy, flip-sequence diary that lay there.

I shouldn't. I knew it was wrong to look. *Well, I guess it won't hurt anything.* Feeling just a little guilty, I cracked open the diary to the first entry...

Dear Diary, this is Rae. My dad left the house for good and he took my dog Iggy. I hate him for taking Iggy. Iggy needs me and I need him. He is my best friend and I have no idea where he is now or if my dad will bring him back. I hate my dad for leaving but I miss him too. Why is he doing this to our family? He stole my favorite blanket!!!! I told my mom about the blanket and she said she told him not to, but he did anyway, and that he is a total disappointment. That same stupid word she uses with me and Teo sometimes when we make a mistake. God I hate that stupid word. And now my mom hates my dad, too, which makes me hate her. She calls him 'my ex.' I'm not sure if that means he's my 'ex dad' too? I hope he is not mad at me. I hope this is not my fault. I hope he didn't leave because I messed up last week and got a C on my math test. Mom helped me study for it because dad had to work late. Dad is better at math even though mom thinks she knows everything about everything. Or maybe dad left because Teo didn't make the A team for basketball this season. We are not perfect kids. I suppose we could have tried harder. Maybe if me and Teo were better at stuff, our parents wouldn't have fought so much and dad would still be here, with Iggy, and with us.

Oh no, baby, it's not your fault. It is all his fault—your lying, no-good father!

My eyes instantly wet with tears, I quickly flipped through the diary pages and saw Rae had made consistent entries. Sometimes, there were days or weeks in between, but there were fairly consistent entries since the day Luke had left the house.

> Dear Diary, this is Rae. My dad is still gone and Iggy too. My mom is a total stress case but it is nice there is no more fighting in the house between my parents. Mom keeps talking about Attorney of the year and how much money she is costing. Mom finally told us that her and dad are getting a divorce, duh! She thinks me and Teo are idiots I guess. Grandma told us our parents were getting a divorce a long time ago, that my dad had smartened up and was going to finally divorce mom. Mom hates grandma now, too, mom is always mad. And I don't think grandma likes mom much either, or ever really liked her at all. At least according to both of their Facebook pages. My family sucks!

I can't believe his mother is talking to my kids behind my back!

> Dear Diary, this is Rae. We have to move from our house because of my stupid parents divorce. None of this is fair. My life is ruined!

My heart nearly stopped in my chest. *It's your father's fault we had to move. I tried to keep the house but he made us sell it, and I am doing my very best for you and your brother.*

My anger suddenly front and center, I considered ways to beef up my assault on Mr. Disappointment. *I'll have to change my Facebook password to keep Rae out of there, and then let it really rip. A mass email maybe to all of our friends and family outing my ex. Hell, maybe I'll even contact the Dr. Phil show or Jerry Springer.*

Dear Diary, this is Rae. We moved to a little apartment with mom, but I still have my own room. I'm in here right now. It's not too terrible. I saw some cute boys down by the pool. There's a pool and a playground. My dad lives downtown now, in the city, in a haunted house. It is weird. His apartment number is 666. We go there on the weekends. Ozzy is finally home with me!!!!!!!!!!!!!!!! He says woof woof.

Cute boys?! I gulped loud enough for the neighbors to hear through the wall.

And then, I turned to the final page she had written just the night before. Every cell in my body hurt as I read her words and felt my sweet daughter's pain oozing off the page.

Dear Diary, this is Rae. I think my parents are aliens or aliens came and took my real parents away and left these different versions of them. I miss the old ones. Everybody is mad all the time. My mom has been making all these projects, like book reports or something about all the terrible things about my dad. She thinks me and Teo don't know her hiding spots for those naughty notebooks she made, or the password to the computer where her files are stored, but we do. We have seen everything that she put together for some lady she is going to go and see tomorrow. I even noticed she had Teo's old shoe packed up in a suitcase, and some of my jeans that are now too small. Why is this happening? Why can't she just be nice? She said we have to go and see this lady too, I'm not saying a word to some stupid stranger lady, no way!

We hardly ever see my dad except on some weekends. I really miss him. I know my mom wants Teo and me to be on her side, and sometimes we pretend to be because it's just easier that way. But really we love our dad and want to see him more than a couple of days every month. We love our mom too, but she is acting all crazy since he left. Every time I get a scratch or bruise mom takes a picture of it even though I tell her not to cause it's embarrassing. And she wrote some terrible stuff on Facebook about my dad and their divorce. I overheard some of the other girls' moms talking about it at school. My life is a joke. I want to crawl into a cave and live like a bear, or run away and join the circus. Wait, I'm already in the circus, my family is an act right out of Barnum + Bailey. At least I'm a strong girl and have Issy to lean on. Teo has been super cool to me too. My teacher said I needed a theme song, something that would help me focus on the good stuff and things that are special about me. Obviously, I picked "This Is Me!"

I cued up iTunes on her iPod that sat on the nightstand and played my daughter's chosen theme song. As the melody started, tears thundered down, and I reflected on my recent bad behavior and the two hours I had just spent tearing down her daddy in every possible way in a session with the court-appointed evaluator who was helping to decide my daughter's future.

I should probably apologize to Rae for all of this and find a counselor for her so she has a safe place to talk. She has always been so dramatic. Stupid judgmental mothers at school. I'll be having some words with them. But, Dr. Phil might still be able to help us. How in the world did the kids get the computer password? I'll need to change that, if I can figure out how.

I put the diary back just as I had found it, closed up the iPod, and sat in complete silence—drained and feeling like a Mac truck had just run me over at 65-miles-an-hour. I was dumbfounded that this could possibly be my life and at what had become of our once-loving family.

Ugh, I gotta go! My two hours were up. I needed to collect the kids from school. *How am I going to look her in the eyes?* I was a little bit scared to face her, having this new insight.

I wonder what's going on in Teo's head? He has always been quiet. I figured he was doing fine, besides getting into a little trouble at school, but now I don't know.

As I drove toward their schools, I thought about all the things I could do to make it up to them. This past year and everything about the divorce had really been rough. I'd been so focused on gathering evidence to crush my ex in this evaluation, that I'd overlooked the kids' needs.

Their wish is my command tonight. Whatever they want for dinner, I'll make, or maybe take them out to their favorite restaurant, Olive Garden, for some of those delicious breadsticks. We'll make special plans for this weekend—mom and kid time. Whatever their little hearts desire. Mommy needs to get back in their good graces before they talk to the child custody evaluator.

I grabbed Teo from school first, and we had a little time before Rae was done for the day. FroYo after school always lightened the mood, so I drove us to our favorite place. After loading his bowl with frozen yogurt, his favorite gummy sharks, and a chocolate brownie on the side, he sat down next to me as I started in on my sorbet and sprinkles.

"How was your day, buddy?" I asked, trying to not make it obvious that I was digging for information. I really wanted to find out if he felt the same way Rae was feeling.

A shrug of his shoulders and familiar grunt were all he gave me. Teo had never talked very much but had become even more withdrawn and isolated since his dad left the house. He had gotten into a couple fights at school and spent time in detention, which is totally out of character.

Not only did his dad leave all of us, but he forced us out of our family home. Of course my teenage son is struggling.

"What are you thinking about, Mom?" His question, thick with contempt, startled me out of my angry daydream.

"About your father and everything he has done to ruin our lives. I'm so sorry your dad is such a disappointment, honey."

Teo exhaled loudly, rolled his eyes, got up from the table, his metal stool scraping against the tile floor, and tossed his cup of uneaten froYo into the garbage. He stormed out of the yogurt shop with me hot on his heels, sorbet and sprinkles still in hand.

"Teo, wait up! What's the matter?" I yelled, running after him.

He beat me to the car, got in the front seat, and locked the door. The windows were closed so I tried talking to him through the glass, but his hoodie was up, and his arms were wrapped tight around his long legs hugged up against his chest. I could tell he was crying.

"Buddy, please open the door. I'm so sorry. I want to help make this right. Please talk to me. What can I do to make it better, bud?"

He flipped me the bird.

"Teo, that is not acceptable." I unlocked the door myself with the key fob since my son, now acting like his father, clearly did not intend to. I walked around the front end of the car and slipped into the driver's seat. We sat in silence for a couple of minutes, and then I handed him a Kleenex®. Finally, he looked up, mad but defeated.

He stands taller than me now, and his jawline has hardened. His baby face is no more. This is a young man sitting beside me.

I reached over to wipe a tear from his cheek, and he pulled away so I couldn't touch him. "Teo, please talk to me. What did I do to upset you?"

And with that one question, the floodgates opened. My otherwise even-tempered son let loose. "You and dad have ruined my life! Rae's too! Why do you have to hate each other and act like such immature stupid brats? We want our old life back. We miss our house and hate having to move between your and Dad's boring apartments. Why can't you guys work it out like adults? When you call dad your 'ex,' it's hurtful to us. He is not our ex-dad. And he's not a disappointment to us, so stop saying that! The more you hate him, the more we hate you. And who is this lady we have to talk to? I am not going there and talking to her. That ridiculous suitcase of filth you packed up—did you seriously show all of that to a stranger? You are such a loser, Mom. And I want my favorite shoe back—the one with a hole!"

I had no defense and made an effort to close my mouth that had somehow dropped open.

Teo continued on. "Dad says you can end it all right now, but are making us go to a custody evaluator. You're always complaining about not having any money but Dad says this evaluation costs a fortune. What is your problem, Mom? Can't you just be nice?"

That did it. My rage took over. "Your dad isn't telling you the truth, Teo. Everything is his fault, not mine. And you *will* go talk to the evaluator. You and your sister. We have to pick her up from school now. Buckle up, buddy. And watch your tone with me."

I saw my son sink deeper into his seat. We left froYo in silence and pulled into the carpool line at Rae's school. She hopped in, singing a new song she had learned in choir that afternoon. But Rae, being the barometer of our family's emotions and very aware of how other people feel, quickly assessed the atmospheric temperature in the car and asked us what was wrong.

"Nothing, sweet girl. Teo is having a hard day."

He shot me a look of pure evil.

Rae reached forward and patted her brother's shoulder. He shrugged away from his sister, too, and curled into the smallest ball possible with his 5'8" athletic frame. No one spoke another word on the drive home. When we arrived, the kids couldn't get out of the car and into their bedrooms fast enough. Both of them used more force than necessary in closing their doors.

My second meeting with the evaluator was only a couple of days away, so I decided to sit down at the computer and document the horrible impact of this divorce on my children. Mid-sentence, while journaling the day's events, I remembered I needed to change the computer password.

No more snooping, you little hackers. Got it! Maybe this technology stuff is not so hard after all.

Neither one of them wanted to eat at Olive Garden, or eat at all, so it was early to bed for all of us. My brain hurt, and my nerves were fried.

The days passed uneventfully until my second evaluation appointment. I was glad to see her again. Maybe she would have some advice about making things better for the kids, or just maybe she had talked some sense into my ex when they had their meeting.

I decided to leave my suitcase at home this time, but brought along a copy of the daily journal I was using to document all the troubling things the kids have said and done as well as the ongoing drama with Mr. Disappointment. I continued to collect plenty of dirt on him. He was never a disappointment in *that* department—a reliable screw-up.

The second evaluation meeting was different from the first. I was greeted in the same way, and we went to the comfortable back office; but once we were seated, the evaluator told me she had an agenda. Today would be more of a structured interview than the first. There were lots of questions about my parenting, daily routines in my household, the kids' healthcare and dental care, extended family relationships, holiday traditions, activities, their friendships, and school. We walked through my thoughts about the best parenting plan and why I thought it would work for Teo and Rae. That part was easy. Minimal time with Luke and the rest with me.

The evaluator then said it was time for her to share Luke's parenting concerns, so we could sort through some of the disagreements, and she could hear both sides of the issues.

It was so hard to hear and respond to all of his lies. When we finally made it through the litany of his BS, I reminded the evaluator of his narcissism and saw her make a note. I took extra time at the end to really lay it on thick—emphasizing all of his worst characteristics. I needed her to know what a fool my ex is, and how terrible it would be for him to get custody of the kids. It would be a disaster if they spent more than every other weekend with him. After twenty minutes, I was satisfied that I had crushed him as well as any angry, scorned, rageful, soon to be ex-wife could.

She best be getting the picture!

We scheduled our third evaluation meeting for two days later. This meeting would include interviews of the children at her office. I asked what I should tell them about the appointment, and let her know Teo was not into it. She assured me teenagers can be resistant, but getting to the office was the hardest part. The evaluator suggested I tell them a little bit about her and her office, to let them know that their father and I have both talked to her, have them take an online office tour, and assure them that they do not have to talk about anything they don't want to. She told me the burden of this process is not theirs, and she never asked kids where they want to live because it is not their decision to make. The evaluator assured me that she did not poke and prod at children for information they don't want to share. She did not fact-check me or their father's concerns through the children, but was interested in getting to know them a bit. I was told not to "coach" the children about what they should or should not say.

Oops, too late for that! I have to make sure they tell her they want to live with me and only visit their father every other weekend. To hell with "parenting time!" He's no parent at all. I need them to say all the good stuff they can about me—tell her how close we all are and how much we love and need each other. We'll need to revisit some horrible memories of their father. Even though Iggy's home now, I'll remind Rae how terrible she felt when her father dognapped him.

After school that day, I invited the kids to our kitchen table to take the online tour of the evaluator's office.

Teo sat arms crossed, obviously disinterested. Rae spotted the toys and was open to going in and meeting the "nice-looking" lady. Finally, Teo said he would go if he had to, but was not saying anything.

Good enough for me. She's an expert in this stuff and can surely figure out what to do with an angry, shut-down, increasingly defiant teenager.

The evening before our family meeting with the evaluator, we finally had dinner at Olive Garden. A much-needed night out with my kids at their favorite place. We swung by the mall afterwards, and I bought Teo a new pair of basketball shoes and Rae some new clothes.

I want them to speak positively about me, and nothing works better than the bribe of cool new stuff. Plus, they'll look fresh for the meeting.

We stopped for haircuts before heading home, too, so we would all look our best for the evaluator. I had the lady braid Rae's hair so she didn't look disheveled. Homework was done without incident, and we hit the sack early so we would be well-rested for the big day.

I picked the kids up a little early from school so we could make the 3:00 p.m. meeting at the evaluator's office. When we walked in, she was ready for us.

"Hi there!" she welcomed. After introducing herself to Teo and Rae, she invited all of us into the back office. This time, there was a large white piece of paper sitting on the little table and colored pencils, markers, crayons, watercolor paints, and stickers neatly stacked in piles. "Teo, you're so tall, here's a bigger chair for you." He gave her a crooked smile, appearing to feel comfortable, the same way I had felt during that first meeting several weeks ago. "Alrighty, so here's what I'd like for you to do first. I want you to create a family picture together—a favorite family memory or vacation, or anything you wish—where everyone in the picture is doing something."

All three of us nodded as the evaluator backed out of our space so we could get started. Music started playing in the background, which helped to lighten the mood.

"How about we draw our new apartment, or us eating delicious breadsticks and our trip to the mall last night?" I suggested.

Both of them shook their heads at me, so I proposed drawing other good family memories with just the three of us and Iggy.

Rae finally spoke up. "Let's make a Christmas scene around the tree at our old house—when we all lived together and everyone was still happy."

I cringed and tried to gently dissuade her, but Teo piped in, in the critical tone inherited from his father, "Yah, Mom, let's make a picture of when everyone was still happy and being nice to each other."

I couldn't bite my tongue fast enough and the words spilled out, "I am not the one who has been unkind, Teo. Your father is the one who broke up our family—not me." I looked over and saw the evaluator writing something on her notepad, and then looked up at Teo in time to see tears welling in his eyes as he stood up and stomped out. Rae was looking down at the paper and pretending not to notice. She just kept drawing with the red crayon.

The evaluator was quickly on her feet and headed after Teo. She walked past Rae, put a gentle hand on her shoulder, and said she would be right back. Just before leaving the room, she set a box of Kleenex on the table. When my daughter looked up, I noticed she was crying, too.

What a disaster! Why can't the kids grasp the fact that their disappointment of a father is responsible for all of this pain and suffering—not me! I do everything for them and always have while their father sits back and watches. He just shows up for the fun stuff!

With the evaluator and Teo out of the room, I took Rae's hand and asked if she was okay. She looked back at me, solemn and teary-eyed. "Why can't you and Daddy just get back together? Why do we have to be here? Why can't everything just go back to normal?"

"Rae, this will all work out," I promised, stroking her hand gently. "But I need you to do something for me. When the evaluator comes back in, it's important that you tell her that you want to live with me and *not* your dad. Remember how your dad took Iggy away, and your favorite blanket, too, when he left us? Plus, you said his new apartment is creepy. And this lady has the power to make you live there and not with me if you do not speak up."

The tears stopped, and Rae looked a little scared. She nodded in agreement and looked back down at the big piece of drawing paper.

Well, at least she understood that!

After fifteen minutes or so, the evaluator returned with Teo.

"Rae, would it be okay for Mom to sit out on the comfy couch for a while, so the three of us can play a game of UNO™?"

My daughter looked up at me, seeking permission with only her eyes.

"I will be right outside the door." I kissed the top of her head, collected my purse, smiled at Teo, who seemed more at ease, and left my children with this court-appointed professional.

Please tell her all the right things, so I can win custody in court and continue taking care of you as usual— protecting and keeping you safe from your father.

I sat on the couch, sweating every minute they were behind the closed door with our evaluator. At one point, I tried to listen in but there was music playing in both rooms and a loud white noise machine whooshing away. I could not make out anything concrete, except for random laughter. At least they were having a good time.

When the three of them emerged from the back office, my children looked at peace and Teo was even smiling. Rae gave the evaluator a big hug, who then directed both of them to a treasure box of cool stuff. Each of them picked something before she finished by saying, "I'll see you guys Friday with your dad. I'm excited to see you at home, too, and to meet Iggy."

Rae had to stop at the restroom, and Teo headed right to the car. Before I followed her into the ladies' room, I saw that he was already texting someone on his phone.

"Rae, how did it go?" I asked.

"Fine," she answered matter-of-factly from behind the stall door. I didn't want her to feel pressured but was dying to know what they had talked about. The evaluator had provided me with some tips and tricks for insulating and protecting the kids through this process—one of which was not to ask questions about their conversations—but I was their mom and knew best.

Surely, asking about their session couldn't hurt anything. Besides, I need to run damage control if they didn't say all the right things I told them to.

"Baby, now is not the time to go silent. What questions did she ask you guys? Did you tell her you wanted to live with me and not Dad? Did Teo say good stuff about me? It's really important I know what was talked about."

She flushed and came out of the stall to wash her hands. "Mom, she said what we talked about with her was none of your and Dad's business. That unless we said something that would cause worry for our safety, she does not, and we do not, have to report back to you. She also said that she is not on your side or Dad's side. She said she knew that you and Dad both love us very much and that going through the divorce of your parents is a really, really hard thing for kids. She said she was on *our* team—me and Teo—and her job is to make sure that we have two comfortable homes and will always see both of our parents."

"That all sounds good, honey. What did you guys tell her?" I prodded in the most gentle and sincere voice possible.

"Mom!" She turned the faucet off, wiped her hands, and left the restroom.

As we were approaching the car, I could see my son in the front seat with his phone, smiling and laughing. At least he was in a better mood. After Rae and I got into our seats and buckled in, I started the car, and Teo connected the Bluetooth. We drove home, windows down, listening to whatever noise that my teenager was into these days.

They seemed much happier than they had in a while and scurried off when I said I was going to make dinner. A few minutes later, I could hear them, both in Teo's room, with the door closed.

It's weird that he let her in. They must be conspiring. I sauntered down the hall as quietly as possible and put my ear to the door. *They are talking about the meeting! Perfect. No music or white nose machines here at home.*

But then I heard it. They were joking and making fun of me—mocking my tone and anger towards their father. *I cannot believe this is happening! He must be brainwashing them against me!*

Just then, I lost my balance and smacked my forehead against the door. The door flung open and four intense eyeballs were staring me down.

"Um, hi guys! Just came down here to let you know dinner is almost ready." Right on cue, the smoke alarm started blaring at that awful pitch, and I looked down the hall of our little apartment to see flames on the stovetop. "Crap!" I ran down the short hallway back into the kitchen, turned off the burner, and started whacking the flames with a wet towel. Rae was yelling for Teo to "call 911," and he just stood there with that smug look on his face.

"Mom, if you keep eavesdropping on us, you are going to burn down this home, too."

Ha, very funny, son! And what exactly does that mean anyway?

"New plan. Let's go out for burgers and fries!" I said, ignoring his smug statement and all of the questions that bubbled up as a result.

We went out for dinner, and then they got ready for a weekend with their dad. The next day was Friday. I would drop them off at school in the morning, and their dad would collect them at the end of the day and take them to the evaluator's office. I would not see them again until Monday afternoon, after school, when the evaluator was due for the home visit at our place.

Hopefully that goes better than today did. It's me and Iggy for the weekend. Thank goodness for our furry beast. He always has love to give, I thought as I tucked Rae into bed and said goodnight to Teo from the doorway.

Even though things are hard with the kids right now, and Teo is usually mad at me, I sure miss the heck out of them while they are away for the weekend, I thought to myself as I finished cleaning up the fire mess in the kitchen. *Although, it is nice having a little time, too.*

I had rediscovered books and begun jogging again. I also used this newfound time to beef up my journal. I had been documenting everything—every phone call, text message, transition snafu, things the kids said, things my ex said, things I saw on Facebook posted by my mother-in-law.

My counselor worked on Saturdays, so I saw him on weekends when my kids were with their dad. He kept suggesting I had deep-seated anger to work through, patterns of passive-aggressive behavior, and that I was projecting negative feelings about Mr. Disappointment onto the children. He said it was essential I resolve those negative feelings in a productive way, so they do not become emotional burdens, and eventually scars, my children will end up having to carry.

I like seeing the counselor, but I don't always understand what he's talking about.

Monday arrived, and the apartment was spic and span for the home visit with our evaluator at 4:00 p.m. I had even given Iggy a bath, baked cookies, and put a vase of fresh flowers by the door. Luckily, Teo and Rae were both in a good mood when I picked them up from school. I asked how the weekend with their dad was and got the standard responses: "good" and "fine." They never shared about anything that happened during their dad's weekends. Actually, they never talked about him at all. Not wanting to upset them before the home visit, I left it alone.

The evaluator arrived with her usual friendly disposition. Rae gave her a quick tour of our apartment, and they ended up talking in her room. The door was open, so I could hear some of the conversation.

"That's a nice picture of your family," she said.

"Yeah, but look at these pictures. My mom cut my dad's face out of all of them." Her voice was full of anger and a hint of sadness. "My mom hates my dad now."

Gulp. *How does she even have those?* I wondered as I walked back down the hall.

Teo was in his room on his phone and invited the evaluator in for a short talk. He showed her his cool new basketball shoes and all of his basketball trophies and medals. I heard her ask if he wanted to talk about anything else and Teo answer, "No."

Iggy stayed glued to this lady the whole time, like he had known her all of his doggie years even though he usually shies away from strangers.

Weird. My kids and the dog really like this lady. I wonder how well she's getting along with my ex? I hope he has not fooled her with his ridiculous charm.

"Alright, Vanessa," she said as she walked into the living room where I was waiting impatiently. "You have a nice home here. I should be wrapping up the report

Prove He's an Idiot | 91

for Teo and Rae in the next few weeks and will be in touch." She collected some paperwork from me that she'd asked I have ready, shook my hand, gave Iggy one last pat, and waved goodbye. As I closed the door, an instant sense of relief washed over me. The process, for better or worse, was complete.

I emailed Attorney of the Year with some frequency in the following days, to see if the evaluation report was out yet. We had a trial date on the court docket just one month away, and I was hopeful we could at least get custody and parenting time settled without having a judge decide the future of our children. Finally, two weeks after the home visit, the subject line of an email from my attorney read: "Evaluation for Teo and Rae, attached." I clicked the email and immediately saw a PDF. Attorney of the Year's email message read, "Please make an appointment with my office at your earliest convenience. We need to talk about this."

I immediately picked up the phone and called the law office to schedule a meeting. Ms. I've Got All My Shit Together answered in her usual perky voice and offered a meeting at 3:00 p.m. that afternoon. Since that was pick-up time from school, I asked for an alternative. The next day at 9:30 a.m. would have to do. I spent that afternoon reading through the evaluator's report line by line, and could not believe some of the conclusions she made about me: "angry parent, hateful of children's father, demonizes father, limited insight into children's need for a healthy ongoing relationship and bond with both parents, narrow capacity to support relationship with father."

Well duh! Their father is a complete and total disappointment. What does she expect? Of course I hate that bastard for ruining our family!

I printed the report, pulled out my best highlighter pen, and got to work, making notes next to all the sentences and statements that were just plain wrong. This would help Attorney of the Year put together our case for court.

I'll seek justice for my kids from the judge and have my day in court! This report had better not cause too much of a problem for me. Some of the things in here are unbelievable and make me seem like a completely uncaring and insensitive mother to the two children who I love more than life. Who does she think raised them?

There were some conclusions about how my kids are feeling, specifically about my anger and the bad things I say about their father. I told them not to tell the evaluator these types of things and tried to run interference during the evaluation, but I guess I failed.

I can't believe they would do this to me.

I shook my head as I read through all the services and therapies and educational courses that were recommended to improve communication and parenting insights.

Who has time or money for all that?

Then I saw the line: "Father is to be involved in all areas of the children's lives. Teo and Rae are to enjoy equal parenting time between their two homes."

No way am I agreeing to that! This is a complete disaster!

I put on my running shoes and left the apartment to sweat out some of the anxious energy caused by reading the evaluation report. The statements in the report were so off-base. The next day's meeting with Attorney of the Year could not come fast enough!

Prepared with my highlighted copy of the report in hand, I sat down across the cherry wood desk promptly at 9:30 a.m.

"Have you had a chance to read the report?" she asked.

Well, yah, like fifty times!

I nodded affirmatively, and she continued. "Have you been meeting regularly with the therapist I recommended?"

I affirmed with another nod, gulping down the giant lump in my throat.

"There is a lot noted in the evaluation that will not be favorable to our position. It will be best if we try to settle this along the lines of the evaluator's recommendation." Her tone was very matter-of-fact, and her brown eyes were sad and frustrated.

I'm sure I looked like a deer in the headlights, and my mouth was hanging wide open again. Somehow, I managed to articulate the question: "That means

Teo and Rae will see their dad more than every other weekend? That's not okay! He is going to ruin them!"

Attorney of the Year leaned toward me, lowered her voice, and with the utmost kindness and respect offered, "According to the evaluation, it seems you have been doing a pretty good job of ruining them yourself, with all the anger and hatred and blame."

Immediately defensive, I opened my mouth to say something but then the true weight of my attorney's words knocked me over. Tears flooded in, and I was a blubbering mess.

This cannot be happening. How can this be happening?

The assistant from the front office appeared with a warm cup of tea and a fresh box of Kleenex. She also placed a small package of dark chocolate in front of me.

Looks like my "congratulations on your divorce gifts" have finally arrived. I pulled myself together, sipped the tea, and popped in a small piece of dark chocolate.

Attorney of the Year and I spent some time writing up a settlement proposal. She said she would finalize it and send it to Mr. Disappointment's attorney later that day. We would wait and see what their response was; we would either reach an agreement or a judge would decide.

This anger everyone thinks is such a problem for me is nothing compared to how I'm feeling right now!

I seethed all the way home and stomped into the apartment, where I spotted Teo's phone that he had forgotten on the kitchen table.

The urge to snoop overwhelmed me, and I picked it up. It was password protected, but at least he did not have facial recognition on his older version iPhone. The first two password attempts failed, and then I remember his PlayStation gamertag and entered it:

RimRocker12. Voila! I was in and went right to his text messages.

Wow, so much chatting with his father and his bestie, Ethan. His language has become raunchy. When did that happen? Teo and Ethan sure know a lot more about girls than I realized, I guess we missed the opportunity for a birds and bees talk. So many distractions—I wonder what else we missed. So much venom about me, which his father doesn't necessarily encourage but does not shut down either. He's so angry. He totally gets that from his dad!

One text communication with his father stood out amongst the sea of others.

Teo: "mom hates you dad, she says terrible things about you, like all the time, and blames you for everything. What did you do to her anyway? She says you're a 'fraud' and 'a total disappointment.'"

Dad: "sorry bud I'm trying to get more time with you and your sister, so you don't have to be around Negative Nelly so much. That must suck. I am not a perfect man, and I have made mistakes, but I'm your dad, kid, for better or worse, and I always will be. I love you."

What an ass! I am going to have to tell the kids the awful truth about all of it so they understand. I'll show them all the evidence I collected for the evaluator so they can see the things their father has done—so they understand the truth about who he really is. We are going to have a real pow-wow tonight kids, a tell-all, get-real, come-to-Jesus moment. Kid gloves are off, time to see the forest, or the tress in the forest, or look through the forest... Whatever! Time to pull back the curtain and see your father for who he really is!

When the kids sat down for dinner that night, I whipped that curtain back with full force, the suitcase at my feet and a fresh copy of the evaluation printed off for each of them. We sat around the kitchen table, and I let my children in on all of their father's dirty little secrets. Rae asked questions and cried a lot. Teo mostly defended his father, proving that their alliance was stronger than I realized. Neither of my children were hungry after the show. They both wanted to be left alone in their rooms.

I know it was a lot for them to hear, but I sure feel a lot better now that they know the "truth," I thought as I drifted off to sleep that night.

The next morning after getting the kids off to school, I fired up my computer and found an email from Attorney of the Year. It was marked "urgent."

Uh oh. My stomach sunk and my heart began to race.

The email read:

Dear Ms. Smith,

Last night around 5:00 p.m., I received the counteroffer to our settlement proposal. It was favorable, just a few small areas to work out. However this morning, I received notice from the other party that all offers are off the table, and they will see us in court. Did something happen between last night and this morning? I feel it is urgent that we meet today if possible.

Possible! Hell yes, it is possible! I will be right there! I dialed the office, spoke to the perky assistant, and was told to come right down. *On my way. Yes, ma'am!*

I threw myself together and drove just above the speed limit to my attorney's downtown office. The greeting I received was cordial, though less enthusiastic than usual, and I was escorted right to the corner office where the ace-up-my-sleeve sat, arms crossed, looking troubled.

"Ms. Smith, please sit," she offered with a wave of her hand. No warm tea or Kleenex® or dark chocolate today. "Did anything happen between you and the children's father between last night and this morning?"

How much should I tell her? How in the world could their father and his attorney possibly know about my pow-wow with the kids? The thought hit me like a ton of bricks. *Teo! He must have sent a text to his father! He must have made our conversation sound worse than it actually was.*

"Ms. Smith?" Her voice brought me back to the corner office.

"I... I think I know what might have happened." I shifted in my seat, unable to get comfortable.

"Well, could you please enlighten me?" my attorney prodded.

"I thought it was time the kids knew who their father really is, the truth of it all, so I sat them down at the kitchen table last night..." The whole ugly truth about what I had done came out, and I could tell by the expression on my attorney's face that I had really messed up big time.

"Well, Ms. Smith, being awarded legal custody and primary residence of the children is now a long shot. Your behavior will be seen as detrimental to the children, because it is. This is a real-time example of what the evaluator described in her report, effectively demonstrating the limited insight you have into Teo and Rae's emotional safety, welfare, and well-being. It's possible that your children may end up in their father's sole legal custody because of the terrible choices you have made. This is the reason I urged you to work on your anger with the therapist."

"What can I do?" I pleaded with a shaky voice, a faucet of tears already flowing.

"Get in to see your counselor as soon as possible and talk this through. Apologize to the children, shred all printed copies of the evaluation report, and secure the electronic version. Say absolutely nothing that could be interpreted as negative or bad, condescending, belittling, or hurtful about their father. You are to 'zip it' when it comes to discussing anything with Teo and Rae that has to do with their father. Off limits. Bite your tongue until you taste blood if necessary."

I nodded to let her know that I understood, holding back the tears.

There was nothing to do but wait for a judge to hear our case and make a decision about the most important two people in my life—my beautiful babies.

Teo and Rae's futures are now in the hands of a stranger—a judge who has the power to decide. I can't believe this is happening.

As I slumped out of the attorney's office, guilty heat flushed my skin from head to toe. But by the time I made it back to the car, the anger had bubbled back up to the surface, and I was fuming again.

If he wants a fight, I am going to give him one.

Many months had passed since Mr. Disappointment left me, the kids, and our home. Months of high conflict, change, compound losses, upset, attorneys, moving from our family home, and what was sure to be bankruptcy with the additional cost of this trial.

I entered the courthouse in my best clothes, Attorney of the Year by my side. She had one neatly packed rolling bag, and I had brought all of the three ring binders along, Rae's too-small pants, and the heavily soiled socks. Unfortunately, Teo had taken back his favorite shoe with the hole. On the way to the courtroom, we passed the evaluator sitting in the hallway. She waved hello.

We didn't subpoena her. So, the other side must have? That cannot be good.

My ex was already sitting at the courtroom table with his attorney, Bulldog, whose name was fitting insomuch as I understood. I also noticed my mother-in-law sitting in the back of the courtroom. She glared at me and snickered something under her breath as we passed by.

I didn't think to bring anyone along. I'm not sure who would have come anyway. No one has really been supportive through this. In my hour of need, they abandoned me.

After a few minutes, a clerk in front of the judge's bench authoritatively instructed: "All rise." My attorney nudged me, and I followed her lead.

The judge entered the courtroom and recited our family name, the case number, and made record of who was in attendance. What followed were some of the worst hours of my life.

I was called to the stand to testify, where my ex's attorney was aggressive and downright mean to me. He didn't speak a lick of the truth, and I ended up looking incompetent. The evaluator went next and spent quite a bit of time answering questions from both attorneys and the judge. She beamed with positive accolades when speaking about Teo and Rae, and then used a much more serious and critical tone when describing her concerns about me and Luke.

We took a break for lunch and then were right back at it. My ex testified last. He should have been an actor with his Oscar-worthy performance. By 4:30 p.m., I hardly knew my own name. This had been the most stressful, exhausting, and expensive day of my life. It was surreal to be there, doing battle with the man I'd slept next to half of my life.

After Mr. Disappointment left the stand, the judge asked if there were any additional witnesses. There were none. He heard closing arguments from our lawyers, and I was grateful for Attorney of the Year's eloquent summation of our family and the primary role I'd always had with Teo and Rae. Bulldog lived up to his name—he was scrappy, accusatory, and nasty-toned in his conclusions about me. He made my ex sound like the saint he definitely is not.

I had no idea what the judge was going to do—what choices he would make for my children based on all the evidence presented. The lump sum of my twenty-year marriage had been laid out by two attorneys who had played the day like a game of chess, one methodical move after another, strike and counterstrike. My children's lives had been filleted open in this court of law, before a man who has never met them but was charged with deciding their future.

When closing arguments were finished, the judge leaned back in his chair, crossed his arms over his round belly, took a deep breath, and looked somewhat distressed. Silently, he removed his glasses, rubbed his eyes, put the glasses back on, and then sat forward and made eye contact—first with me and then with Mr. Disappointment, sitting to my right. Tension in the air was palpable.

"I have been sitting on this bench the last twenty-three years, listening to disputes and gripes between divorcing parents about the very children each of them says they are here in this courtroom to protect. Reality is, folks, being here and fighting with each other, tearing each other down, does not offer any amount of protection to your children.

"I have not heard one shred of evidence today that convinces me either of you is a physical threat to your children's well-being. Both of you have made some terrible choices. Your choice," he said, looking directly at me, "in divulging the ugly marital history to these children was inconceivably foolish, ill-advised, and most importantly hurtful to Teo and Rae. While I am relatively certain both of you will meet their basic daily needs, I do not feel confident in mother's capacity to nurture their emotional health or support an ongoing relationship with their father. I am ordering that Teo and Rae be enrolled in counseling within thirty days, so they have assistance going forward—someone who can help them adjust and learn to cope with the flaws in this family system. A professional will be assigned to the children to help mitigate the inevitable harm that the bickering between the two of you has caused and will continue to cause unless you both intentionally work to change the thinking, behavior, and conduct that has landed your family here today."

He took a deep breath and let out a huge sigh before continuing with his decision. "Your anger towards the children's father, Ms. Smith, is harmful and hurts the children. Repeat exposure to conflict and anger harms children."

He paused another few moments, as if trying to find the right words. "I believe that both of you, mother and father, would jump in front of a bus for your children. Am I right?"

He stared both of us down. We both nodded in agreement.

"You love them so much that it would not even be a second thought to jump right out in front of a moving bus. Hear me now when I tell you that *you are the bus.* Mr. and Ms. Smith. You are the biggest threat to your children. The conflict between you harms them more than anything else. The acts of bitterness and name-calling, finger-pointing, blaming, blame-shifting, and gaslighting are ruining your children. I cannot stop you from doing those things. Only you have the authority to choose differently. Only you can protect Teo and Rae, through the myriad of daily choices you make about your own behavior, especially your behavior and attitudes towards one another."

My stomach turned. That was it. The scolding was finished. He listed off the court's findings and his ruling came next: "The evaluator provided a roadmap for educational and reparative services that mother and father are hereby ordered to participate in, including individual therapy, a high-conflict parenting course, co-parent training, and use of the online communication platform for high-conflict families, *Our Family Wizard*…"

It was somewhere around then that I checked out, until I heard the judge say that we were to share parenting time equally and Mr. Disappointment was granted major decision-making authority—"legal custody" of my children!

Apparently, the judge viewed the children's father as the more emotionally stable parent, who was best able to foster a positive relationship between the children and me than I was in the reverse. He completely missed all the reasons I am so angry.

The judge continued, looking straight at me, "Ms. Smith, I am deeply concerned about your anger and hatred for the children's father. Referring to him as 'Mr. Disappointment' or 'my ex' is hurtful to your children. And they are *not your* children, not possessions at all. I hope you will do the work before you for the sake of your children. They need you to do the work."

This was not the way I had envisioned my big day in court. This did not feel like justice at all, but nonetheless it was a legal and binding court order, our dissolution judgment, and the final say about how we were to move forward with our children and the new structure of our lives.

Below are two choices Vanessa can make at this point.

Follow the judge's orders.
Turn to page 106 to find out what happens when Vanessa makes this choice.

Fight for my children.
Turn to page 110 to find out what happens when Vanessa makes this choice.

🌀 Two Years after Vanessa Followed the Judge's Orders

"Did she give you her birthday wish list?" Luke asked me as we walked toward our cars, parked next to one another in the back of the dark school lot. We had just finished Rae's sixth-grade parent teacher conferences and were walking out into the cool evening air, fallen leaves crisp and crunching beneath our feet.

It had been about twenty-four months—two whole life cycles through the calendar year—since our dissolution judgment was final, and things were beginning to feel "normal" again. Teo was driving, and Rae was off to middle school. Time was moving fast, and we knew their childhoods were fleeting, so we were both working hard to establish new traditions and make positive memories during the time they spent with each of us.

Luke was less of an asshat, and somewhere along the way, I started to feel comfortable around him again. We even sat together at Teo's basketball games and Rae's choir concerts and dance recitals. I had done what the judge said, and what Attorney of the Year had instructed from the start: I resolved my anger. The less angry I became, and the more negativity I let go, the happier *our* kids were. I could see it in everything they did. They were thriving at school, in their relationships, and with their activities. They loved their dad, and they loved me. We gave them permission to love and be loved by everyone, including both of their opinionated grandmothers. Iggy even traveled with the kids between their two homes. It was not the life I signed up for when Luke and I got married, but it was turning out alright—this season of calm that followed the storm.

"Yep!" I couldn't help but chuckle out loud as I remembered reading Rae's birthday wish list earlier that morning.

"LEGOs are easy enough," he started. "I'll get her the big set she asked for—you think she's ready to build the entire Death Star?"

"Oh yeah, she can handle it. I'll get the few items of clothes and fancy high heels she wants," I said, glancing over to see Luke's eyebrows pull together in concern. "Don't worry, overprotective Daddy, they're not that high."

As we stopped short of our cars, Luke touched my shoulder before asking me the question I knew inspired this conversation. "She wants a family birthday party, with both of us, her big brother, and her grandmothers—my mother and yours. Lord help us, do you think our mothers are ready?"

Both of Luke's strong hands dropped to his hips as he tilted his head back and looked up at the starry sky, obviously stressed by the idea of both our mothers in the same room together. I grinned while remembering Rae's #1 wish that she had written in bubble letters, and colored bright pink with glitter sprinkled over the top for full effect. I was sure it had made both of us choke back a wave of anxiety:

#1: A FAMILY BIRTHDAY PARTY – EVERYONE I LOVE INVITED, LOVING ME UP GOOD THE WAY A GIRL SHOULD BE LOVED ON HER 12TH BIRTHDAY.

Luke turned his gaze from the sky toward me with something other than anxiety. "That kid—she's really something. Smarter than any of us. Our girl is well on her way to ruling the world, if that's what she wants." I saw pride beaming in his eyes.

This man standing in front of me is the one I fell in love with—compassionate and caring.

"Yes," I agreed. "And I'm sure that she will handle her grandmothers' behavior with all of that cleverness and grace."

"You're right. I'm sure it will be fine. Good night, Vanessa." He gave me a little wave and a genuine smile and got into his car.

Driving home, I thought about how far I had come. I absolutely hated this man just two years ago, but today, I knew the truth: I still loved Luke, but not in a wife-loving-her-husband kind of way. I loved him as the father of our children, a co-parent, sharing the very most important work of our lifetimes—raising Teo and Rae to be good and happy human beings. For them, I knew Luke and I could do absolutely anything, even manage our difficult mothers so Rae can enjoy the best family birthday party ever.

Teo had really come around, too, and would appreciate this family-focused time. He'd told me recently that he was "proud" of us—his dad and me— for finally sitting together at basketball games and being kind to each other. We had all learned through our counseling that being nice was a subjective term; but kindness and respect, these were the standards which our family agreed to value and uphold. Teo was tearing up the floor on his high school basketball team, had amazing friends, and was getting decent grades. Our son was growing into a wonderful young man, and benefitted from spending the amount of time he had with his dad and with me. He had his daddy's good looks and the sweetest girlfriend who he planned on taking to the winter formal.

It took time and lots of hard work, on both of our parts, and skilled professionals who earned every cent we paid them to educate us about healing our family: Teo and Rae were worth it. Our children were worth every effort it took to think, behave, and act in the new ways that have become second nature for us now—two years past the divorce.

I know things could have turned out so differently, based solely on our choices. Looking back, I am now grateful for the evaluator, her recommendations, the judge's order to engage in services, and the road map it all provided to get here. Our son is thriving, and our baby girl is about to turn twelve and wants all of us there to celebrate her birthday. My heart is full, our kids are happy, and I'm really looking forward to the next chapter.

☸ Two Years after Vanessa ☸ Disregarded the Judge's Orders

"Can you believe that teacher?" Luke asked me as we walked towards our cars parked in dark school lot. We had just finished Rae's sixth grade parent teacher conferences, and were walking out into the cool evening air, fallen leaves crisp beneath our feet. It was the first time we had attended conferences together in years, and it was awful. Middle school did not permit separate times, like elementary school had always accommodated.

It was about twenty-four months—two whole life cycles through the calendar year since our judgment. Attorney of the Year had passed me off to an appellate attorney when I insisted on appealing the judge's decision. I had fought tooth and nail for my children for two years—all to no avail. The appellate court affirmed the lower court's decision.

Things had continued to be tumultuous between Luke and me, even worse I think, since he had been granted custody and wielded it over me like a weapon. After everything we had been through, we had agreed we did not have the time or money to participate in those court-ordered services the judge had prescribed, and our kids appeared to be having some problems.

Teo had gotten criminal charges brought against him after the last fight at school. When he was arrested, the cops found weed in his pocket, and now he has a juvenile counselor and community service hours. He was unable to get his driver's license as a result of his delinquency. And Rae was off to middle school and apparently failing all of her classes, according to the teachers we had just met. She was terribly thin and often refused to eat. I wanted to get her in with the doctor, but with Luke having legal custody, I am not supposed to be the parent who schedules medical appointments for our children.

I was really worried about her—about both of them.

Time was moving fast, and I knew their childhoods were fleeting and their futures were not looking so bright. I was thinking of filing a modification in court to try and win back legal custody from their father, but that was expensive and I was broke.

Teo had stopped playing sports in favor of video games and smoking weed. He had a whole new crowd of friends in high school and could not pass a class to save his life. *Maybe if he actually attended class...* At this rate, he was headed to be a dropout. Rae had become the class clown and was totally boy crazy. I'd caught her by the pool several times, making out with different boys. Her dad pays no attention when she is at his house. He totally favors Teo, and Rae just stays in her private space at both our houses.

When I wasn't worrying about the kids, I was mad as hell—at the kids, at Luke, at his mother, at my mother. The kids moved between houses when we told them to, like robots. They had stopped complaining about the transitions, but I knew they despised it. Rae has snuck out through her bedroom window a couple of times, and Teo prefers his friends' couches to either of our places. Iggy had to be re-homed because I just didn't have the money to take care of him anymore. One more thing Rae hated me for. She told me that I have ruined her life and that she wanted to emancipate from the family.

"Yah, she's a real peach," I responded to Luke, "saying Rae has problems. The only problem our daughter has is spending so much time with *you*. The kids were just fine until you up and left. You destroyed all of our lives, Luke. You're such a selfish asshole."

Luke responded in the same annoyed tone as usual, "Whatever Vanessa, it's all my fault, right? Nothing's ever good enough—never will be with you."

I was not in the mood for button-pushing. The natural impulsiveness that I used to keep at bay was now less controlled, and I shoved him with all my might. He stumbled but outweighed me by fifty pounds and was completely fine.

A shit-eatin' grin instantly emerged, putting me on-guard. Of course, he had his phone in hand and was video recording—something he told me a while back that his attorney had advised whenever he was alone with me. I watched as he dialed 911 and listened to the

BS story that he told dispatch so that police cars came screaming into the school lot as other parents looked on. We had gotten to be on a first name basis with most of the local police force over the past years, as they responded to our "domestic disputes" with regularity and had more recently become familiar with Teo and Rae, too. Luke showed them the video of me shoving him just a few minutes ago. The officers gave us another stern talking to, instructed Luke and me to part ways immediately, and go home.

As I drove home, not knowing if the kids would be there or not, the tears started flowing. I wondered how life had gotten so off-course, why my kids seemed to be self-destructing, and if there was any hope for us.

Suddenly, words from the evaluator's report rang in my ears:

We know that children exposed to ongoing conflict, negative information about the other parent and unstable home lives, *always* have long-term emotional problems. Children who are exposed to ongoing parental conflict *will* have adjustment problems in their preadolescent and teen years that most commonly manifest in extreme defiance and anger, delinquent behavior, substance abuse, teen pregnancy, eating disorders, suicide attempts, failing grades, and high dropout rates at school. It is one of the only certainties in the professional literature and surely not the legacy these parents wish for Teo and Rae.

Could this really be Teo and Rae's fate? Have their father and I sentenced them to these kind of unhappy lives with our poor choices and all the ongoing anger between us? I wish there was a do-over—a mulligan—for my kids. I know there is not a reset button, but maybe, just maybe, their father and I can choose better, and we can still turn things around.

"Numbing the pain for a while will make it worse when you finally feel it."

~*Albus Dumbledore*~

GET HAPPY AGAIN

Rediscover myself and create a new, improved version of me. If I'm happy, my kids will be happy.

REFILLING MY WINE glass, I had reached a decision—a clear choice about the best way to move forward. It was time to stop letting my ex control my feelings and start enjoying life again.

I need to plan my time wisely and lean on the people I have in my life. My tribe will understand and support me. Juls, my best friend gets it, even though her husband, Mike, is still besties with Mr. Disappointment. I'm sure he'll take my side once he hears the truth—the "real" story. Thank heavens for Juls and our BFF, Margarita Mondays.

I pulled out my calendar and picked up the pencil Rae had left on the table.

Tuesdays, I could go out with Sally from the gym. She has firsthand experience with the same evaluator and has been through this with her own kids.

Taking another sip of vino, my belly starting to warm, I moved on to the next day of the week.

Wednesdays, I could hit up the girls from work! My new job at the coffee shop has some perks over being a SAHM (stay-at-home mom). Most of the coffee shop girls are young and single. I'll help them make sure they do not settle for a Mr. Disappointment of their own.

I smiled, proud of myself for saving others from this type of pain.

Thursdays, the sitter is not available, so I'll dedicate this night to Teo and Rae while also capturing years of old emails and text messages to print for the evaluator.

I shook my head, momentarily wondering what I ever saw in Mr. Disappointment.

Hello, weekend! I'm not missing an opportunity to meet Mr. Right. I deserve to be happy, and my kids need a mom who is happy. So, I'll take this little bit of Me Time to rediscover who I am without a husband.

It had been many months since that little twerp had served this divorce lawsuit on the front stoop of our old house, and the day of my first evaluation meeting had finally arrived. I was ready for all of this to be over so I could just move on. Attorney of the Year said the evaluation would help get this divorce finalized, which I am all for—an end to this feeling of being in limbo.

It was a Tuesday morning, and I woke up thinking that maybe Juls and I should not have stayed out so late, even though I *was* nervous about the first evaluation meeting and needed to blow off some steam. I pulled my numb body and pounding head upright and sat on the edge of my bed. For a moment, I admired the gorgeous man still sleeping there.

Maybe I shouldn't have brought this guy home either. Yet, Mr. Disappointment would lose his mind to see this Adonis laying where he used to sleep.

I had started to enjoy myself again the way I had with Mr. Disappointment early on in our relationship, back when things were simple, and he was cool. After the kids were born, I had taken my parenting responsibilities seriously and stopped going out altogether. Luke never quite got there. In fact, he was like having kid number three around the house. These last few months of letting go (of him, such big responsibilities, and the constant pressures of parenthood) have made me feel totally alive again—dancing, socializing with a younger crowd, and looking for my soulmate.

Well, if not my soulmate, at least a really good time. I glanced at Adonis once again, remembering our midnight delight.

I smiled and then wrestled last night's hunk out of my bed before the sun came up so I could get the kids off to school without them knowing a man, not their daddy, had spent the night at our apartment—again. We said goodbye with a quick smooch before I'd sent him out the bathroom window so the neighbors wouldn't notice him leaving my place at 5:00 a.m. Then I crawled back into bed for another hour. Unfortunately, I was still drained when I got up to shower, dress, and wake the kids to begin our new morning routine. With our new and improved schedule, they are ready fast and eat a quick breakfast in the car.

I'm sort of a genius with figuring things out. I should probably start my own Amazing Mommy podcast. My kids are smart and have always gotten good grades. They're probably happier without me helicoptering around all the time. They need their space now, and seem to enjoy more independence without me in their business all the time. Neither one has asked for help with schoolwork in months.

"Bye, kids. Have a great day!" I chirped as they both slammed their doors and walked toward their friends.

Kids dropped off at school, check.

Shower, check, check.

Attempt to look my best, check, check, check.

Giant glass of water, guzzle, and repeat.

On time for 10:00 a.m. evaluation meeting, che—or, wait, was it scheduled for 9:00 a.m.?!?

Quickly, I scanned through the deleted emails on my iPhone, looking for the evaluator's appointment confirmation notice. A wave of relief struck when I saw I was on schedule.

Phew. I hopped back into the car empty-handed. *Bummer that I couldn't find those emails and text messages I printed off. It's like they just up and walked away.*

I stopped for coffee, pulled into the parking lot of the evaluator's office, parked my car, and then checked my appearance in the visor mirror. Nothing a quick swipe of lip-gloss, spritz of perfume, and breath mint couldn't fix.

Hopefully, the evaluator can see that I have been the sole responsible parent who has managed every meaningful aspect of Teo and Rae's lives and that Mr. Disappointment has been missing in action.

I opened the door to the evaluator's office. *Nice place*, I thought until the scent of an earthy candle immediately turned my stomach. Hastily, I asked the lady sitting at the front desk where the bathroom was. Before she finished answering, I headed in the direction her finger was pointed and hustled down the corridor near the speed of LeBron James sprinting down the basketball court. I flung the door open, burst into the nearest stall, and dropped to my knees in front of the toilet. After emptying the contents of Margarita Monday from my stomach, I felt much better.

Glad I chose strawberry last night. Still smells fruity, unlike the time the kids got the flu at midnight and launched their spaghetti dinner everywhere. What a terrible, stinky mess that was.

Still kneeling in front of the toilet I chuckled, as only a mother could, remembering how disgusting it was to pick noodles out from between my toes after stepping in spaghetti barf puddles while chasing the kids on their way to the bathroom of our old house.

Only a truly dedicated and amazing mom could look back and laugh at that dreadful memory.

With Teo and Rae at the forefront of my mind, I cleaned myself up and returned to the front desk, signed a disclosure form, secured a copy for my own records, and paid my portion of the professional fee. I accepted a glass of cold water the nice lady had offered me. And with that, the cheerful, sales-rack-dressed evaluator emerged from the back office and introduced herself with a firm handshake. She had kind eyes, a warm smile, and what looked to be Pop-Tarts® crumbs on her shirt.

While introducing myself to this woman, I kept a fair distance. *Hopefully, this wad of gum is enough to cover any lingering odor.*

After releasing my hand, the evaluator led me into our meeting space. It felt inviting and was flooded with soft light, which my tired eyes appreciated. There were two comfortable chairs along with her standup desk and a treadmill.

Awesomeness. This is way less intimidating than I expected. It smelled like home, and I quickly felt safe. There was an area to my right set up for kids with toys, art, books, LEGOs, chalk, magnets, and even a little table just Rae's size.

The kids will not mind coming here. Is Rae still into LEGOs? I've not noticed any new creations around the house lately.

We took our places in the overstuffed chairs and the evaluator apologized for her casual dress, explaining that she had been volunteering in her daughter's classroom that morning. She spotted the crumbs on her shirt and lightly brushed them off with a quiet giggle. Suddenly, a vivid memory of snack time at my kids' pre-schools flashed in my mind, immediately causing tears to well up out of nowhere. The evaluator pointed to the tissue box next to my chair.

"Don't worry. Plenty of tears are left in this office, Vanessa." When I had dabbed my eyes dry, she continued, "Most parents are a bit nervous meeting me for the first time, although usually they feel much better by the end of our two hours together. I know it has probably been a long road leading up to today, and you're likely emotionally and financially exhausted. Add to that the constant worry about your children, and a parent can really start to feel like they have been swept down the proverbial rabbit hole.

"Good news is that this evaluation is an opportunity to step back from the adversarial high conflict that litigation often creates between two parents, as we fully explore and concentrate on the needs of your children. We'll be discussing the strengths of each parent and both parents' concerns, and then put our big brains together to design the best plan for Teo and Rae." Her body language was relaxed and poised. With raised eyebrows, head tilted slightly to the right, she made eye contact, clearly looking for my buy-in to this process that the court had ordered my family participate in.

That sounds reasonable. My big brain and your big brain, working in tandem, for the benefit of my kids.

I replied, "Okay," while nodding my agreement.

Then she kept talking about working *together* as a "team"—her, me, and Mr. Disappointment. "I have never met a parent who didn't love their child. Mothers and fathers come to this process, both wanting what they believe is in their child's best interest. They both want their children to win the game but are working from different playbooks. My hope is to bring you and the children's father 80% of the way toward the middle, and then provide enough guidance and direction that the two of you can finish off the last 20% by infusing the final plan for your children with specific details to meet the unique needs of your family.

"When both parents are invested in the final plan, and both parents feel heard and that they had a say in what's best for the children, the plan is far more likely to work versus a legal and binding judgment imposed on your family by the court. Make sense?" Again, she paused and waited to make sure I understood.

I nodded in agreement to be polite while really feeling a bit confused. I was in a custody battle with my ex. Wasn't he supposed to be enemy #1?

After fifteen minutes of listening to the evaluator prattle on about kids needing both parents and this process focusing on reaching a mutual agreement while avoiding a courtroom trial, I wished I had at least taken time to visit her webpage or prepared a timeline or maybe just told my BFF Juls that I needed to stay home last night.

My head is pounding, was all I could think as I mostly just nodded and tried to choke back the tears that kept threatening to explode from my eyeballs.

"Vanessa, the goal of our time today is for you to educate me about the story of your family. How you got from point A (meeting the children's father) to point B (a custody litigant). Only a small percentage of divorcing parents ever participate in an evaluation. I'm curious to learn all about why your family is here and begin to understand ways in which I can best assist your children and family moving forward."

She paused before giving me further instruction. "It would be helpful if you could go down memory lane. Relay information in chronological order—paint a picture of the most significant events in your family's timeline. Throughout the story, please highlight the most important details of your children's lives (residential moves, school/academics, friendships, important relationships, activities/sports/music, health, religion, special needs, services, successes, areas where they struggle and excel, etc.)."

She paused *again* for emphasis.

"In addition to learning as much as possible about your children's lives, it is necessary that we identify and understand patterns of conflict between you and the other parent. Patterns of conflict are important to uncover because embedded within them are often your parenting concerns; and unless we make an effort to understand and mitigate the unhealthy patterns of conflict that exist now, those unhealthy patterns will perseverate, harm your children, and continue to cause trouble for your family after the divorce. Exposure to conflict is detrimental to Teo and Rae and will inflict irreparable psychological harm over time." She repositioned a little straighter in her chair and picked up a notepad and pencil. With that, she gestured to me, as if offering me the floor to start talking.

I uncrossed my legs, reached over to the side table, took a big draw from my water glass, and started bawling. Ugly, uncontrollable bawling!

"I'm so sorry..." I choked through the tears as the sip of water gurgled down my throat.

"It's okay. Do you want to step out and get a breath of fresh air?"

I nodded and left the office. Wasting no time, I headed back to the bathroom and promptly fished a prescription medication bottle out from the bottom of my purse.

This will help settle my nerves.

I took two anxiety pills for good measure and waited about ten minutes for them to kick in. With pharmaceutically-enhanced courage, I returned to the office and pieced together my story for the nice lady who was going to help me keep my kids.

By the end of our two hours, I was feeling pretty good, but the evaluator looked a little frayed. She had hardly spoken a word since I'd returned from the bathroom and jumped right into the story of the shit-show our family had become, all because of Mr. Disappointment.

Seeing her expression, I hoped I hadn't shared too much. After telling her about Mr. Disappointment's many affairs, I didn't want her to think I could not hold my own in the dating scene, so I had also elaborated on the ongoing search for my soulmate, and the hunk that I was currently seeing.

Geez, did I actually say out loud that he could be a terrific new dad for the kids? He does seem to have so much more to offer than Mr. Disappointment. I'm glad I said it. When the evaluator talks to my ex about all of this stuff, he'll be so upset that I plan to replace him with a new and improved model. Plus, a stable relationship will probably look best for court.

"Vanessa, thank you for sharing your story with me. We will plan to meet again next week after I have talked with Teo and Rae's father. I'll send you an email with some possible dates and times." She stood up, commented on the warm sun shining outside her large bay of windows, and politely walked me to the door.

"Great. Next time, I would like to meet on a Friday, if that's possible?" I asked.

Thursdays are my quiet nights at home with the kids, so a Friday meeting ought to go a little better.

"Okay, we'll find a good time next Friday. I'll be in touch," she said.

I grabbed my purse and got the heck out of there.

I'm so tired of this divorce! I complained to myself as I walked to my car. *That could have gone better, but it probably doesn't matter that much. There is no way Mr. Disappointment is getting the kids over a stay-at-home mom. This should be a slam-dunk.*

I phoned Attorney of the Year from the parking lot, as I had been instructed. After summarizing the meeting, we scheduled a meeting of our own for the next day, at her office to discuss possible ways of fixing the mess Attorney of the Year insisted I had just made.

"Wait right where you are and an Uber will arrive in a few minutes to take you home," was her firm declaration before she hung up.

She's always overreacting.

While I waited for the Uber, I wondered what the evaluator thought of me.

I'm sure it wasn't nearly as bad as Attorney of the Year thinks. The evaluator doesn't know that I've been using a little alcohol and a few anxiety pills to deal with the stress of this divorce. I mean, I can't be a blubbering mess or a raging monster when my kids are around.

Just then, the Uber pulled up.

Oh, look, it's Marvin, our Uber driver from last night. Ha! What a coincidence!

"Over here, Marvin," I waved enthusiastically. As I got into the SUV, I glanced up at the bay of office windows facing the parking lot and saw the evaluator staring down at me. She waved with a friendly smile, and I told Marvin to floor it.

She doesn't know that I drove here, does she? I mean, maybe I can just say my car wouldn't start if it ever comes up.

Marvin and I had a casual chat on the drive back to my place. He claimed to be happily married and kept a picture of his three children proudly displayed on the dash. I shared about the awful evaluation appointment I'd just endured, and he was a good listener. When my rant was finished and we had pulled into the apartment complex, Marvin took the liberty of reminding me that even though Mr. Disappointment sounded like a total loser, my kids surely love him and need their dad, too, regardless of his unsavory behavior.

Whatever, Traitor! I got out in a huff and gave Marvin a dismissive wave before I walked into my little apartment two full hours before I had to pick up the kids from school.

This place is a mess! I shook my head as the evaluator's speech floated through my head. *She said that at some point, she would be making a home visit, so I suppose I should get started straightening this place up. But first...*

The anxiety pill from earlier was starting to wear off, so I grabbed one more pill out of my purse. After swallowing it down with a swig of soda, not the beer I had started reaching for (*see, I have some self-control!*), I cranked up some music and got to work. First, I poured bleach into the toilets and then the sinks, and filled those with warm water.

Man, how I used to love that smell every Saturday morning when I cleaned the family home. Nothing was better than a clean house and fresh pancakes to start the weekend.

My heart clenched a moment, but the medication kicked in, and I turned my attention to searching for the vacuum, which I found buried under the winter coats in the hall closet. Turning it on, I started working my way around the apartment.

When I opened the door to Teo's room, a wave of gym stink almost knocked me over. I quickly picked up the food wrappers and the dirty laundry that was scattered all around, opened the window, sprayed some musk body cologne that was sitting on his dresser, and called it good.

Now, for Rae's room.

When I opened her bedroom door, an appreciative smile stretched across my face. Rae's room was much tidier than her brother's and the rest of the house. It smelled good, too. She had lots of stuff, but liked everything to be organized. Her clothes were sorted by color in her closet, and her books were placed on the shelf in alphabetical order. She loved art and had her slime-making supplies stacked on her desk next to pictures of her besties. A picture of our family—all four of us and Iggy—had been placed inside a homemade frame Rae had made at camp one summer and hung above her bed.

I paused and remembered the day it was taken.

It wasn't that long ago, but the kids looked so much younger and happier. Me and Mr. Disappointment even seemed to be in love. We had some good times together, for sure.

My eyes trailed down to the little bedside table and Rae's fuzzy, flip-sequence diary.

I shouldn't. I knew it was wrong to look. *Well, it won't hurt anything.* I cracked open the diary to the first entry...

Dear Diary, this is Rae. My dad left the house for good and he took my dog Iggy. I hate him for taking Iggy. Iggy needs me and I need him.

He is my best friend and I have no idea where he is now or if my dad will bring him back. I hate my dad for leaving but I miss him too. Why is he doing this to our family? He stole my favorite blanket!!!! I told my mom about the blanket and she said she told him not to, but he did anyway, and he is a total disappointment. That same stupid word she uses with me and Teo sometimes when we make a mistake. God I hate that stupid word. And now my mom hates my dad, too, which makes me hate her. She calls him 'my ex.' I'm not sure if that means he's my 'ex dad' too?

I hope he is not mad at me. I hope this is not my fault. I hope he didn't leave because I messed up last week and got a C on my math test. Mom helped me study for it because dad had to work late. Dad is better at math even though mom thinks she knows everything about everything. Or maybe dad left because Teo didn't make the A team for basketball this season. We are not perfect kids. I suppose we could have tried harder. Maybe if me and Teo were better at stuff, our parents wouldn't have fought so much and dad would still be here, with Iggy, and with us.

Oh no, baby, it's not your fault. It's his fault—your lying, cheating SOB father! He is the Disappointment, not you and your brother.

My eyes wet with tears, I quickly flipped through the diary pages. Rae had made consistent entries. Sometimes, there were days or weeks in between, but there were fairly consistent entries made since Luke had left us.

> Dear Diary, this is Rae. My dad is still gone and Issy too. My mom is a total stress case and had to get a job. She's gone a lot of nights now, working I guess. The sitter is nice, and I like that there is no more fighting in the house between my parents. Mom finally told us that her and dad are getting a divorce, duh! She thinks me and Teo are idiots. Grandma told us our parents were getting a divorce a long time ago, that my dad had smartened up and was going to finally divorce mom. Mom hates grandma now, too. And I don't think grandma likes mom much either, or ever really has.

I can't believe his mother is talking to my kids behind my back!

> Dear Diary, this is Rae. We have to move from our house because of my stupid parents divorce. None of this is fair. My life is ruined!

My heart nearly stopped in my chest. *It's your father's fault we had to move, baby girl. I tried to keep the house and am doing my very best for you and your brother. It's not like I enjoy working at the coffee shop, but your father won't give me a dime!*

Dear Diary, this is Rae. We moved to a little apartment with mom, but I still have my own room. I'm in here right now. It's not too terrible. I saw some cute boys down by the pool. There's a pool and a playground. My dad lives downtown now, in the city, in a haunted house, it is weird. We go there on the weekends. Iggy is finally home with me!!!!!!!!!!!!!! He says woof woof.

Cute boys?! Girl, slow down. We better have the birds and the bees talk real soon. I wonder where Teo is with all that stuff?

Dear Diary, this is Rae. Mom has been "sneaking" guys into the apartment and thinks me and Teo don't know LOL. Sometimes I sit outside her bedroom door in the middle of the night and listen to whatever it is they are doing in there. I am not so sure I ever want to get a boyfriend because I've heard mom making all kinds of weird noises behind her locked bedroom door. Teo caught me spying, said mom was fine, and told me to go back to bed.

Obviously, Teo is familiar with the birds and the bees.

Teo told me today that he was up really early to use the bathroom and he found the window wide open, and the screen off. There was a man size, flip-flop shoe floating in the toilet, right under the open window, and he saw some one-shoed guy running away from the apartment. My brother did not seem too concerned, but now I think someone is going to break into the apartment, or maybe already has! I told mom we need a security system but she says we cannot afford one because this divorce is costing her a fortune. She is always complaining about not having any money but she goes out and leaves us home with a babysitter, or with grandma. Grandma told us she is not always at work. Grandma is the only one who cleans up around here besides me. Mom cannot find anything she's looking for and then blames us. She used to be a neat freak like me, but not anymore. Our apartment is disgusting, I never have friends over because it's so embarrassing.

Oh shit! I'll need to be far more discreet. Maybe the babysitter can just stay overnight with the kids and I can go elsewhere. I could get home before school.

Dear Diary, this is Rae. My Aunt Juls and Uncle Mike are taking sides. Everyone is talking about my parents divorce all the time. Everywhere I go. At school my mom's friend Sally's kids are a total nightmare. Sally has three kids. They are obnoxious and the little one keeps sitting by me in the lunchroom, like she wants to be besties or something. No thanks! She told me they went to see the same evaluator lady that me and Teo have to go and see. She said the lady was nice, but I ain't buying it.

Taking sides? I bet Mike and Mr. Disappointment are downing their brewskies and shooting the shit in front of the kids. I'll have Attorney of the Year write his attorney a letter about that, and I'll ask Sally to tell her kids to lay off mine at school.

Dear Diary, this is Rae. I'm pretty sure my mom has lost her mind. Sometimes she is super happy, other times she just sits around crying, and some days she is totally out of her mind crazy. She never plays with us anymore at all and didn't even notice the new huge LEGO set I built. And I keep getting in trouble for being late to school. I think it's like 24 times now this year. My mom never wakes up on time and she keeps running into the mascot sign outside my school with our car, which is all crashed up now. At least no one sees her run into stuff at school because we are always late! She is so embarrassing. The days we get there on time, she yells and honks her horn and even gives other moms the finger. What's wrong with her? The teacher says its "disruptive" to the whole class when I'm late, like it's my fault. Mom won't get up in the morning and she even makes us wear our school clothes to bed now, so we can hustle right out the door. She make us eat Poptarts every morning, it's so gross. She never cooks dinner anymore since dad left. Mom used to volunteer in my classroom and go on field trips but says she does not have time now. She has plenty of time to go out at night, every night! She spends time with everyone but us. Teo is really pissed (sorry I know that's a bad word but it's what my brother is, pissed!)

I had to look up from the diary for a moment. I couldn't believe what I was reading.

I know that I am not in the running for Mother of the Year right now, but...

And then, I turned to the final page she had written, just the night before. My heart pounded as I read her words and felt my little girl's pain oozing off the page.

Dear Diary this is Rae. I think my parents are aliens or aliens came and took my real parents away and left these different versions of them. I miss the old ones. No one is paying attention to me and my stupid brother, although he has been amazingly less stupid lately. Our house is a disaster, my mom never picks up or cleans anymore. My dad's apartment is super small and creepy and maybe even haunted. I don't like going there but miss him. My parents hate each other and are constantly saying bad things about each other, except me and Teo are the only ones to hear it. My mom is always talking about "your father..." and my dad is always talking about "your mother......" I hate it, I hate all of this!

Everybody is mad all the time and moms acting weird. I found a whole bunch of old emails and text messages Mom had printed off and clipped together like evidence from a crime scene. I hid them, so she could not use them for whatever they were for. All of them made my dad look bad, and he is not bad. He just gets angry at her sometimes because she is crazy, he says.

We hardly ever see my dad except on some weekends. I really miss him. I know my mom wants Teo and me to be on her side, and sometimes we pretend to be because it's just easier that way. But really we love our dad and want to see him more than a couple of days every month. We love our mom too, but dad is right. She is acting crazy since he left and I see her drinking alcohol all the time. She stays out all night and leaves us with the babysitter and grandma. My life is a joke. I want to crawl into a cave, or run away and join the circus. Wait, I'm already in the circus, my family is an act right out of Barnum & Bailey. At least I'm a strong girl and have Iggy to lean on. Teo has been nicer to me lately too. My teacher said I needed a theme song, something that would help me focus on the good stuff and things that are special about me. Obviously I picked "This Is Me!"

I cued up iTunes on her iPod that sat on the bedside table and played my daughter's chosen theme song. As the melody started, tears thundered down and I reflected on the choices I'd been making over the last year—worse yet, the two intoxicated hours I had just spent in a session with the court-appointed evaluator who was helping to decide my daughter's future.

I need to get my shit together, or maybe Rae's just being dramatic, and it's not really that bad?

Either way, my sweet baby was hurting, and that hurt me. I put the diary back just as I had found it, closed up Rae's iPod, and glanced at the clock.

Ugh, I gotta go! My two hours were up. I needed to collect the kids from school. *How am I going to look her in the eyes after snooping in her diary?* I was scared to face them, having this new insight. *I wonder what's going on in Teo's head? He has always been quiet. I figured he was doing fine, but now I don't know.* I picked up my keys, ready to head out.

Crap! My car is still at the evaluator's office. Think, Vanessa, think.

I grabbed the AAA membership card out of my wallet and used it to call a tow. This was a free service, and one I had become familiar with as of late. My car would be back home in no time, so I sat down and sent some overdue text messages I had been ignoring.

Remarkably, I was en route to the kids' schools on time and thought about all the things I could do to make them feel better. This past year and everything about the divorce had really been rough. *Maybe I've been so focused on my pain, on getting through this myself, that I've overlooked a few things.* I pulled my shoulders back with determination to change—to do better.

Their wish is my command tonight. Whatever they want for dinner, I'll make. Or maybe take them out to their favorite restaurant, Olive Garden, for some of those delicious breadsticks. We'll make special plans for this weekend—mom and kid time. Whatever their hearts desire. Mommy needs to get back in their good graces, especially before they talk to the child custody evaluator in a couple of weeks. We'll need to work on that starting now.

I grabbed Teo from school first, and we had a little time before Rae was ready. FroYo after school always lightened the mood, so I drove us to our favorite place. After loading his bowl with frozen yogurt, his favorite gummy sharks, and a chocolate brownie, he sat down next to me and my sorbet and sprinkles.

"How was your day, buddy?" I asked upbeat, trying not to be obvious that I was digging for information. I really wanted to find out if he felt the same way Rae was feeling.

A shrug of his shoulders and grunt were all he gave me. Teo never was one to talk very much but I had noticed he'd become even more withdrawn since his dad left the house.

Not only did his dad choose to leave all of us, then he forced us out of our family home. Of course, my teenage son is angry.

"What are you thinking about, Mom?" His question, thick with contempt, startled me out of my angry daydream.

"Your father and everything he has done to ruin our lives. I'm so sorry your dad is such a disappointment, honey."

Teo exhaled loudly, rolled his eyes, got up from the table, his metal stool scraping against the tile floor, and tossed his cup of uneaten FroYo into the garbage. He stormed out of the yogurt shop with me hot on his heels, sorbet and sprinkles still in hand.

"Teo, wait up! What's the matter?" I yelled, running after him.

He beat me to the car, got in the front seat, and locked the door. The windows were closed so I tried talking to him through the glass, but his hoodie was up, and his arms were wrapped tight around his long legs hugged up against his chest. I could tell he was crying.

"Buddy, please open the door. I'm so sorry. I want to help make this right. Please talk to me. What can I do to make it better, bud?"

He flipped me the bird.

"Teo James Smith, it is not acceptable to flip off your mother!" I unlocked the door myself with the key fob since my son, now acting like his father, clearly did not intend to let me in. I walked around the front end of the car, tripped over the bumper that was hanging a little low, and slipped into the driver's seat.

We sat in silence for a second before I started. The medication I'd taken earlier was still coursing through my veins, making me feel braver than I naturally was. Teo looked up, locked eyes with me, and I saw hatred steadily flowing in my direction.

He stands taller than me now, and his jawline has hardened. His baby face is no more. This is a young man sitting beside me, staring me down, wanting to do me harm.

I reached over to wipe a tear from his cheek, and he pulled away so I couldn't touch him.

"Teo, please talk to me. What in the world did I do to upset you?"

And with that one question, he let me have it. My otherwise even-tempered son came unglued. "You and Dad have ruined my life! Rae's, too! Why do you have to hate each other and act like such immature stupid brats? We want our old life back. We miss our house and hate having to move between your and Dad's boring apartments. Why can't you guys work it out like adults? And who is this lady we have to talk to? I am not going there and talking to her. All those emails and text messages you printed off and left lying around—who do you think found those? Rae cried her eyes out and then lit them on fire in the dumpster—you know, the one you ran into and wrecked the front end of the car?!" His eyes bugged out at me in that sarcastic "duh" kind of way. "Were you really going to give all of those hateful messages between you and Dad to a stranger? You are such a loser, Mom, and an alcoholic. I can smell margaritas on you right now. Is that from last night?!?!"

I had no defense but made an effort to close my mouth that had somehow dropped open.

Teo continued on. "Dad says you can end this, but are making us go to a custody evaluator. You're always complaining about not having any money, but Dad says this evaluation costs a fortune. What is your problem, Mom? Can't you just be nice for once and stop acting crazy?"

That did it. My rage took over. "Your dad isn't telling you the truth, Teo. This is all his fault, not mine. And you *will* go talk to the evaluator. You and your sister. We have to pick her up from school now. Buckle up, pal. And watch your tone!"

He sunk deeper into the seat. We left FroYo in silence and pulled into the carpool line at Rae's school. I made an effort to be on my best behavior. She hopped in, singing a new song she had learned in choir that afternoon. But Rae is the barometer of our family's emotions and very aware of other people's feeling. In fact, she is always trying to make everyone happy and has really picked up her efforts to nurture me and make sure I'm doing alright lately. True to her nature, she quickly assessed the atmospheric temperature.

"What's wrong? Did something happen to Dad? To Iggy?" the concern in her voice was palpable.

And what about me? She didn't even consider that something had happened to me!

"Nothing, sweet girl. Teo is having a hard day." I choked out the words, with my anger increasing with every passing moment.

Teo shot me a look of pure evil from underneath his hoodie and atop the sunglasses. Rae reached forward and patted her brother's shoulder. He shrugged away from his sister, too, and curled into the smallest ball possible with his 5'8" frame.

No one spoke another word on the drive. When we arrived, the kids could not get out of the car and into their bedrooms fast enough. Both of them used more force than necessary in closing their bedroom doors.

My second meeting with the evaluator was a couple days away, so I decided to document everything that just went down. I grabbed half a glass of wine and sat at the computer.

A real alcoholic would surely pour her glass full to the top. He has no idea what he's talking about.

Neither one of them wanted to eat at Olive Garden that night, or eat at all, so it was early to bed. At least I think they went to bed. Neither of them ever left their rooms. My brain hurt, and my nervous system was fried from this wild day, so I finished off the bottle of wine in bed while texting my man. He always made me feel better. I told him he could come over, but not stay the night. And to wear tennis shoes. No more flip flops that could accidently get left behind.

The following days passed with the usual routine, but Rae's diary and Teo's outburst had opened my eyes to some new things. Teo found himself in detention again for skipping class. He was also caught rolling a joint in the boys' locker room. Apparently, he was now experimenting with drugs. I think he has been into my stash of booze, too. Rae seems to be wearing eye shadow in the mornings now. I think she looks cute but have received a not-so-nice email from her teacher about it.

Everyone is so uptight all the time, just like I used to be.

My next meeting with the evaluator was scheduled for Friday. I didn't leave things too great with her, and I was ready to make a better impression at our second session. Attorney of the Year had given me some great pointers when we met, and I vowed to not party the night before and attend the meeting from start to finish, completely sober. I also promised her there would be no more intoxicated driving, ever, and especially with the kids in the car.

Things seem to have calmed down between Luke and me. He sends nasty text messages every now and again about what a crazy and unfit mother I have become, how worried he is about my choices, and letting me know with no uncertain terms that he is scared for the kids' safety due to my "partying." He regularly threatens that he and the judge are going to take the kids away from me very soon. I mostly ignore these messages, but keep them as evidence that he is a jerk.

The second evaluation meeting was different from the first. I was greeted in the same way, and we went to the comfortable back office; but once we were seated, the evaluator told me she had an agenda today. It would be more of a structured interview than our first. She had lots of questions about my parenting, the daily routines in my household, the kids' healthcare and dental care, extended family relationships, holiday traditions, their activities, friendships, and school. We walked through my thoughts about the best parenting plan and why I thought it would work. That part was easy. The kids should stay with me and only visit Luke every other weekend. That's how it's always been for kids with divorced parents. Live here, visit over there.

The evaluator then said it was time for her to share the father's parenting concerns, so we could sort through some of the disagreements, and she could hear both sides of the story.

It was so hard to hear and respond during this part of the interview. By the time we had made it through the litany of Luke's BS, I was ready for a stiff one, probably two. I took some extra time at the end of our session to show the evaluator the nasty messages on my phone. I needed her to know what a fool my ex was, and how terrible it would be for him to get custody of the kids or for them to visit with him more than every other weekend. After twenty minutes, I was satisfied that I had crushed him as good as any soon-to-be ex-wife could.

We scheduled our third evaluation meeting for two days later. This meeting would include interviews with the children at her office. I asked what I should tell the kids about the appointment, and let her know Teo was not into it. She assured me teenagers can be resistant, but getting to the office was the hardest part. She suggested I tell them a little bit about her and her office, let them know that their father and I have both talked to her, have them take an online office tour, and assure them that they do not have to talk about anything they don't want to. She told me the burden of this process is not theirs, and she never asks kids where they want to live because it is not their decision to make. She ensured that she does not poke and prod at children for information they don't want to or are not ready to share. She was simply interested in getting to know them a little bit and advised that I not coach them in any way.

Back at the apartment, and after school that day, I invited Teo and Rae to our kitchen table to take the online tour of the evaluator's office. Teo sat arms crossed, obviously disinterested. Rae spotted the toys and was open to meeting the "nice-looking" lady. Teo said he would go if he had to, but was not saying anything.

Good enough for me. She's an expert in this stuff and can surely figure out what to do with an angry, snotty, shut-down, increasingly defiant teenager.

The evening before our family meeting with the evaluator, we had dinner at Olive Garden, which had always been the kids' favorite. I resisted the urge to order a glass of wine, not wanting them to mention how much I had been drinking since me and their father split. We swung by the mall afterwards, and I bought Teo a new pair of basketball shoes and Rae some new clothes, hoping to score some last-minute brownie points.

We even stopped for haircuts before heading home, so we would all look our best for the evaluator. Homework was done without incident, and they hit the sack early to be well-rested for the big day. After they were asleep, my man snuck in. We shared a couple midnight cocktails, got our groove on, and even talked about introducing him to the kids soon. Our relationship was ready for the next level, since we had been together for more than a month now. He was a great guy, and I just knew the kids were going to love him as much as I was starting to.

I picked the kids up a little early from school so we could make the 3:00 p.m. meeting at the evaluator's office. When we walked in, she was ready for us.

"Hi there!" the evaluator welcomed. After introducing herself to Teo and Rae, she invited all of us into the office. This time, there was a large white piece of paper sitting on the little table and colored pencils, markers, crayons, watercolor paints, and stickers neatly stacked in piles. "Teo, you're so tall. Here's a bigger chair for you." He gave her a crooked smile, appearing to feel comfortable the same way I had felt during that first meeting several weeks ago. "Alrighty, so here's what I'd love for you to do first. I want you to create a family picture together—a favorite family memory, or vacation, or anything you wish—where everyone is doing something in the picture."

All three of us nodded as the evaluator backed out of our space and started playing some music in the background, so we could get started.

"How about we draw our new apartment, or the meal we had at Olive Garden last night?" I suggested.

Both of them shook their heads at me, so I proposed drawing other good memories with just the three of us and Iggy.

Rae said, "Let's make a Christmas scene around the tree at our old house—three years ago when we all lived together, and everyone was still happy."

I cringed and tried to dissuade her, but Teo piped in, in that critical tone he inherited from his father, "Yah, Mom, let's make a picture of when everyone was still normal and happy."

I couldn't stop the words from spilling out, "I am not the one who has changed, Teo. Your father is the one who broke up our family and is acting crazy—not me." I looked over and saw the evaluator writing something on her notepad, and then looked up at Teo in time to see tears welling in his eyes as he stood up and stomped out. Rae was looking down at the paper and pretending not to notice. She just kept drawing with the red crayon.

The evaluator was quickly on her feet and headed after Teo. As she walked by Rae, she put a gentle hand on her shoulder and said she would be right back. Just before she left the room, she set a box of Kleenex on the table. When my daughter looked up, I noticed she was crying, too.

What a disaster! Why can't the kids grasp the fact that their disappointment of a father is responsible for all of this pain and suffering—not me! I really wanted them to tell the evaluator what a great mom I am and have always been, and what a complete loser their father is.

With the evaluator and Teo out of the room, I took Rae's hand and asked if she was okay. Rae looked back at me, solemn and teary-eyed. "Why can't you and Daddy just get back together? Why do we have to be here? Why can't everything just go back to normal?"

"Rae, this will all work out," I promised, stroking her hand gently. "But I need you to do something for me. When the evaluator comes back in, it's important that you tell her that you want to live with me and not your dad. Remember how your dad took Iggy away, and your favorite blanket, too, when he left us? Plus, you said his new apartment is creepy. And this lady has the power to make you live there and not with me, if you do not speak up."

The tears stopped and Rae looked a little scared. She nodded in agreement and looked back down at the paper.

Well, at least she understood that!

After fifteen minutes or so, the evaluator returned with Teo.

"Rae, would it be okay for Mom to sit out on the comfy couch for a while, so the three of us can play a game of UNO™?"

My daughter looked up at me, seeking permission with only her eyes.

"I will be right outside the door." I kissed the top of her head, collected my purse, smiled at Teo, who seemed more at ease, and left my children with this court-appointed professional who seemed to have the power to decide their future.

I sat on the couch, sweating every minute they were behind the closed door. At one point, I tried to listen in, but there was music playing in both rooms and a loud white noise machine whooshing away. I could not make out anything concrete, except for random laughter. I could hear Teo's deep baritone voice prattling on and on about something, more words than usual coming out of his mouth. I tossed down an anxiety pill for good measure.

This cannot be good. He decides to talk now, in this moment, to this person.

When the three of them emerged from the back office, my children looked at peace, and Teo was even smiling. Rae gave the evaluator a big hug, and she directed both of them to a treasure box. Each of them picked something while the evaluator said, "I'll see you Friday with your dad. I'm excited to see you at both your homes, too, and to meet Iggy."

Rae had to stop at the restroom, and Teo headed right to the car. Before I followed Rae into the ladies' room, I saw he was already texting someone on his phone.

"Rae, how did it go?" I asked.

"Fine," she answered matter-of-factly from behind the stall door. I didn't want her to feel pressured but was dying to know what they had talked about, especially what Teo had said. The evaluator had told me it was important to protect the kids through this process and not to dig for information about their conversations— but I was their mom and I knew best.

"Baby, now is not the time to go silent. What questions did she ask you guys? Did you tell her you wanted to live with me and not Dad? Did Teo say good stuff about me? It's really important I know what was talked about."

Rae flushed and came out of the stall to wash her hands. "Mom, she said what we talked about with her was none of your and Dad's business. That unless we said something that would cause worry for our safety, she does not, and we do not, have to report back to you. She also said that she is not on your side or Dad's side. She said she knew that you and Dad both love us very much and that going through the divorce of your parents is a really, really hard thing. She said she was on *our* team—me and Teo—and her job is to make sure that we will always spend time with both of our parents."

"That all sounds good, honey. What did you guys tell her?" I prodded in the most gentle and sincere voice possible.

"Mom!" Rae turned the faucet off, wiped her hands, and stormed out of the restroom.

As we were approaching the car, I could see my son in the front seat with his phone, smiling and laughing. At least he was in a better mood. After Rae and I got into our seats and buckled in, I started the car, and Teo connected the Bluetooth. We drove home, windows down, listening to whatever music my teenager was into these days.

They seemed much happier than they had in a while and scurried off when I said I was going to make some dinner. I covertly poured a vodka sour into my water bottle, then re-hid the bottle of booze before I popped in another prescription pill. A few minutes later, I could hear the kids snickering, both of them in Teo's room, with the door closed.

It's weird that he let Rae in. They must be conspiring. I sauntered down the hall as quietly as possible and put my ear to the door. *They are talking about the meeting! No music or white nose machines here at home.*

Then I heard it. They were joking and making fun of me—mocking my tone, anger toward their father, late nights out, and my new man.

That does it! They do not get to make fun of someone they have never even met! He could be their stepdad one day. My children have no shame. They used to be so much more respectful.

Just then, I lost my balance and smacked my forehead against the door. The door flung open, and I saw four intense eyeballs staring me down.

"Um, hi guys! Just came down here to let you know dinner is almost ready." Right on cue, the smoke alarm started blaring at that awful pitch, and I looked down the hall of our little apartment to see flames on the stovetop. "Crap!" I ran down the short hallway back into the kitchen, turned off the burner, and started whacking the flames with a wet towel. Rae was yelling for Teo to "call 911," and he just stood there with that smug look on his face.

"Mom, if you keep eavesdropping on us, you are going to burn down this home, too."

Ha, very funny, son! And what exactly does that mean anyway?

"New plan. Let's go out for burgers and fries!" I said, ignoring his smug statement and all of the questions that bubbled as a result.

We grabbed burgers at the drive-thru, and when we got home, they got things ready for a weekend with their dad. The next day was Friday. I would drop them off at school in the morning, and their dad would collect them at the end of the day for their meeting at the evaluator's office. I would not see them again until Monday afternoon, after school, when the evaluator was due for the home visit to our place.

Hopefully that meeting goes better than today. It's just me, Iggy, and my hunky man for the weekend, I thought as I tucked Rae into bed and said goodnight to Teo through his closed door. I was looking forward to time off from the daunting responsibilities of never-ending Mom Duty.

I thought about cleaning up the fire mess in the kitchen but didn't have the energy. I took a fresh vodka sour to bed, texted my man goodnight, and fell asleep watching a rerun of *Jerry Springer*.

My weekend was amazing, and I felt rejuvenated. My mother had come over and helped me clean the apartment for the home visit with our evaluator at 4:00 p.m. on Monday. I had even sprayed some doggie spritz on Iggy and bought a couple of those wall plug-ins that smell like a Hawaiian Breeze. Luckily, Teo and Rae were both in a good mood when they got into the car. I asked how the weekend with their dad was and got the standard responses: "good" and "fine." They never shared about anything that happened with their dad. Not wanting to upset them before the evaluator's visit, I left it at that, and we headed home.

The evaluator arrived on time with her usual friendly disposition. Rae gave her a quick tour of our cozy home, and they ended up talking in her room. Through the open door, I heard Rae tell her the house was usually a complete mess, and that Grandma had probably come over to help.

"That's a nice picture of your family," I heard the evaluator say. I assumed she was talking about the one above Rae's bed.

"Yeah, but look at these pictures. My mom cut my dad's face out of all of them." Her voice was full of anger and sadness. "And she spilled a bottle of wine on my baby book."

How does she even have those? That wine spill was a total accident.

Teo invited the evaluator into his room once she and Rae had finished up. After he showed her his cool new basketball shoes and all of his basketball trophies and medals, I heard her ask if he wanted to talk about anything else. Teo answered, "Yes, can we take a walk?" The evaluator asked my permission, which I gave, because it would be totally weird to say "no." They were gone about twenty minutes, and when they got back, she checked in with Rae to say goodbye.

"Alright, Vanessa. You have a nice home here. Very... clean! I should be wrapping up the report for Teo and Rae in the next few weeks and will be in touch if I need anything else." She collected some paperwork, shook my hand, gave Iggy one last pat on the head, and waved goodbye on her way out the door. Instant relief washed over me as I watched her disappear. We were done with the evaluation, and I had done my part, the best I could with what I knew.

I emailed Attorney of the Year with some frequency in the following days, to see if the evaluation report was out yet. We had a trial date on the court docket just one month away, and I was hopeful we could get this settled without having a judge decide Teo and Rae's future.

Attorney of the Year replied several days after the home visit, with instructions that I needed to report to a forensic lab for urine and hair follicle testing for substances. My heart raced.

The email instructed me to report to the lab within twenty-four hours and provide "samples" as requested in the referral letter. There was a phone number, address, directions to the lab and instructions to bring my driver's license and payment of $400.

What? How am I supposed to come up with that kind of cash in twenty-four hours?

I picked up the phone and called Attorney of the Year. Luckily, she had a minute to chat (at the rate of $250 per hour).

"Vanessa, there is no way around this request. You have to comply," she said matter-of-factly.

When I didn't respond, she asked, "Is this going to be a problem—have you been using alcohol, THC, or street drugs since I advised you to stop? Or have you taken any medication in the last ninety days for which you cannot show an active prescription from your physician?"

"Define *using*," I prodded, trying to keep my voice from shaking.

"Vanessa," she started with that annoyed tone. "I advise you to get to the lab as the evaluator has requested. If you need professional help, it is time to get some. The children need a sober mom. They need you to be strong and resilient, and neither is possible if you are abusing substances. I'll let you know when I hear back from the lab." With that, she ended our call.

No way can I pass a urine test! I had hit it hard the night before and was already a few drinks into this day. *Maybe I could use someone else's urine?* I Googled "fake urine" and found all kinds of stuff, but no time to wait for delivery. *Shoot! Maybe I could get some pee from the kids?* I wondered. *No, that would be awkward and Rae cannot keep a secret.* Hair was going to be even more difficult to fudge, and then I had an amazing idea. *Maybe if I bleach my hair, I could pass the test?*

Flustered, I called my man for reassurance. He was a smart guy and gave me a stellar idea. Iggy! Of course! I could get some urine from Iggy and pass it off as my own. He would be happy to stop by later for moral support, too.

But the kids are with me tonight. Well, now seems as good a time as any for an introduction!

I was going to the lab at noon, picking the kids up around 3:00 p.m., and Blade said he would bring us takeout at 5:00 p.m. A little Mo Goo Gai Pan and egg rolls ought to butter up my kids. I told him to bring some cupcakes, too—for good measure.

I made my way to the bathroom and got out the bottle of household bleach.

How hard can this be? Blade said the lab takes hair right at the scalp. The "follicle" of the hair is what they want. I stared at the bottle and then at myself in the mirror. *Oh, fuck it.*

I poured bleach into the sink—the rest of the bottle—and added a little bit of water. I flipped my head over and dunked it in, all the way to the follicles.

Best to be thorough. For a good fifteen minutes, I sat there upside-down, scalp fully immersed in bleachy sink water. Breathing in the noxious fumes was a bonus buzz. When it seemed like I had soaked long enough, I wrapped my hair up in a towel and went looking for Iggy.

"Iggy, here boy. Iggs, Momma needs you. Come here, boy."

Always such a lover, Iggy came running out of Rae's room. Expecting a biscuit, he stared at me for a second and then sat.

"Let's go potty. You need to tinkle?" I led him outside to a small patch of grass where he always does his business. Iggy sniffed around, looked up at me, and then plopped down on his belly, looking to enjoy a rest in the warm sunshine. With an empty plastic dish in hand, I cheered him on. "Igg, come on, buddy. Go potty. Get up." He was not in a cooperative mood, so I called him back inside and lured him over to his bowl. "Drink, buddy. Have some nice, cold water."

Iggy looked at me like I was the crazy fool everyone had been saying I was, and I wondered if he might be right. But then another brilliant idea struck. *Iggy loves beer.* Mr. Disappointment always thought it was funny to give the dog beer. He would let him lap it up right from his dish and Iggy would pee like crazy. I dumped out Iggy's water bowl, cracked a beer from the fridge, and dumped it into his bowl. Iggy the lush dove right in, his big ol' tongue licking a million miles a minute. He did not step back until the bowl was empty.

"Come on, boy. Ready to go potty now?"

Iggy wobbled behind me toward the door but stopped short and lifted his leg on the couch. Fortunately, I was lightning fast with the plastic dish, and he filled that sucker to the top.

Good boy!

Iggy looked confused, and drunk, so I helped him to the door and outside to his favorite patch of grass. He plopped down and passed out, four paws skyward and his tongue hanging out.

Best to leave him out here, I guess. I got his collar and leash and secured him safely to a tree. Then I left a bowl of cold water and his dish of food, so no one would call the doggie police on me. That's all I needed right about now.

I secured the lid on the plastic container of urine and placed it carefully into my purse. Then I headed to the bathroom to check out my new golden locks. I removed the towel and saw a tangled rats' nest of light rust-colored hair. It looked like Ronald McDonald met Beetlejuice. Frantically, I started brushing through it as best I could. I used Rae's leave-in conditioner, got out the blow dryer, and used the hair straightener. After ten minutes, I decided it was good enough, or just not getting any better.

Time to visit the lab. I drove, heart racing, hoping that all of my clever tactics would work. *I can't lose my kids over this!*

At the lab, I was sent into a restroom with a small cup for my urine where I carefully poured what I had collected from Iggy into the sample cup. When I returned, the technician was ready to cut off some of my hair (a bigger chunk than I expected!). She asked if I had chemically treated my hair recently, which of course I denied. When she got what she needed, I handed her my credit card, crossed my fingers it would not be declined, and left for home.

What a day! God, let it be over soon. How much can a girl take?

I picked up the kids as usual and informed them that a friend was coming over for dinner. When they both looked at me suspiciously, I told them he was an "important friend" and asked Teo to be nice. He rolled his eyes at me. And then Rae was upset when she saw Iggy tied to a tree outside the apartment, but I assured her that he had needed some fresh air and sunshine.

At 5:00 p.m. sharp, Blade knocked on the front door. I opened it to see his fine self standing there in the setting evening sun—a true Adonis. We chuckled at the awkwardness of him using the door, instead of the bathroom window. Quickly, I looked behind me to make sure the kids were still in their rooms before I planted a big one on him.

As he set the food on the table, I started down the hall and found Rae peering around the corner. She had tears in her eyes and took off for her room. I stopped at Teo's door, which was locked, and asked if he was hungry. A resounding "no" is all I got until he followed up with, "Go away!" I continued on to Rae's room and could hear her muffled sobbing.

When I opened her bedroom door, I saw Rae's face down in the pillow, hugging her favorite stuffie. "Sweetheart, why are you crying?" I sat down beside my daughter and rubbed her back. "Honey, someone is here that wants to meet you."

Rae lifted her head and spun it around like the exorcist before spitting out, "I already have a dad! Tell him to go away!"

"He brought egg rolls," is all I could think of to say.

Rae planted her face back into the pillow and kicked at me so I would leave.

"We'll be in the kitchen if you want to eat, okay?" I said as I stood up to leave.

When I turned, Teo was there, blocking the door, clearly pissed. Without saying a word, he moved to the side so I could pass. "Bitch," he muttered and then walked into his sister's room, slammed the door, and locked it.

Blade was already making his way down the hallway in my direction. I'd never seen him upset before, but he looked angry. "Are you okay? Did your kid just call you a bitch and slam the door in your face?" he asked protectively.

My knight in shining armor riding in on his white horse.

Blade began pounding on Rae's bedroom door, and then my man was standing toe-to-toe with my adolescent son. They were both yelling about this, that, and another thing—the F bomb bouncing back and forth. I was about to jump in between them, but Rae beat me to it! My two guys towered over Rae by almost two feet, but she stood her ground and was using brute strength to physically push them apart. Iggy stumbled down the hall, late to the party, still drunk, and attempted a protective growl. Of course, it came out more as a slurred woof, followed by one heck of a doggie fart. Iggy smiled with his drooling jowls, leaned up against the wall, and closed his eyes, apparently passed out again.

I had the good sense to pull Blade by the arm, down the hallway and away from Teo, and my son picked up Iggy and went with Rae into her room.

This was not how I imagined the evening would go.

I apologized to Blade and told him we'd talk later that night. He was really upset, with himself mostly, for losing it on my kid. We quick-kissed goodbye and parted ways. I stopped in the kitchen for a shot of vodka and grabbed a pill from my purse.

Now, for these kids!

After a little sweet talking from the hallway, Teo and Rae let me into the bedroom, where they were both fussing over Iggy.

"Did you kick that asshole out?" Teo asked as soon as I entered. "I cannot believe you are hanging around a total prick like that dude."

I was speechless. Rae buried her face in the pillow again with her arm around Iggy, who was snoring and drooling on her pillow.

"Mom!" Teo barked. "Is he gone?"

"Yes, I asked him to leave."

"Good! Now, what the hell is wrong with Iggy? Why is he acting drunk?" Teo demanded.

"Well, I..." I started. *Oh good god!* "I had to, well, today, earlier the evaluator..."

Time to fess up. I hoped they might find some humor as I told them about the day, about the evaluator's request for a lab sample, and about needing clean urine so they were not taken away from me and forced to live with their dad in his downtown studio apartment.

When I finished with the story, Rae finally lifted her head and yelled over her shoulder. "Stop it! I want my 'old mom' back! I hate you!"

I had no idea what she was talking about and tried to comfort her, but she jumped up, ran into the bathroom, and locked the door. Teo was on his feet too, and said he was calling his dad to come get them. He said he wanted to live with his dad and that Rae wanted to leave me, too.

Are you kidding me? I'm doing all of this for you!

I told Teo to go ahead and call his dad. I didn't want him around the way he was behaving anyway. And truthfully, I'd rather spend the night with Blade.

Of course my ex was over in a flash, feeling victorious over this one bad night between me and the kids. Teo and Rae left with him, without a word. And they took Iggy, too.

Finally, two weeks after the home visit and lab testing, the subject line of an email from my attorney read: "Evaluation for Teo and Rae, attached." I clicked the email immediately and saw a PDF. Attorney of the Year's email message read, "Please make an appointment with my office at your earliest convenience. We need to talk about this."

I immediately picked up the phone and called the law office to schedule a meeting and then spent hours reading and rereading the evaluator's report line by line, crying my eyes out. I could not believe some of the conclusions she made about me: "demonizes father, limited insight into children's needs, safety risk, irresponsible, fractured parenting capacity due to heavy substance use."

I printed the report, pulled out my best highlighter pen, and got to work, making notes next to all the sentences and statements that were just plain wrong.

I shook my head in disbelief as I read the lab results: Urine – *temperature outside of range, *positive* for ETG (alcohol) Hair Follicle – *altered sample, *positive* for opioids, *positive* for amphetamine, *positive* for ETG (alcohol), *positive* for benzodiazepines.

What the hell? I ruined my hair for nothing?

And then it hit me, "The beer!" I gave Iggy beer so he would pee but did not even consider that it would register in his urine.

Rookie mistake.

There were services and therapies and educational courses recommended to improve communication between homes and both of our parenting insights.

Who has time or money for all that?

Then I saw the line: "Mother is to immediately participate in a substance abuse assessment with a qualified processional and follow all recommended treatment services. Intensive outpatient and/or inpatient care is likely indicated by the vast data collected through this process."

I grabbed a bottle of wine, dialed up my man, and sobbed. The statements in the report were so off-base. The next day's meeting with Attorney of the Year couldn't come fast enough.

Prepared with my highlighted copy of the evaluation report in hand, I sat down across the cherry wood desk promptly at 9:00 a.m., Blade by my side for moral support.

"Who's this with you today, Vanessa?" she asked, obviously assessing him.

I introduced them briefly. "He's here to support me. There's nothing you cannot say in front of him. I want him here so please do not ask him to leave."

"Okay well, have you had a chance to read the report?" she continued, clearly not happy that I had brought him with me. I nodded yes, and she continued. "We need to talk about the lab results." I affirmed with another nod because there was a giant lump in my throat. "There is a lot noted in the evaluation that will not be favorable to our position. The positive lab supports your husband's concern for the children's safety. It will be best if we try to settle this along the lines of the evaluator's recommendation." Her tone was even and steady. "I've never seen a urine test out of range for temperature *and* positive for alcohol. What happened?"

I told Attorney of the Year the sad story about collecting Iggy's urine, the whole truth and nothing but the truth, hoping that it would set me free. No luck. She looked horrified.

"Does this mean that Teo and Rae will see their dad more than every other weekend? That's not okay! He is going to ruin them!" I nearly screamed.

Attorney of the Year leaned in, lowered her voice and, with the utmost kindness and respect, offered, "According to the evaluation, it seems you have been doing a pretty good job of ruining them yourself. We need to get you scheduled for a substance abuse assessment right away and then started in the proper treatment program so you can get back on track with Teo and Rae."

I opened my mouth to defend myself but then the true weight of my attorney's words knocked me over. Tears flooded in, and I was a blubbering mess.

This cannot be happening. How can this even be happening?

Blade tried to console me by rubbing my back and kissing the side of my head. The attorney's office assistant appeared with a warm cup of matcha tea and a fresh box of Kleenex. She also placed a small package of dark chocolate in front of me.

Looks like my "congratulations on your divorce gifts" have finally arrived. I pulled myself together, sipped the tea, and popped in a small piece of dark chocolate.

Together, Attorney of the Year, Blade, and I wrote up a settlement proposal that she said was reasonable. She'd send it over to Mr. Disappointment's attorney later that day and then wait for their response. We would either reach an agreement or have a judge decide two weeks from now.

I really do not want a judge to see the evaluator's report, and I am not going into some stupid treatment facility. What a cluster!

We stood up to leave, and right before we reached the door, my attorney asked, "Blade, have you met Teo and Rae?"

Blade looked to me in silence and before either of us said a word, Attorney of the Year cautioned, "Now is not the time to introduce anyone new into the children's lives. They need time to heal and adjust."

We turned around quickly and left. Blade drove us out of the city, and we stopped by the local bar to drown my sorrow in a couple of cold drinks. When Blade dropped me off at the apartment a while later, I saw Teo's phone sitting on the kitchen table and picked it up. It was password protected, but his PlayStation gamertag worked! I was in and went right to his text messages where I spent the next ten minutes holding my breath with every surprise that awaited me.

Wow, so much chatting with his father, and his bestie, Ethan. His language has really become raunchy. When did that happen? So much venom about me, which his father doesn't necessarily encourage but does not shut down either. He gets that anger from his dad. Teo and Ethan sure know a lot more about girls than I realized. I guess we missed the birds and bees talk. So many distractions during this time of absolute chaos.

One text communication with his father stood out amongst the sea of others.

Teo: "mom hates you dad, she says terrible things about you and blames you for everything. What did you do to her anyway? She says you're a 'fraud' and 'a total disappointment.' I think she is going to drink herself to death. She is out of control."

Dad: "sorry bud I'm trying to get more time with you and your sister so you don't have to be around your drunk and impossible-to-please mother so much. That must really suck. I am not a perfect man, and I have made mistakes, but I am no fraud. I'm your dad, kid, always will be, and I love you. Protect your sister, and never get into the car with your mom if she is drunk or is acting like a lunatic. Got it?"

What an ass! I am going to have to tell the kids the awful truth about all of it so they understand. I'll show them evidence in all those emails and text messages their father wrote so they understand who he really is. And who is he to worry about my drinking? He was drunk most of our marriage. Thank God I've found Blade. A real man who is going to make a great dad.

The next morning after getting the kids off to school, I fired up my computer and found an email from Attorney of the Year. It was marked "urgent."

Dear Ms. Smith,

Last night around 5:00 p.m., I received the counteroffer to our settlement proposal. It was favorable, just a few areas to work out. I planned on arranging a meeting with you to discuss. However this morning, I received notice from the other party that all offers are off the table, and they would see us at trial. Did something happen between last night and this morning? I feel it is urgent that we meet, today if possible.

Gosh, no drama last night. Blade didn't even sneak in and out. What is going on now?

My thoughts were interrupted by a knock on my door. Iggy came with me to answer and discover a young woman was standing there, with a police officer. "Yes?"

"Ms. Smith my name is Mary and I am with the Department of Human Services, Child Welfare. This is Officer Timothy. We received a report of possible violence and substance abuse in the home and need to speak with you, please, about Teo and Rae. May we come in?"

My heart almost jumped out of my chest. "Sure."

We sat together, the three of us, in the small living room, and I answered all of their questions. Someone had reported the yelling between Blade and Teo, and Rae's high-pitched voice as well. Along with that report was a copy of my recent lab testing and photos of my banged-up car. Mary explained that her job was to ensure the safety of children, and that a child's witness to violence and substance abuse were a concern to the agency. I assured her this was all a misunderstanding, gave her the name of my attorney, and let her know I had stopped drinking and intended to seek treatment. Satisfied for the moment, she and Officer Timothy, who looked bored out of his mind, got up from the couch and left my home.

I immediately dialed the attorney's office, spoke to the perky assistant, and was told to come right down. *Yes, ma'am!*

I threw myself together and drove plenty over the speed limit to the downtown office. The greeting I received was cordial, though less enthusiastic than usual. I was escorted to the corner office where the ace-up-my-sleeve sat, arms crossed, looking troubled.

"Ms. Smith, please sit," she offered with a wave of her hand. No warm tea or Kleenex or chocolate today. "Do you have any insight to what might be going on? Did anything happen with you and the children's father between last night and this morning?"

I don't know where to start. How much should I tell her? What should I tell her?

"A child welfare lady came to my house this morning," I blurted.

"Well, could you please enlighten me as to why?" Attorney of the Year prodded.

"A few nights ago, I tried to introduce Blade to the kids and things went poorly. Teo was being difficult, downright rude, and Blade stood up for me. There was yelling." I could tell by the expression on my attorney's face that I had really messed up big time. I immediately felt sick.

"Well, Ms. Smith, being awarded legal custody and primary residence of the children is looking less and less likely. Your behavior, and Blade's, will be seen as detrimental to the children and possibly abusive—a real-time example of what the evaluator described in her report, only this takes it to a whole new level of concern for their safety, welfare, and well-being. It's highly possible that your children will end up in their father's sole legal and primary physical custody because of the choices you have been making—fueled at least in part by substance abuse."

"What can I do?" I pleaded, my voice shaky and a faucet of tears already flowing.

"Abstain from alcohol and pills and get to the substance abuse assessment ASAP. Follow the treatment recommendations. Apologize to the children and say absolutely nothing that could be interpreted as negative or bad, condescending, belittling, or hurtful about their father. You are to 'zip it' when it comes to discussing anything with the kids that has to do with their father. Off limits. Bite your tongue until you taste blood if need be. And stop seeing Blade. He is not to be around the children at all after the scene you described that now has the child welfare agency involved. They could see you as an unprotective parent and remove the children immediately."

I nodded to let her know that I understood and wiped tears from my cheeks.

There was nothing to do but wait for a judge to hear our case and make a decision about the most important two people in my life.

Teo and Rae's futures are in the hands of a total stranger—a judge who has the power to decide. I can't believe this.

As I slumped out of the office, I was riddled with guilt. But by the time I made it back to the car, I was fuming angry, too, and had one heck of a headache. I reached for the bottle in my purse, considered what the attorney had just said about abstinence, and then popped in a pill.

Stop seeing Blade? No way! He is the only positive thing in my life. I love him. The kids will learn to love him, too. If my ex wants a fight, I am going to give him one.

Many months had passed since Mr. Disappointment left me, the kids, and our home. Month after month of high conflict, compound losses, upset, attorneys, selling our home, and what was sure to be bankruptcy with the additional cost of this trial.

I entered the courthouse in my best clothes, but my hair was still an awkward shade of rust from the at-home bleach job. Attorney of the Year walked by my side. She had one neatly-packed rolling bag, and I had brought a bunch of those old nasty email and text messages and Blade.

On the way to the courtroom, we passed the evaluator sitting in the hallway, next to Mary, the lady from child welfare who had visited my home. *We didn't subpoena either of them, so the other side must have. That can't be good.*

My ex was already sitting at the courtroom table with his attorney, Bulldog, whose name was fitting insomuch as I understood. He didn't look up at me. I noticed my mother-in-law sitting in the back of the courtroom, who glared at me and snickered something under her breath when we passed by. Attorney of the Year told Blade to go and sit out in the hallway until we were finished.

After a few minutes, a clerk in front of the judge's bench authoritatively instructed: "All rise." My attorney nudged me, and I followed her lead.

The judge entered the courtroom, a commanding presence in his long black robe, obviously a no-nonsense kind of man. He recited our family name, the case number, and made record of who was in attendance. What followed were some of the worst hours of my life.

I was called to testify, and Luke's attorney was not only aggressive but downright mean to me. He also didn't speak a lick of the truth. The evaluator went next and spent quite a bit of time answering questions from both attorneys and the judge. She beamed with positive accolades when speaking about my children, and then used a much more serious and critical tone when describing the strengths and concerns about me and Luke. Mary, the child welfare caseworker, followed her, telling the judge about her concerns for the children's safety in my home based on the reports her agency had recently received.

We took a break for lunch, and then were right back at it afterwards. My ex testified last. He should have been an actor with his Oscar-worthy performance. By 4:30 p.m., I hardly knew my own name. This had been the most stressful, exhausting, and expensive day of my life. It was surreal to be there, doing battle with the man I'd slept next to half my life.

After Mr. Disappointment left the stand, the judge asked if there were any additional witnesses. I asked my attorney if Blade should testify as a character witness, to which she sternly replied, "No!" The judge heard closing arguments from each of our lawyers. I was grateful for Attorney of the Year's eloquent summation of our family and the primary role I'd always had with Teo and Rae, but Bulldog lived up to his name. He was scrappy, accusatory, and nasty-toned in his conclusions about me. He made my ex sound like the saint he definitely is not.

I had no idea what the judge was going to do— what choices he would make for my children based on all the evidence presented. The lump sum of my twenty-year marriage had been strategically laid out by the attorneys had played the day like a game of chess, one methodical move after another, strike and counterstrike. My children's lives had been filleted open in this court of law, before a man who has never met them but was charged with deciding their future.

When it was all over, the judge leaned back in his chair, crossed his arms over his round belly, took a deep breath, and looked somewhat distressed and a-lot-a-bit mad. Without any words, he removed his glasses, rubbed his eyes, put the glasses back on, and then sat forward and made eye contact—first with me and then with Mr. Disappointment, sitting to my right. Tension in the air was palpable, thick enough to cut with a knife.

"I have been sitting on this bench the last twenty-three years, listening to disputes and gripes between divorcing parents about the very children each of them says they are here to protect. Reality is, folks, being here and fighting with each other, tearing each other down instead of focusing on improving yourselves, does not offer any amount of protection to your children. Both of you have made some terrible choices. Your choice," he said, looking directly at me, "to suddenly entertain a lifestyle of substance indulgence is foolish, ill-advised, and most importantly dangerous for Teo and Rae. Twenty-four times tardy in one school year is not acceptable, Ms. Smith. While I can see you have not yet been picked up for driving intoxicated, that seems only a matter of time by the look of your vehicle and other evidence of your substance abuse provided to this Court today. I see a window of opportunity following today's hearing for you to get some help, Ms. Smith.

Your children need you to sober up and re-engage as the mother they miss."

He paused for a moment. "Neither of you parents elicits much confidence in me about your capacity to nurture the children's emotional health, well-being, and proper adjustment during this sensitive time. Especially so with you," he said, looking at me again, "while inebriated, electing to leave them so often with other people, and having the poor judgment to introduce someone new into their lives so early, before this divorce is even final. I am ordering that Teo and Rae be enrolled into counseling within thirty days, so they have assistance going forward—someone who can help them cope and learn to deal with the flaws in this family system. I am ordering a professional assigned to the children who can help mitigate the inevitable harm that all the bad behavior I heard about today has caused and will continue to cause unless both parents intentionally work to change the thinking, behavior, and conduct that has landed your family in my courtroom."

He leaned forward even further, looking at the evaluator's report in his hand.

"The court-appointed evaluator has provided a roadmap for educational and reparative services, which mother and father are hereby ordered to participate in, including a substance dependence evaluation followed by any and all recommended treatment services for mother. Both parents will participate in individual therapy, a high-conflict parenting course, and co-parent training. They will start using the online communication platform, *Our Family Wizard*."

Releasing the evaluator's report, he clasped his hands together and paused for a moment before asking us one last question: "I believe that both of you, mother and father, would jump in front of a bus for your children. Am I right?" He stared both of us down. We both nodded in agreement and he continued. "You love them that much it would not even be a second thought to jump right out in front of a moving bus. Hear me now when I tell you both that *you are the bus*. Mr. and Ms. Smith, you are the biggest threat to your children. The conflict between you harms them, substance abuse harms them, exposing them to arguments and yelling harms them. The acts of bitterness and name-calling, finger-pointing, blaming, blame-shifting, and gaslighting are ruining your children. I cannot stop you from doing those things. Only you have the authority to choose differently, in the moment, every day. Only you can protect Teo and Rae, through the myriad of choices you resolve to make with regard to your personal thinking and conduct, and especially your behavior and attitudes toward one another."

And that was it. The scolding was finished. He made some findings, and his custody ruling came next. We were to share parenting time equally, once I participated in a substance abuse assessment and finished treatment, and Mr. Disappointment was granted sole major decision-making authority—"legal custody" of my children! My life was ruined. *How could I have lost custody of my children?*

Apparently, the judge viewed the children's father as the more "stable" parent, capable of reliable decision-making, and better able to foster a positive relationship between the children and me than I was in the reverse. The judge had told me, with no uncertain terms, that referring to Luke as "Mr. Disappointment" or "my ex" was hurtful to our children, and to stop. He made sure I understood that Teo and Rae were not "my" children, that they were not possessions to be claimed, but human beings with a mom and a dad—they were "our" children.

This was not the way I had envisioned things going. This did not feel like justice or how I had imagined my big day in court. Our legal system is so broken! But, it is a binding court order, our dissolution judgment, and the final say about how we are going to move forward.

Below are two choices Vanessa can make at this point.

Follow the judge's orders.
Turn to page page 180 to find out what happens when Vanessa makes this choice.

Fight for my children.
Turn to page page 185 to find out what happens when Vanessa makes this choice.

☉ Two Years after Vanessa
☉☉ Followed the Judge's Orders

"Did she give you her birthday wish list?" Luke asked me as we walked toward our cars parked in the back of the dark school lot. We had just finished Rae's sixth-grade parent teacher conferences, and were walking out into the cool evening air, fallen leaves crisp and crunching beneath our feet.

It had been about twenty-four months—two whole life cycles through the calendar year since our judgment—and things were just beginning to feel "normal" again. After the hearing, Attorney of the Year drove me to a treatment facility she recommended and I was admitted that day—kicking and screaming, of course. I finally surrendered and allowed myself to feel and heal all the hurt and pain that had accompanied my marriage, and our divorce. Luke had even brought the kids to family therapy at the residential treatment facility during my stay. Today, I am sober, and an active member of the recovery community. Blade got bored waiting for me while I was in treatment and took off to another state with some other gal which was probably for the best.

"Our" kids, me, and my e—Mr. Dis—the "children's father" somehow managed all those appointments and classes. Paying for them sucked, but we did it. Luke and I acquired all kinds of tools for working together as divorced co-parents, just as the judge had instructed. Teo and Rae were transitioning more smoothly between their two homes without being witness to any conflict, arguments, or bad attitudes between us. The kids each saw their own therapists now, and Teo seemed to be talking more. The court closed his juvenile case, and he was doing better in school. Rae was less angry and seemed free to love and be loved by everyone. I was focused on me, truly reclaiming myself (which, trust me, cannot be found in a club or a bottle)—an actual improved version of me, which means being the best mom possible as my sole and only priority.

Teo was driving, and Rae was off to middle school. Time was moving fast, and we knew their childhoods were fleeting, so we were both working hard to establish new traditions and make positive memories. Luke was pretty cool now, too. We even sat together at Teo's basketball games and Rae's choir concerts and dance recitals. I did what the judge said, what Attorney of the Year had instructed from the start: I stopped blaming Luke and pointing fingers elsewhere. The more aware I became, the more present I was to my own stuff, and the happier our kids were. I could see it in everything they did. They were thriving at school, in their relationships, and with their extracurricular activities. They loved their dad, and they loved me. We gave them permission to love and be loved by everyone, including both of their opinionated grandmothers. Iggy even traveled with the kids between their two homes. It was not the life I signed up for when Luke and I got married, but it was turning out alright—this season of calm that followed the storm.

"Yep!" I couldn't help but chuckle out loud as I remembered reading Rae's birthday wish list earlier that day.

"LEGOs are easy enough," he started. "I'll get her the big set she asked for—you think she's ready to build the entire Death Star?"

"Oh yeah, she can handle it. I'll get the few items of clothes and fancy high heels she wants," I said, glancing over to see Luke's eyebrows pull together in concern. "Don't worry, overprotective Daddy, they're not that high."

As we stopped short of our cars, Luke touched my shoulder before asking me the question that I knew inspired this conversation. "She wants a family birthday party, with both of us, her big brother, and her grandmothers—my mother and yours. Lord help us, do you think our mothers are ready?"

Both of Luke's strong hands dropped to his hips as he tilted his head back and looked up at the starry sky, obviously stressed out by the idea of both our mothers in the same room together. I grinned while remembering Rae's #1 wish that she had written in bubble letters, and colored bright pink with glitter sprinkled over the top for full effect. I was sure it had made both of us choke back a wave of anxiety:

#1: A FAMILY BIRTHDAY PARTY – EVERYONE I LOVE INVITED, LOVING ME UP GOOD THE WAY A GIRL SHOULD BE LOVED ON HER 12TH BIRTHDAY.

Luke turned his gaze from the sky toward me with something other than anxiety. "That kid—she's really something. Smarter than any of us. Our girl is well on her way to ruling the world, if that's what she wants." I saw pride beaming in Luke's eyes.

This man standing in front of me is the one I fell in love with—compassionate and caring.

"Yes," I agreed. "And I'm sure that she will handle her grandmothers' behavior with all of that cleverness and grace."

"You're right. I'm sure it will be fine. Good night, Vanessa." He gave me a little wave and a genuine smile and got into his car.

Driving home, I thought about how far I had come. I absolutely hated this man just two years ago. But today, I knew the truth: I still loved Luke, but not in a wife-loving-her-husband kind of way. I loved him as the father of our children, a co-parent, sharing the very most important work of our lifetimes—raising Teo and Rae to be good human beings. For them, I know Luke and I can do absolutely anything, even manage our difficult mothers so Rae can enjoy the best family birthday party ever.

Teo had really come around and would appreciate this family-focused time. He'd told me recently that he was "proud" of us—his dad and me—for finally sitting together at basketball games and being kind to each other. We had all learned through our counseling that being nice was a subjective term; but kindness and respect, these were the standards, which our family agreed to value and uphold. Teo was tearing up the floor on his high school basketball team, had amazing friends, and was getting decent grades. Our son was really growing into a wonderful young man, and he benefitted from spending as much time with his dad that the judge had ordered. He had his daddy's good looks and the sweetest girlfriend who he plans on taking to the winter formal.

It took time and lots of hard work, on both of our parts, and skilled professionals who earned every cent we paid them to educate us about how to heal our family: Teo and Rae were worth it. Our children were worth every effort it took to think, behave, and act in the new ways that have become second nature for us now—two years past the divorce.

I know things could have turned out so differently based on our choices. Looking back, I am grateful for the evaluator, her recommendations, the judge's order to engage in services, and the road map it all provided to get here—right now at this very moment—when our son is thriving, and our baby girl is about to turn twelve and wants all of us there to celebrate her birthday. My heart is full, our kids are happy, and I'm really looking forward to the next chapter.

Two Years after Vanessa Disregarded the Judge's Orders

"Can you believe that teacher?" Luke asked me as we walked toward our cars parked in dark school lot. We had just finished Rae's sixth grade parent teacher conferences, and we were walking out into the cool evening air, fallen leaves crisp beneath our feet.

It had been about twenty-four months—two whole life cycles through the calendar year—since our judgment. Before His Honor was even done speaking that day in the courtroom, I was whispering to Attorney of the Year about filing an appeal. Mr. Disappointment was not getting custody of my children, not during this lifetime. And no way was I going into some nasty gross treatment facility. I certainly couldn't afford all those expensive services the judge ordered us to participate in. He said Teo and Rae needed a counselor, but I knew he really wanted a "spy" to watch over them—logging and recording their traitorous thoughts. Attorney of the Year said I was stuck with the judge's ruling and passed me off to another attorney who specialized in appeals. The appeal is still pending, and things continued to be tumultuous between Luke and me.

It wasn't any better for the kids either. Time was moving fast, and I knew their childhoods were fleeting and their futures were not looking so bright. Teo had stopped playing sports in favor of video games and smoking weed. He had a whole new crowd of friends in high school and could not pass a class to save his life. *Maybe if he actually attended class...* At this rate, he was headed to be a dropout. He was also supposed to be driving, but was still in trouble with the law and not able to get his license as a result.

Rae was off to middle school, apparently failing all of her classes, according to the teachers we had just met. She had become the class clown and was totally boy crazy. I'd caught her by the pool several times, making out with different boys. Plus, she was terribly thin and often refused to eat. I wanted her to see a doctor, but Luke has legal custody, and I am not supposed to be the parent who schedules medical appointments.

I hadn't done anything the judge ordered and was still drinking and popping pills. Luke had filed contempt charges against me; apparently, now he thought the kids' time with me should be supervised. I was mad as hell all the time and had needed the booze and pills to numb the pain. The kids moved between houses when we told them to, like robots, and hated it. They compartmentalized everything and barely said a word to me when they were home. Iggy had to be re-homed because I just didn't have the money to take care of him anymore.

One more thing Rae hates me for.

"Yah, she's a real peach," I responded to Luke, "saying Rae has problems. The only problem our daughter has is spending so much time with *you*. She never gets her homework done at your place. You cannot even handle the simplest things, Luke."

Luke responded in the same nasty tone as usual, "Whatever, woman. It's all my fault, huh? Nothing's ever good enough, right, Ms. High and Mighty?"

I was not in the mood for button-pushing tonight. So, I shoved him with all my might. He stumbled but outweighed me by fifty pounds and was completely fine.

His Cheshire Cat grin instantly emerged, putting me on-guard. Of course, he had his phone in hand and was video recording. I watched as he dialed 911 and listened as he fabricated and totally out-of-proportion story until police cars came screaming into the school lot as other parents looked on after leaving their child's conferences. Officer Timothy was there with several others. We had gotten to be on a first-name basis with most of the local force. Luke showed them the video of me pushing him. The police gave us a stern talking to and instructed us to part ways immediately and go home.

I drove home, where Blade was waiting, and wondered where things had gone so wrong, why my kids were self-destructing, and if there was any hope for us.

Suddenly, the words of the evaluator's report rang in my ears:

> We know that children exposed to ongoing conflict, negative information about the other parent and unstable home lives, *always* have long-term emotional problems. Children who are exposed to ongoing parental conflict *will* have adjustment problems in their preadolescent and teen years that most commonly manifest in extreme defiance and anger, delinquent behavior, substance abuse, teen pregnancy, eating disorders, suicide attempts,

failing grades, and high dropout rates at school. It is one of the only certainties in the professional literature and surely not the legacy these parents wish for Teo and Rae.

Could this really be Teo and Rae's fate? Have their father and I sentenced them to these kind of unhappy lives with our poor choices and all the ongoing anger between us?

I wish there was a do-over—a mulligan—for my kids. I know there is not a reset button, but maybe, just maybe their father and I can choose better and still turn things around.

"Believing takes practice."

~Madeleine L'Engle~
A Wrinkle in Time

BE THE BETTER PARENT

Demonstrate why the kids will be better off with me, since I have always been their primary parent.

I TRADED MY wine for a mug of warm herbal tea and reached a decision about preparing for the custody evaluation. Opening my laptop, I searched for the evaluator's website.

When I clicked on the "how to prepare" tab, a dropdown appeared and, with one more click, I found printable worksheets and questionnaires, lots of suggested resources, and creative ideas for getting into the right mindset before our first meeting.

I sipped my sweet tea and kept scanning through tabs on the evaluator's website. Eventually, I picked up a pen and legal pad and got busy outlining my thoughts with the help of the parent questionnaire. Then, I created a timeline of important family events per her suggestion.

Pausing, I thought to myself, *I'll set a special meeting with Attorney of the Year and learn the best legal approach to the evaluation, too.*

After perusing the evaluator's website and jotting my thoughts down, I was feeling a little more confident and ready to tackle what had initially seemed like a massive undertaking. Before closing my computer, I ordered the suggested reads and bookmarked some webpages about divorce and the impact of high conflict on children.

There is a lot to consider for Teo and Rae—so much I can do myself to help them through all the changes happening in their lives.

With a deep sigh of relief, I finished my cup of tea.

We're going to be alright, I thought to myself as I turned off all the lights and crawled into bed that night.

The next few days were spent focused on the worksheets and parent questionnaires I'd found on the evaluator's webpage. Several of the suggested books I'd ordered arrived in record time, and I was busy reading those as well. Per the advice from the website and the books, I made sure the kids and I were consistent with counseling appointments, and that we were all eating well and getting good rest. Homework was done on time, they kept up with their activities, and we regularly saw our family and friends. I decided to stay off social media altogether for the time being; and, quite frankly, the break was refreshing. I focused on making sure we kept life as predictable as possible, so the uncertainty of these uncharted waters didn't close in and threaten to drown us.

At my pre-evaluation meeting the following week, Attorney of the Year helped me understand the legal statutes in our state with regard to custody and parenting time:

1. emotional ties between the child
   and other family members,

2. interest of the parties in and attitude
   toward the other child,

3. desirability of continuing an
   existing relationship,

4. the abuse of one parent by the other,

5. preference for the primary caregiver, and

6. willingness and ability of each parent
   to facilitate and encourage a close
   and continuing relationship between
   the other parent and the child.

She told me that custody is not determined by isolating any one factor, but that #6 was really important to children's ability to properly adjust and thrive after divorce.

She urged that I keep practicing compassionate self-care during the stress of all this so I could model emotional steadiness for Teo and Rae—ensuring their worlds would not feel so upside-down: "Just like on the airplane, be sure to fasten your own oxygen mask before assisting those you love. If you cannot breathe, you are not going to be of any use to others that are depending on you for help," she reminded me.

She said I was ready and the limited number of well-organized and indexed email and text messages I'd collected to support my parenting concerns were just the right amount to get my point across without overwhelming the evaluator with the ocean of paper I could have printed off. My attorney congratulated me on a job well done for my kids since the separation from their father, and I left feeling rather proud of myself.

Many months had passed since I had been served the divorce lawsuit on the front stoop of our old house, and the day had finally arrived for me to meet our court-appointed evaluator at her professional office.

This year has not been easy. In fact, I would not wish it on anyone. I experienced such intense emotions swirling around inside, all the time, sometimes going from happy to sad to angry in the same hour. Then this often repeated, for days and weeks at a time.

The books I'd ordered had really started to set me straight. Some of my favorite, game-changing reads were *Joint Custody with a Jerk, People Can't Drive You Crazy If You Don't Give Them the Keys,* and *Loving Your Children More Than You Hate Each Other.* But the books were just the beginning.

Without such good legal counsel, my therapist, the rock-solid support of our family and friends, Teo and Rae's amazing teachers and counselors, and the kids' steady involvement in organized activities and sports, I imagine things would be quite different right now in our family. Assembling this team of support had made a world of difference.

Luke had not made anything easy, and it was hard not responding to his BS. In counseling, I'd learned how to keep my power by setting boundaries and holding firm. I'd learned how not to engage when he was provocative. Most of all, I'd learned that I had the power to insulate and protect the kids by not saying bad things about their father, addressing and letting go of my anger, and doing everything on my end that I could to put some armor on them so they, too, could feel empowered.

Boy, I am a different person than when all of this started, I thought to myself, casually driving to the evaluator's office.

I glanced down at the one small notebook I was taking to the meeting and the picture of our family on the front. Yes, Luke is in the picture, too, with the kids hanging all over their daddy. I had a timeline of important family events and a few notes in case I got nervous and forgot some of the most important things about life with my kids. I had completed the required paperwork and listed the requested number of personal references, even though I wanted to give far more than the three she requested.

I am so ready to advocate for Teo and Rae and move our lives forward.

I'd had a good night's sleep, enjoyed a morning walk with Rae and Iggy (Teo slept in), cooked a good breakfast for us, and was as ready as I would ever be for this very important day. Feeling a little shy and somewhat embarrassed to be in this situation, though grateful for the help, I opened the door to the evaluator's office.

Nice place, I thought as I walked in. *Nothing like Attorney of the Year's corner suite on the tenth floor, but it is comfy in here.*

There was a harmless looking, sensible-shoe-wearing, middle-aged lady with naturally curly hair at the front desk. She welcomed me and offered coffee or water. Almost as soon as I signed the disclosure form, secured a copy for my own records, and paid my portion of the professional fee, the cheerful, sales-rack-dressed evaluator emerged from the back office and introduced herself with a firm handshake. She had kind eyes and a warm smile, and made me feel welcome.

Not intimidating at all. A genuine person. She looks like a mom, too. I wonder if she has kids. I immediately felt justified in my optimism.

After releasing my hand, the evaluator led me into our meeting space which was flooded with soft light. There were two comfortable chairs along with her standup desk and treadmill. *What a great idea!* I thought as we passed it.

The room smelled like home and I quickly felt safe. There was an area to my right set up for kids with toys, art, books, LEGOs, chalk, magnets, and even a little table just Rae's size. Teo's knees might be a little too tall, but he'd adapt.

They are going to love coming here and seeing some of the same familiar things they use at their counseling meetings.

We sat down together, and a wave of absolute relief came over me when the evaluator smiled, asked me how I was doing, and began outlining the process ahead. This was the same humble professional her webpage portrayed. She was here for my kids.

"Vanessa, most parents are a bit nervous meeting me for the first time, although they usually feel much better by the end of our two hours together. I know it has probably been a long road leading up to today, and you're likely feeling emotionally and financially exhausted. Add to that the constant worry about your children, and a parent can really start to feel like they have been swept down the proverbial rabbit hole.

"The good news is that this evaluation is an opportunity to step back from the adversarial high conflict that litigation often creates between two parents, as we fully explore and concentrate on the needs of your children. We'll be discussing the strengths of each parent and both parents' concerns, and then put our big brains together to design the best plan for Teo and Rae." She gave me a settling smile, confident in her conviction to do what's right for the kids.

Well, that sounds promising and exceptionally reasonable. My big brain and your big brain, working in tandem, for my children's benefit.

She kept talking about working *together* as a "team"—her, me, and Luke—which was a little confusing at first, but then she explained: "I have never met a parent who didn't love their child. Mothers and fathers come to this process, both wanting what they believe is in their child's best interest. They both want their children to win the game, but they are working from different playbooks.

"My hope is to bring you and the children's father 80% of the way toward the middle, and then provide enough guidance and direction that the two of you can finish off the last 20% by infusing the final plan for Teo and Rae with specific details to meet the unique needs of your family. When both parents are invested in the final plan, and both feel heard and that they had a say in what's best, the plan is far more likely to work versus a legal and binding judgment imposed on your family by the court. Make sense?" Again, she paused, making sure I was tracking with her.

Make sense? Oh my goodness, why didn't we do this evaluation months ago? I nodded enthusiastically in agreement while legitimately understanding that we were in fact a team here—team Teo and Rae—all working together for their best interest.

After fifteen minutes of hearing her talk about children needing both parents, and this process being focused on reaching a mutual agreement while avoiding a courtroom trial, I emphatically knew this was the right way to ensure the best outcome for our family— for Teo and Rae's family, even though we look a little different now than we used to.

"Thank you," I offered. "I appreciate this opportunity to participate in a child-focused process and to move our family in the best direction possible."

"I'm glad to hear that, Vanessa. The goal of our time today is for you to educate me about the story of your family. How you got from point A (meeting the children's father) to point B (a custody litigant). Only a small percentage of divorcing parents ever participate in an evaluation. I'm curious to learn all about why your family is here and begin to understand ways in which I can best assist your children and family moving forward." She paused before giving me further instruction.

"It would be helpful if you could go down memory lane. Relay information in chronological order—paint a picture of the most significant events in your family's timeline. Throughout the story, please highlight the most important details of your children's lives (residential moves, school/academics, friendships, important relationships, activities/sports/music, health, religion, special needs, services, successes, areas where they struggle and excel, etc.)."

She paused for emphasis.

"In addition to learning as much as possible about your children's lives, it is necessary that we identify and understand patterns of conflict between you and the other parent. Patterns of conflict are important to uncover because embedded within them are often your parenting concerns; and unless we make an effort to understand and mitigate the unhealthy patterns of conflict that exist now, those unhealthy patterns will perseverate, harm your children, and continue to cause trouble for your family after the divorce. Exposure to conflict is detrimental to Teo and Rae and will inflict irreparable psychological harm over time."

Her body language was relaxed and poised. With raised eyebrows, head tilted slightly to the right, she made eye contact, clearly looking for my buy-in to this process that the court had ordered my family participate in. She repositioned a little straighter in her chair, picked up a notepad and pencil, and gestured to me, as if offering me the floor to start talking.

I repositioned, too, took a deep breath, and vividly recalled meeting Luke in college. "We were so young and unburdened by the demands of adulthood, although at the time felt mature and in love, ready to get married, and start a family as soon as we earned our degrees. That's precisely what we did. At the ripe ages of twenty-two and twenty-three years old, we said, 'I do' and never imagined two decades later we would say, 'I don't.' When the kids were born, we decided I would stay home while he worked as the sole wage earner. He was hired on with a good company and has since received several promotions."

I paused, noticing that I still sounded proud of his accomplishment.

"We were happy—the all-American family. A suburban home, two cars, two kids, and our beloved dog Iggy joined the family five years ago. On paper and to any outsider, we looked to have it all. Then life happened. Unpredictable as it is. Highs, lows, celebrations, and heartbreaks. Mother-in-laws, the drama created by other family members, and triangles of friends. All the things you never consider when you are in college, in love, and fantasizing about your life to be—the fantasy life you eventually realize was created by childhood storybooks, movies, and the belief in a happily-ever-after..."

I walked the evaluator through our whole family history, making sure to focus on Teo and Rae and the relationship we share, along with their strengths and struggles in life.

"Teo is a rock-star athlete in middle school—a basketball player. He is not academically gifted, but tries hard and earns good marks. He is on task, wants to please, has a sensitive heart, is a loyal friend, and doesn't say too much unless there is something important to be said. Rae is fiery, loves life, and tries everything. She is artistic and musical, a hip-hop dancer, gymnast, and brown belt martial artist. In the winter, she plays basketball; and come spring, she switches to softball. Academics come easily for her. My girl can really talk! Everyone loves Rae, and Rae loves everyone. This has been the hardest on her—her family falling apart..."

I also told her about their father's strengths, what he does well, along with the areas that give me concern for the children's well-being while in his care. I confidently painted a realistic picture, careful about separating my feelings for Luke from my concerns about our children's time in his care. The evaluator affirmed what I was saying all along through her body language and a few "Atta girl" remarks, particularly when I told her about not responding to the snarky and provocative text messages my ex sent late at night. Sharing all of this was cathartic, and I knew the course I had chosen for the kids and myself this past year had been a healthy one—to do what is right and best for them. It has not been easy for me, but it has been best for them.

I feel a million pounds lighter, I noticed while thanking the evaluator. We scheduled our next appointment, and I bounced out of the office toward my car in the parking lot.

I called Attorney of the Year from the parking lot and got one more "Atta girl!" before heading off to the coffee shop for my afternoon shift. I felt good knowing the kids would be with their dad the next night. He is a flawed human being (same as us all, I suppose), but I know he adores them the same as I do. Teo and Rae really miss their dad, and I have come to learn and appreciate that they need his influence, equal to mine.

Their daddy would take them to their Friday activities and then out for pizza, and they'd spend the weekend in his new place. I tried to push the thought of *her* out of my mind, knowing he had brought someone new (actually a few new someone's) into the kids' lives so soon. It was no surprise to me that Luke didn't pay close attention during the court-ordered parenting class we both sat through. The knowledgeable facilitators emphasized the need for children to heal and for parents to wait before starting a new relationship. Alas, paying attention was never Luke's forte, nor was patience.

Not like he's ever listened to anyone before, or is about to start to now, I guess. I softly scoffed to myself and shook my head. *It's not surprising that he's already snagged himself another woman, and Teo's best friend's mother of all people. At least I know she'll be good to our kids. At the end of the day, that's really all that matters to me.*

I sighed out of frustration and concern, and then quickly reminded myself: *We are all the simple sum of our choices. None of us can control the choices other people make. I have learned that children need one safe place, and one safe parent, to come out of this okay; and I am resolved to be that for them. That much, I can control—the endless choices I make every day about the way I conduct myself. It is the emotional safety I create for my kids in my home that has helped them to adjust and thrive.*

When I arrived at the coffee shop, there were already four girls on shift. The manager on duty happily informed me I was not on the schedule for today. *Hallelujah!* I gave the girls a smile and quick wave, said hi to several of the regulars, and headed back to my car. The sun was shining bright with blue sky all around and the warmth felt good on my face as I drove home with the windows down and my favorite music streaming on Spotify®. When I arrived to our little apartment complex, there was extra time to appreciate the flowers in full bloom and the vibrant green color of the grass. Extra time was a rarity these days, and I chose to use what I had wisely.

The house could use a quick clean. Maybe I'll even bake some cookies.

I preheated the oven to 350 and pulled some overpriced (but worth it!) gluten-free break-n-bake cookies from the freezer so the dough had time to thaw. While the oven heated up, I straightened the couch pillows, folded a few blankets, unloaded the clean dishes, and loaded in the dirty ones left over from breakfast.

Beep. The oven was ready for cookies. I set the timer for twenty minutes and headed down the hall where the cleaning supplies were stored.

I poured bleach into the toilets and the sinks, and filled them with warm water. Then I grabbed the vacuum and worked my way around every corner of the apartment, careful not to suck up stray earrings, LEGO pieces, or hair ties. Iggy's dog hair was everywhere.

It sure is nice for Rae to have her dog here with us. I still cannot believe Luke took her best buddy with him when he first moved out. Just glad he came to his senses and let Iggy come home, though I do wonder if Iggy is maybe not allowed at his downtown apartment? That's probably it. He can't have Iggy there and probably got himself into trouble not following the rules of his lease. Some things will never change.

When I opened the door to Teo's room, a wave of gym stink almost knocked me over. I quickly picked up the dirty laundry and candy wrappers that were scattered on the floor by his unmade bed, opened a window, sprayed some Febreze, and called it good.

Now, for Rae's room.

When I opened her bedroom door, an appreciative smile stretched across my face. Rae's room was much tidier than her brother's, and it always smelled good. She had lots of stuff, but liked everything to be organized. Her clothes were sorted by color in her closet, and her books were placed on the shelf in alphabetical order. She loved art and had her slime-making supplies stacked neatly on her desk next to pictures of her besties. A picture of our family—all four of us, and Iggy—had been placed inside a homemade frame Rae had made at camp one summer and hung above her bed.

Suddenly overwhelmed, I paused and remembered the day it was taken.

It wasn't that long ago, but the kids looked so much younger and we all looked happy. It has been a time of learning, grieving, and overcoming—for the kids and for me.

My eyes trailed down to the little bedside table and her fuzzy, flip-sequence diary.

I shouldn't. I knew it was wrong to look but decided it wouldn't hurt anything. I cracked open the diary to the first entry...

Dear Diary, this is Rae. My dad left the house for good and he took my dog Iggy. I hate him for taking Iggy. Iggy needs me and I need him. He is my best friend and I have no idea where he is now or if my dad will bring him back. I hate my dad for leaving but I miss him. Why is he doing this to our family? Mom says he is a disappointment. He even stole my favorite blanket. I told my mom about the blanket and she said she would ask dad for it back, along with Iggy. I wonder if I will ever see my dad again. Mom says I will always see both her and dad but everything is so weird right now I do not know if that's true. I hope this divorce is not my fault. Me and my brother are not perfect kids. Mom keeps saying it's not our fault but I suppose we could have tried harder. Maybe if me and Teo were better at our stuff they wouldn't have fought so much and dad would still be here, with Iggy.

I'm so glad you now know this is no fault of yours or Teo's. Sometimes things just don't work out for moms and dads, but we both love you and your brother to the moon! I'll always love your dad, because he is a part of you, and you of him. Thank goodness the counselor advised me to stop referring to him as Mr. Disappointment!

My eyes wet with tears, I quickly flipped through the diary pages and saw she had made consistent entries. Sometimes, there were days or weeks in between, but there were fairly consistent entries from the day her dad had left the house.

Dear Diary, this is Rae. My dad is still gone and Iggy too. My mom is super concerned about us. Sometimes she hangs around too long, especially at school and it is kinda annoying but I like it when she is there too. It is really nice there is no more fighting in the house between her and my dad. Mom says there are lots of smart people helping to get all the adult stuff sorted out and I do not have to worry about anything except being a kid. Mom told me and Teo there are special people that help kids with their feelings when their parents get divorced. She took me and Teo to see a 'talking person' called a counselor. My counselor is awesome! We do lots of art and play in this cool sandbox sometimes. Both of my grandmas seem really mad about stuff, but mom always jumps in and stops her mom if she starts to say something bad about my dad, or starts to say anything about their divorce. Grandma usually zips it when mom tells her to.

Ugh, Mom, get it together. I hope Luke is handling his emotions, and mouth, and monitoring what other people say when the kids are with him.

Dear Diary, this is Rae. We have to move from our house because of my stupid parents divorce. None of this is fair. My life is ruined!

My heart nearly stopped in my chest. *That was such a hard time. We did our best and I think we are comfortable here now. We'll get a new house, once this is all settled. A real nice home with a fenced backyard, where you and Iggy can play.*

Dear Diary, this is Rae. We moved to a little apartment with mom, and I still have my own room. I'm in here right now. It's not too terrible at all, I actually like it. There's a pool and a playground but mom does not let us go down there alone without her. My dad lives downtown now, in the city, in a haunted house. It is weird, but at least I get to see my dad. We go there on the weekends and eat lots of pizza. Iggy is finally home with me!!!!!!!!! He says woof.

I need to keep helping her with these transitions between our two homes. Why did Luke have to move to an apartment numbered 666? I don't know how else to convince her it is just a silly superstition and not actually a haunted house.

I heard the oven timer beep and took Rae's journal to the kitchen with me so I could keep reading. It was almost time for school pickup, so I flipped to the last page.

Dear Diary, this is Rae. I miss our family being together, and sometimes wish everything could go back to the way it used to be but I know this is the way things are now and my parents are not getting back together. My counselor says it is normal for kids to feel this way and she helps me a lot. She says I am a strong girl and it takes time after a big change for things to feel normal again. We see my dad on weekends and during the week at our activities and mom takes good care of us on school days. They are even nice to each other now when we are all together. I see them laughing together sometimes. Teo has been cool to me since all of this happened, he is a good big brother most of the time, except when he is playing video games for hours or on his stupid phone. My counselor said I should think of a theme song, something that would help me stay focused on all the good stuff, a song that reminds me of how special I am and how much both my parents love me. I picked This Is Me from the Greatest Showman..."I am brave, I am bruised, I am who I'm meant to be, This Is Me!!!" xoxoxoxoxo Rae

My sweet girl, I know this has been hard on you.

I walked back to her room, cued up iTunes on an iPod that sat on the bedside table, and played her chosen theme song. As the melody started, tears thundered down, and I reflected on our last year and the challenge it has been for all of us. I was filled with gratitude for having found my way to the right people and resources that have helped us all get through this difficult year. It wasn't easy, but I was doing my best to keep our kids happy and healthy while learning to co-parent with Luke.

I don't know what life would be like if I hadn't put the kids at the center of my world during this past year. I might have really gone off the deep end with a few bad (and tempting) choices, and I bet that this diary would look a lot different. Rae's obviously feeling the pain and grief of her parents' divorce, but at least she knows we're trying.

I glanced up at the pink clock on her desk and realized my time was up. The diary was placed back as I'd found it, and I hustled to the kitchen where I packed up some fresh-baked, gluten-free cookies and grabbed two cold bottles of water from the fridge before I headed out to collect them from school.

It seemed like a productive day, and a sense of calm filled me as I navigated the familiar streets to their schools.

Maybe we should go out for their favorite dinner tonight. I'll let them choose.

Teo got released from school first. He was always ready to roll, and found me parked down the road under an oak tree that had become our pickup spot. He jumped into the front seat, eyeballed the cookies, and gave me a loving grunt before stuffing his face. I asked how his day was, and he let me know things were "all good, mom." He didn't have much to say but I could tell by his mood, positive friendships, steady grades, and focus on basketball that he was doing well. He had goals and was working toward them. He was after a college scholarship in basketball—the sport that he loved.

We enjoyed happy chit-chat for fifteen minutes or so in the car and then eased into the carpool line at Rae's school, where several familiar faces offered a smile and wave. Sally, from the gym, was there with her three kiddos. I remembered that she too was divorced last year, and knew she used the same child custody evaluator. The thought of consulting with her had briefly flashed through my mind, and then I thought better of it.

Sally's kids are having problems at school, and she seems to be having a rough go of it herself. In the hallway at school recently, I had heard her belittling her children's father. After reading about the damage this causes to children, I had made a very conscious choice never to engage in that type of conduct. It seemed best to keep my distance from Sally and surround myself with positive people, and only happily divorced people who co-parent their children with kindness and co-parenting respect. They were few and far between, but they did exist.

Right on cue, Rae came skipping out of the building with her school bag slung over her shoulder and one shoe untied. She jumped into the back seat, talking a million miles a minute about her "om-azing" day while I smiled at the glitter tattoo on her arm.

"I smell cookies!" Rae has the nose of a bloodhound and demanded to know where the cookies were without ever seeing them. Her brother teased that they were already gone, so she kicked his seat and socked him in the arm. "Give 'em up, pal!" Teo laughed and handed her what was left in the bag.

Man, I love these two. For them, I will continue to make even the most difficult sacrifices.

Their satisfied faces and Rae's fast-moving stories, interrupted momentarily by a bite of cookie here and a bite of cookie there, warmed my heart. I knew it was going to be okay—better than okay. I had assembled the help we needed to get us through this major family change. I had been and would continue to do what was right for them. The second evaluation meeting was a couple days away, and I looked forward to it.

The second meeting with our evaluator was different from the first. I was greeted in the same way, and we went to the comfortable back office; but once we were seated, the evaluator told me she had an agenda. It would be more of a structured interview than our first. She had lots of questions about my parenting, daily routines in my household, the kids' healthcare and dental care, extended family relationships, holiday traditions, their activities, friendships, and school. We walked through my thoughts about the best parenting plan and why I thought it would work. That part was easy. The kids needed ample time with both parents and permission to love everyone, although I thought it would be best that they continue to spend school nights with me. My goal was to create a safe bridge between houses, allowing them to ebb and flow between with ease.

The evaluator then said it was time for her to share Luke's parenting concerns, so we could sort through some of the disagreements, and she could hear both sides of the story.

I'm not gonna lie. It was really hard to hear and respond to those critical items Luke brought to the attention of our evaluator. But, I know I'm not perfect and made notes so I could discuss Luke's concerns with my therapist. At least I knew what he was telling the evaluator, and she gave me the opportunity to share my perspective.

We scheduled our third evaluation meeting for early the following week. That meeting would include the children at the office. I asked her what I should tell the children between appointments. She suggested I tell them a little bit about her and her office, let them know that their father and I have both talked to her, have them take an online office tour, and assure them that they do not have to talk about anything they don't want to. She told me the burden of this process is not theirs, and she never asks kids where they want to live, because it is not their decision to make. She also assured me that she does not poke and prod at children for information they don't want to or are not ready to share. She was simply interested in getting to know them a little bit.

I made a few mental notes, thanked her, and headed out.

Back at the apartment, and after school that day, I invited Teo and Rae to our kitchen table to take the webpage-tour of the evaluator's office. Teo's attention span is pretty short, and he seemed distracted by a group-chat on his phone. He asked when the appointment was and seemed only concerned that he would not miss basketball practice. Rae spotted the toys and art and was excited about meeting the "nice-looking lady."

I trust the evaluator knows what she is doing and will take good care of the kids.

On the day of our meeting, I picked the kids up a little early from school so we could grab a quick snack, use the bathroom, and make the 3:00 p.m. meeting at the evaluator's office on time. When we walked in, she was ready for us.

"Hi there!" she welcomed with her warm smile and sing-song voice. After introducing herself to Teo and Rae, she invited all of us into the back office. This time, there was a large white piece of paper sitting on the little table and colored pencils, markers, crayons, watercolor paints, and stickers neatly stacked in piles.

"Teo, you're so tall. Here's a bigger chair for you." He gave her a crooked smile, appearing to feel comfortable the same way I had felt during that first meeting several weeks before.

"Alrighty, so I want to get to know you and your family a little bit today, so here's what I'd love for you to do first. I'd like you to create a family picture together—a favorite family memory or vacation or holiday—where everyone is doing something in the picture. Include whomever you like, your best friends, grandparents, and especially your pets if you have any."

Rae piped right up, "We have a dog named Iggy. Well, he's my dog really."

"Cool!" replied the evaluator. "I love dogs, too. Go ahead and get busy discussing what you want to draw and have at it. I'll give you about fifteen minutes to work together and I'll just stay out of your way."

All three of us smiled at each other and nodded as the evaluator backed out of our space and started playing some music in the background, so we could get started.

"How about we draw a scene at our new apartment, down by the pool," I suggested.

Both of them shook their heads at me, so I proposed drawing other good family memories since the separation, with just the three of us.

Rae said, "Let's make a Christmas morning scene around the tree at our old house—before the divorce."

Teo agreed with the lift of his eyebrows and a slight nod, and I told Rae that was a great idea. We discussed what to put in our picture and divided up the parts of the picture. The evaluator said everyone needed to be doing something, so we chose to draw our family sitting around the kitchen table, eating Christmas morning cinnamon rolls, playing a game of poker. Luke loved to play poker and had taught both the kids to play when they were young. Rae was a real shark.

The kids spoke fondly about their dad and me, and we laughed and made fun of each other's drawings. Teo was good at sketching and Rae was good with color—she made the biggest, most sparkly Christmas tree right in the center of the paper. He added a bright yellow star. I drew Iggy, curled up under the tree on his doggie bed. It was a fun project and our hour was passing quickly.

The evaluator asked if she could join us at the table, and Rae answered with a resounding, "Yes!"

Once seated along with us, she asked about each member of the family, including Iggy. When she asked questions about their dad, the kids answered freely. They were happy to share about their time with both of us. The evaluator noticed an extra person Rae had drawn on the paper near where she sat. Rae said that was dad's "special friend," and Teo looked uncomfortable and rolled his eyes. Rae explained that dad's special friend was Teo's best friend's mom. The evaluator simply affirmed whatever my kids told her and did not probe for more information. I had not mentioned Luke's special friend during our individual interviews, as I did not think it was relevant. I knew who she was, knew she was a good person, and was grateful she treated the kids well.

After a little time together, the evaluator asked the kids if it would be okay for me to sit in the other room, on the comfy couch, while the three of them played a game together. Rae looked up at me, winked, and said, "Yah sure." Teo just gave her an affirming grunt while shuffling the UNO™ cards she had already placed on the table.

"I will be right outside the door," I assured the kids. I kissed the top of Rae's head, collected my purse, smiled at Teo, who seemed perfectly at ease, and left my children with this court-appointed professional who had the grace of a snake charmer.

After grabbing an *Oprah* magazine from the wall rack, I sat down on the couch and appreciated the classical music playing in the reception area. There was a white noise machine whooshing away, which sort of made me sleepy. Faintly, I could hear Teo's deep baritone voice prattling on and on about something, more words than usual coming out of his mouth; and there were intermittent bouts of laughter from all three of them.

I'm proud of you, son. Stepping out of your comfort zone to share, in here, with this professional who wants to help you and our family.

When the three of them emerged from the back office, my children looked at peace and Teo was still talking. Rae gave the evaluator a big hug before she directed both of them to a treasure box. Each of them picked something while the evaluator said, "I'll see you Friday with your dad. I'm excited to see you at both of your homes, and to meet Iggy."

Rae had to stop at the restroom, and Teo headed right to the car. He was already texting someone on his phone, and I wondered who he would want to tell about this unique experience. His best friend? The girl I knew he liked? Or maybe his dad?

None of my business, I suppose.

"Rae, how did it go?" I asked.

"Fine," she answered matter-of-factly from behind the stall door. I was dying to know what they had talked about, but respected her right to some privacy. The evaluator had provided me with guidance about insulating the kids through this process—specifically by not digging for information about their conversations during session, which was the same rule their counselor had provided. I understood that was the best practice.

Rae flushed and came out of the stall to wash her hands. "She was super cool, Mom. She said that she is not on your side or Dad's side in the divorce. She said she knows that you and Dad both love us very much and that going through the divorce of your parents is a really, really hard thing for kids. She said she was on *our* team—me and Teo—and her job is to make sure that we will always see both of our parents and that we are happy, safe, and healthy. I think we passed that test!"

"That all sounds good, honey. I'm glad you felt comfortable here."

She turned the faucet off, wiped her hands, and held the door to the restroom open for me, so I could pass through in front of her.

All that hard work when they were little has paid off. Both of my kids have manners.

As we were approaching the car, I could see my son in the front seat with his phone, smiling and laughing. I was pleased he handled this day so well. After Rae and I got into our seats and buckled in, I started the car and Teo connected the Bluetooth®. We drove home, windows down, listening to their favorite playlist, all three of us singing along.

Both kids said they had some homework to finish before Teo's evening basketball practice, and I headed right into the kitchen to start dinner. Rae and I planned on doing a little grocery shopping while her brother was at the gym.

Homework. Check.

Dinner. Check. Check.

Basketball practice. Right on time. Phew, what a day.

As we pulled into the gym lot, I saw Luke's shiny new muscle car.

"Dad's here!" Rae burst excitedly when she spotted his Mustang from the back seat.

I looked over and Teo was smiling. He scooped up his ball bag and hopped right out.

"Mom, I want to go see Dad," Rae announced, her body already in motion and leaving the backseat of my car.

I rolled down the window and yelled out to Teo to have fun, and that I'd be there when he was finished. He gave me a silent but assured wave and flashed his handsome smile.

Looking up, I caught sight of Rae passing through the front doors on her way into the gym. I was still sitting in the car and contemplated whether I should go in, or just wait for her, giving her the time with her dad that she obviously wanted and needed.

After twenty minutes or so, warring with myself, I decided it was probably best to go in and check on her. I locked the car and headed into the gym where I found her sitting on her dad's lap, watching Teo's practice, and scrolling around on Luke's phone. They looked happy.

Teo was out on the floor tearing it up. *That's my boy!* My heart always swelled with pride when I saw his long, lean body move effortlessly up and down the court.

Although it was not 100% comfortable to do so, I walked over to Luke and said hello. He looked up and smiled, and Rae waved, "Mommy!"

I asked if she still wanted to do some grocery shopping and she said, "No, I want to stay with Dad."

Luke hugged Rae around her tummy, kissed her head, and made eye contact with me. "Would it be okay if I took them for ice cream when practice is over?"

Ugh seriously? He asks in front of the kids so if I say no, I look like the bad guy?

"Come on, Mommy, please. Please can we go out with Dad for ice cream?" she begged.

"Of course, honey. Just make sure they are home by 8:00 p.m., Luke. It's a school night."

He assured me he would, and I told Rae I'd see her later and left the gym, kids now in their dad's care for the next two hours.

Parenting from two homes, with someone you do not necessarily like, leaves a lot to be figured out. All the books I had read reinforced that it was not "my time" and "your time," but all time belongs to the children. This was hard to remember, as an adult, when he just showed up unexpectedly and changed my plans for the night without any warning. I would need to discuss this with him, away from Teo and Rae, at the right time and place. For the moment, I headed to the grocery store alone.

At the store, I collected all the kids' favorite foods, planned a couple of dinners while walking up and down the aisles, and realized as I shopped that it was a nice change of pace to have this quiet time, albeit in the grocery store. I grabbed a solo cupcake for myself from the bakery before checking out and heading home with food for the week.

Just as I finished unpacking the bags in our apartment kitchen, the kids rolled through the front door. Rae had chocolate and a few sprinkles stuck to her face, and Iggy ran to greet them, his tongue licking a million miles a minute.

"Hi, Mom!" Rae pet Iggy's head then ran over and gave me a big bear hug. Teo was right behind her with his basketball bag, and Luke was behind him. Luke stopped in the doorway, respecting my space. He smiled, waved, and said, "Thanks for letting me take them. We all had a good time. Right, kids?"

Yeses all around.

"Sure thing," I said, working hard to keep my tone light. It was strange to feel so awkward communicating with this man after being married to him for twenty years.

"Can I talk to you real quick?" Luke asked, distracted by Iggy now circling his feet, obviously excited to see him, too. "Hi, boy. Yes, Daddy misses you. Go inside, Igg. In yah go. Go find Rae."

"Um yah sure, of course. Rae, take Iggy and go hop into the tub, please, and brush your fangs, girl. You're a chocolaty mess!" Rae hugged her dad, thanked him for the ice cream, called Iggy to follow her, and ran off toward the bathroom.

Teo gave his dad a fist-bump, during which both made an undecipherable grumbling noise, followed by a quick "love yah," and our son headed for his bedroom. Once I heard the tub running and Teo's music start playing down the hall, Luke and I stepped outside and tightly shut the apartment door so the kids could not hear us talking.

"Sorry I put you on the spot tonight. I realize that was not fair of me. I'm trying to get this right. I think I might have screwed up."

What? Insight and taking responsibility? Who is this man?

"Thanks for saying so. It would be good if we exchanged a quick text message and checked in with each other before showing up someplace unexpected and changing the anticipated plan. I'm glad it worked out this time, and the kids are obviously happy. I want them to have both of us at all of their activities and special events, but we need to communicate and be respectful of the children's time in each of our care. "

Luke continued, "Mutual respect and communication. The evaluator has stressed how critical those two variables are for our kids to do well and to thrive. I get it."

I could not agree more!

"Sounds good, Luke. Good night." I opened the apartment door to head back in while Luke started toward his Mustang.

Rae was standing just inside the door, in her robe. "Daddy, Daddy, bye. Olive juice!" she yelled to her daddy.

From the dark parking lot, Luke yelled back, "Olive juice, baby. See you in two days!"

"Olive juice" was something Luke had always said to Rae, at bedtime, ever since she was little. It was their special thing—the funny way "I love you" came out of her mouth when she was a toddler.

Funny how the silliest things stick and become so important.

After her bath and brushing the ice cream and chocolate off her teeth, I tucked Rae into bed. We read a couple pages of her book together, and Iggy lay beside her, in his usual spot. I knocked on Teo's bedroom door, got a "yeah" (his code for "come on in"), opened the door, and found him in his bed, AirPods in, phone in hand.

"Just saying good night, buddy." I sat down on the mattress next to his long legs.

"When do we go to Dad's next?" he asked.

"Day after tomorrow, for the whole weekend. Thursday after school until Monday morning. Everything going okay, at school, basketball, and your dad's place?"

"Yep, all good, Mom," my son answered dismissively. He gave me that knowing look that told me not to pry and that he would share when he felt like it.

"Alright, alright, I'll leave you to whatever you're up to. Don't stay up too late."

"Love you, Mom," Teo said as I was leaving his room. "Thanks for letting us go with Dad. That was cool, and we had a good time."

"You bet. Love you too, buddy—more than you'll ever know."

I straightened up the apartment, brushed my teeth, and hit the sack. I was excited for Monday—the final evaluator appointment, which was our home visit. Things were going well with Luke, and I felt hopeful that with her guidance, we would create a mutually agreeable plan—a stipulated agreement that would keep us out of court. I dozed off as a sense of peace and optimism about our family's future washed over me. No better feeling than knowing your children are going to be okay—way better than okay. They were already thriving and on the path to all good things.

I was super excited to see and pick up the kids Monday after school.

Over the weekend, I had enjoyed time reading, cooking, an evening out to dinner with friends, and a couple of long, bubble baths complete with the homemade bath bombs Rae gave me on Mother's Day. The evaluator was due at 4:00 p.m. The kids were both in a good mood when I picked them up from their schools. When I asked both how the weekend with their dad went, they each shared a couple of funny stories. I reminded them that the evaluator was due to the apartment in an hour, and they seemed fine with this. Rae was excited for her to meet Iggy and to show off all her stuff. She had even made a thank you card for the evaluator.

The evaluator arrived on time with her usual friendly disposition. Rae gave her a quick tour of our cozy home, and they ended up talking in her room for quite a while. The door was open, so I could hear some of their conversation. Rae told her all kinds of good things about this house and the house with her dad, and the one we used to all share.

"That's a nice picture of your family," I heard the evaluator say. I assumed she was talking about the one above Rae's bed.

"I made the frame at summer camp," my daughter replied, clearly proud of her artistic creation.

The evaluator complimented her on her creativity and many talents as Rae showed off her martial arts belts, dance costumes, and her collection of basketball and softball trophies. "You're such a busy girl. Do both of your parents attend all of your activities?"

"Yah, almost always," Rae answered.

"Do both of your parents make sure you arrive to your activities and sports on time, for games and practices?" the evaluator inquired further.

"Yah, for sure, they are pretty good parents," she answered matter-of-factly. "And even last week, Dad was at my brother's basketball practice and we were supposed to be with Mom, but she let us go out for ice cream with him. I got double chocolate, chocolate-caramel bear tracks with chocolate syrup drizzle and sprinkles. Oh my gosh, so good!"

"Wow, that really sounds like something!" the evaluator replied. "I'm so glad to hear they are pretty good parents, Rae. I know they love you and Teo very much. How can *you* tell that they love you very much?"

"Well, I get lots of hugs and kisses, and they make sure to feed us and get us to school. Mom likes to take us shopping and buy us things. Dad makes us laugh. And, they say they love us all the time." Rae's steady flow of thoughts eventually came to an end.

"That sounds about perfect, Rae. Today is the last time I'll see you. Is there anything else you'd like to talk about, or any questions you'd like to ask me?"

"Hum, nope, don't think so. Oh wait, yes, I have one question!" Rae never missed an opportunity to learn something new. "What kind of car do you drive? And are you married or divorced? And do you have kids or any pets?"

The evaluator kindly answered all of my daughter's inquisitions, and I heard them high-five before she headed over to Teo's room. When she knocked on Teo's door, I heard him tell her to come on in and was relieved that he used more manners than his typical "yeah" response.

"Hi, Teo. Cool little pad you have here."

He showed off his basketball awards and medals, which she acknowledged with big accolades. I heard her ask how school was going, about his grades, and his friends. Teo gave her a positive report, a big thumbs up in all primary areas of his life. As she started to wrap up and as she was leaving his room, I heard him ask if he could talk to her about one more thing: "The schedule," I heard him say.

I was not sure how I felt about this, as he was still a kid and did not get to choose; but his opinion mattered, and how he and Rae felt about the divorce and their new life was important, too. I knew I should not eavesdrop, but the apartment was so small that there was no way around it, I justified, mentally giving myself permission to listen in.

"I'd like to see my dad more. Spend more time with him. Rae wants to, too. Not sure if she told you so. We don't want to hurt our mom's feelings and love her lots, but we miss our dad and would like to see him more." He proclaimed it with a measure of authority.

"Ah, okay, thank you for telling me. I am going to be helping your mom and dad with deciding the best schedule for you and Rae, so having your opinion and feelings on the subject is helpful. Ultimately, adults get to decide. It's my job to understand how those decisions affect you and your sister. I will be sure that your feelings are known when decisions are being made. And remember, it is also my job to make sure that kids are happy, safe, and healthy and always spend time with their mom and dad." When the evaluator finished, I hoped my son understood all she had just said.

"Cool, thanks," was his response.

The evaluator walked out of his room and toward the couch I was sitting on.

"Alright, Vanessa. You have a nice home here. I should be wrapping up the evaluation report in the next couple weeks and will be in touch if I need anything else before we finish." She collected some paperwork from me, shook my hand, gave Iggy one last pat on the head, and waved goodbye on her way out the door.

Instant relief washed over me as I closed the door. The evaluation was complete. I had done my part and done it well, advocating for my children. Being the best mom I could under really difficult circumstances, and all the stress of this divorce.

Now, we wait.

I emailed Attorney of the Year to see if the evaluation report was out, and she continued to assure me I would be the first know. Waiting was so hard. We had a trial date on the court docket in a month, and I wanted to get this settled so we did not have to go.

Finally, the subject line of an email from my attorney read: "Evaluation for Teo and Rae, attached." I was so glad the kids were at school when this email was delivered. The kids were scheduled to be with their dad after school, so I opened the message immediately and saw a PDF attached at the bottom. Attorney of the Year's email message read, "Please review and make an appointment with my office so we can discuss."

I knew I had done my very best, and I knew my kids were doing well, but having someone "evaluate" your parenting capacity and the relationship with your children is intense to say the least. I hoped the report said all good things, but feared there was critical feedback that would knock me backwards. And what if the parenting time was not what I wanted? I knew the evaluator's report held a lot of weight. I knew Luke wanted them 50% of the time, and I knew the law favored that outcome.

Before reading a word of what the evaluator had written, I decided to make myself a cup of hot tea. There was dark chocolate in the pantry, and I grabbed two pieces, then a third, just in case. I sat in the most comfortable chair, wrapped in Rae's blanket, with Iggy at my feet. I took a deep breath, summoned my bravery, and double-clicked the attachment.

After an hour with the report, I sat quietly, my teacup empty and all three pieces of chocolate warming my belly. A couple of statements were hard to swallow, but overall, I was impressed that a total stranger could so thoroughly identify the problematic issues for our family, and understand two children with such insight and compassion, in the short amount of time we had been working with her.

Although I respected our evaluator's opinion, and knew she was a child development expert, her recommendation for equal parenting time was not sitting well with me at all. It was what I had feared. I wasn't sure the kids could handle that much time with their dad, or that Luke could handle 50% of the parenting responsibilities that had always fallen 100% on me. Most of all, I wasn't sure I could handle not being a part of Teo and Rae's everyday lives. I would miss out on half of what remained of their childhoods if there was an equal parenting time schedule shared between our two households.

Overwhelmed with this possible reality of our life-to-be, a deep wave of grief settled in and I cried and curled into the smallest ball possible as the weight of that last thought—missing out on half of their childhoods—fully consumed me.

After spending what remained of that day in my favorite pajamas, lying in bed with a pint of ice cream and half a dozen cupcakes, I awoke with a terrible stomachache Saturday morning and hurried to the emergency session I had scheduled with my counselor.

We talked, I cried, and he helped me recenter and see more clearly the benefits to Teo and Rae of having an equal time-share. We would work through my grief together, he said, over the coming weeks, months, as long as it took. I left the counselor's office and did some serious soul-searching the rest of the weekend.

On Monday morning, I sat down across the cherry wood desk with Attorney of the Year on the other side. It was three days after having read the evaluation report. All the kings horses and all the kings men had worked hard putting Vanessa back together again.

Thank God for my friends and family and the allies in my life and support system that has held us together since the separation—possibly the worst time of my life.

The assistant from the front office appeared with a warm cup of matcha tea and a fresh box of Kleenex. She also placed a small package of dark chocolate in front of me.

Looks like my "congratulations on your divorce gifts" have finally arrived. I pulled myself together, sipped the tea, and popped in a small piece of dark chocolate.

Together, Attorney of the Year and I wrote up a settlement proposal that looked a lot like the evaluator's recommendation. I was tearful as we talked it through. She told me we could fight the evaluator's report at trial and ask the judge for a different plan, although in her experience this usually did not go too well. Because the evaluator was a court-appointed neutral expert and advocate for the children, and because she had spent a considerable amount of time getting to know all of us (something the judge could not do), the court typically put a lot of weight on the evaluator's recommendation for children.

I took a deep breath and an image of my children's smiling faces appeared in my mind's eye. There was Rae smiling and waving at me, giving me the "please mom, please, please, please" act. I remembered Teo's last words to the evaluator at our house and how hard that must have been for him to say, knowing I was in the other room and able to hear. And then Luke at our front door that night, taking some responsibility, showing a little awareness of his choices and vowing to do better.

"Many people are better divorced parents, than they were married parents," Attorney of the Year said, breaking the silence and my daydream. "Let me explain," she continued, responding to the perplexed look on my face. "When an adult relationship falls apart, when trust is lost, and emotional distance with one's partner becomes the status quo, an ever-present tension develops in the family home. It lurks and threatens until eventually it becomes palpable, and everyone can feel it; but no one knows what exactly it is, or what to call it."

She paused, tilted her head, and raised one eyebrow to check in and make sure I was following. I nodded for her to continue.

"Some parents ride it out with an occasional blow-up here and there, and there are no giant red flags like violence or alcoholism or major mental health break-downs that would cause other agencies to get involved and be an obvious reason for dissolution. Resentment builds over time between otherwise loving and caring parents, and children are left to grow up in a space of uncertainty, absorbing all that tension and stress res-onating between Mom and Dad until someone finally says, 'Enough.'"

Yeah, that makes sense.

"Vanessa, it's true that Luke went about this in a terrible way, stepping outside the marriage. You need to keep working through the betrayals with your therapist, and that takes time. Separating what Luke did and your feelings about it, from who Luke is as a parent and his relationship with the children is *your* work. They need and love their dad. He is not a risk to them in any way, and while he will not do things the same as you would, or with the detail and precision that you do, he'll get the job done."

On cue, the waterworks started. I knew she was right, and that realization was both painful and relieving all at once.

Attorney of the Year got up from her chair, walked around the big cherry wood desk, and stood in front of me. "Come here, you," she said.

I rose and she gave me the biggest momma bear hug while I sobbed on her shoulder.

Thank God for this woman!

"I'll send our settlement proposal to opposing counsel this afternoon and will be in touch," Attorney of the Year said as she walked with me to the door.

This is really happening, I thought to myself as I got into my car and started driving.

I had time before school pickup that afternoon and needed to pull myself together before then. My car drove itself on autopilot to my favorite place for a pedicure. When Rae came along with me, she always picked out lots of bright colors and asked for "rainbow" toes. I decided to give this a try today. Once my toes were painted, I went to the bakery across the street and ordered a gluten-free chocolate chip cookie instead of my usual cupcake because gluten-free chocolate chip was Teo's favorite. With my rainbow-colored feet and oversized cookie, I found a sunny park bench near a little pond where the kids used to feed the ducks when they were little. The sun was warm on my face and the ducks quacked happily nearby, eyeballing my snack.

I'm not sure how long that bench was underneath my backend, but the cookie was gone, my legs were stiff, and an alarm on my phone reminded me it was time to retrieve the kids from school.

I'm going to wait to tell them about all of this until we finalize the plan.

That evening, Rae had dance class at the same time Teo was at his basketball practice. After dropping both of them off, I had a little more time alone in the car and noticed Teo had left his phone in the front seat cup holder. I couldn't help myself. I wanted to see if Luke had said anything to him about the evaluator's report. I knew his password because that was a hard and fast rule in our home and the kids had been good about it. I typed it in, and the phone lit up.

I tapped his text messages and one text communication with his father stood out amongst the sea of others.

Teo: I told the evaluator we wanted to spend more time with you, dad. I know mom could hear in the other room, but she did not say anything about it. I know she wants us to be here at the apartment with her and that me and Rae being away makes her sad. I hate making mom sad, sometimes I hear her crying, but we miss you, dad.

Dad: Sorry bud, I know all of this is really hard on you and your sister and your mom. Mom and me are getting things worked out and this will be over soon so we can all get on with our lives. You and Rae just keep focusing on school and friends and sports and being kids. Me and your mom's happiness are not your and Rae's responsibility, got it? We are both grownups and will be fine. It's our job to take care of you and Rae, not the other way around. Love you son. Kiss your sister for me and I'll see you guys soon.

I closed Teo's phone, knowing there was nothing more I needed to see. Luke was right, and it seemed he was, in fact, being a better divorced dad than he was a married one, like Attorney of the Year had suggested. While I hated to admit it, Luke's words to our son were spot-on.

Strangely, a wave of calm enveloped me. I tried to "identify the feeling/emotion" as my counselor had been training me. I sat for a moment and realized it was acceptance. Acceptance about the end of my marriage—the end of two decades with someone I considered my best friend. Acceptance that our family looked different now and that Teo and Rae had two homes and two parents who adored them. Acceptance that our children needed equal time to be influenced by their mother and father. I let that sink in for a minute, and my thoughts shifted a bit, allowing me to accept that I was free now, too, to continue reinventing the best version of myself as my own person and as a mom.

A huge smile crossed my face—one that stretched all the way to my eyes and made the skin on my cheeks tighten up. It was like a theater curtain being pulled back to start the show, as if the wonder of heaven's gates opened up before me. The cycle of grief I had learned about in that mandatory parenting class—

what my therapist and the children's therapist had been speaking about—the necessary process everyone travels through denial, anger, bargaining, depression, and acceptance—was finally complete.

I finally get it. I have arrived. I am here, and still standing. And it is time to move forward—for me, for Teo, for Rae, and for Luke.

The next morning, everything just seemed so much lighter in the apartment and easier as the kids, and I went through our usual before school routine. Rae even talked me into a quick dance party in her bedroom, and Teo gave me a big hug and quick kiss on the cheek before leaving. He said nonchalantly, "Happy looks good on you, Mom."

After returning from drop-off, I fired up the laptop and found an email from my attorney.

The email read:

Dear Ms. Smith,

The opposing party has accepted our offer, as it was written here in my office. Please set a time to come down and sign the document. There will not be a need for trial, regarding the children, although we'll need the court to rule on a couple of financial details. We can talk more when I see you in person.

Very Truly Yours,
Attorney of The Year

Many months had passed since Luke left our family home and filed for divorce. Months of change and adjusting to new ways of thinking and doing everything. Attorneys' legal fees, the evaluation, counseling appointments, my new job, a new home, and all of it leading to this end. Our day in court, which Attorney of the Year promised would be "quick and painless," since Luke and I had stipulated to custody and parenting time.

I entered the courthouse in my best clothes, Attorney of the Year by my side. In the courthouse security line, we ran into Luke and his attorney. The two legal professionals evidently knew one another pretty well and started conversing with each another.

"Hi, Luke," I said.

After looking right at me with those big blue eyes of his, the genuine ones I fell in love with two decades before, he said, "Vanessa, I am so sorry we are here at all. Thank you for offering to settle on the evaluator's recommendation, and letting Teo and Rae be with me half of the time. I know that wasn't easy for you."

What in the world? Who is this man?

Luke took a step toward me and continued, "I want you to be financially stable, and the kids to have the best life with both of us in two nice homes. My attorney says I should fight you on the outstanding financials, but I really don't want to or think that's best."

His attorney, known as Bulldog, spun around like the Tasmanian Devil and gave Luke the look of death.

Luke looked straight at him and said, "Give me a minute, man. I'll be up to the courtroom in a sec." He looked back toward me and asked if we could talk outside the courthouse for a minute. Attorney of the Year was alert to what was happening and gave me a quick wink and nod of approval.

Luke and I went outside and, with a hand resting gently on my arm, he began to talk about what he thought was "fair" in splitting our assets, particularly his 401K. I was shocked and elated and could not help myself. I gave him a big hug. He hugged back and we walked, together, through the courthouse security line and side-by-side up to the assigned courtroom where Bulldog was standing with his arms crossed.

"See you in there, Vanessa," Luke said as I pushed open the courtroom door and left him standing in the hallway with his attorney.

I told Attorney of the Year about the conversation, and she immediately got up, told the clerk they would need a few minutes, and then went looking for Bulldog. A few minutes later, both attorneys entered the courtroom and headed into the judge's chambers. They were gone about twenty minutes, giving Luke and me time to chat about how silly all this seemed. We commiserated about how much money had been spent on attorneys and evaluators and agreed those parenting class facilitators were right when suggesting "mediation before litigation is always the best practice for family matters."

We both wished we had tried a little harder in mediation, but recognized that we were both still too angry then. Our path was what it was, and we were here now, having agreed on the best plan for our kids. The attorneys Luke and I were both paying big bucks were in with the judge fighting about what money was left. We chuckled at the irony, wishing they would hurry up so we could stop the clock on their billable hours.

Our attorneys emerged from chambers with the court clerk on their heels who stood in front of the judge's bench and authoritatively instructed: "All rise." I followed my attorney's lead.

The judge entered the courtroom, told us to sit, and recited our family name, the case number, and made record of who was in attendance. He looked like a normal ordinary man in a black robe with the presence of authority.

The judge leaned back in his big chair and looked pleased as he started in, "Mr. and Ms. Smith, I understand that you have stipulated to all issues concerning your children, Teo age 14 and Rae age 10. Congratulations on a job well done."

I felt pride swell and Attorney of the Year triumphantly bumped my elbow with hers and shot me one more of her affirming "atta girl" grins.

The judge continued, "I have been sitting on this bench the last twenty-three years, listening to disputes and gripes between divorcing parents about the very children each of them says they are here to protect. Truth is that justice for children is the result of good choices by their parents. By the people charged with their daily care, health, safety and well-being. By your choices, Mr. and Ms. Smith. You hold the cards to Teo and Rae's future. Their ability to thrive depends on the choices you two make and the life you create for them during the time they will spend in each of your homes and under your care. I figure these are two lucky kids, privileged to have parents that get it, who took them off the table with the other assets from the marriage, such as Mr. Smith's 401K, which we will get to shortly.

"Hear me when I say to both of you, 'Great work!' You're going to make mistakes—lots of them. We all do.

You are going to do things that make each other mad, probably furious, at times. Do not let the emotions you feel for each other contaminate the emotions your children feel for their mom and dad. They need permission to love and be loved by everyone. Period. They need to ebb and flow between you without carrying the heavy, ugly baggage of your marriage. They need to know that you still care for each other. The absolute best way you can take care of your children is to take care of their parents. To take the best care possible of their mom and dad."

I heard Luke's attorney blow out a big sigh.

My attention returned quickly to the judge. "While we are signing off on a plan today that will go into effect immediately, I urge you to keep an eye on the twenty-year plan. How you behave—what you say and do now—has consequences for the twenty-year plan. Kids grow up fast. Before you know it, this chapter will be a distant memory. They will move out of both your homes and focus on relationships of their own. They'll get to choose what relationship to share with you, or not, for the majority of their time on this earth. What you do now matters, in spades. The best gift you can give them is a childhood free from conflict. A childhood from which they do not need to heal. Keep doing the work you need to do to move forward peacefully. Learn the best strategies to co-parent. Do divorce better than you did marriage. Your children are worth the effort."

The judge shuffled some papers on his desk and asked Bulldog to recite the financial agreements onto the record. Bulldog stood up, buttoned his suit coat, and begrudgingly read his client's agreement to allot a generous share of his 401K to me and the kids. He agreed to the highest calculation of child support and five years alimony so I could get back into my field of work—teaching. I'd need time to re-establish my license, which required practice hours and then time to land an actual job.

The future is finally looking bright for all of us—our reconfigured family of four.

Twenty Years Later

Rae was screaming her head off at a pitch I'd never heard any first-time birthing mother yell out in pain before. Our girl always had a special flair for drama when things were uncomfortable and hard or uncertain.

Our Rae, about to be a mommy!

I wanted to soothe her and make the hurt go away but knew that was impossible. "It'll pass, baby, be strong," I kept telling her. She was squeezing my hand on one side and her husband's hand on the other. He looked terrified, probably because my daughter had the strength of an elephant. I swear, I thought she might pinch one of my fingers right off.

Luke and his wife, and Teo and his wife and two kids, were all outside the birthing suite in the waiting area of St. Vincent's Hospital. Luke was having a cup of coffee and chatting with my husband, Jack. My mom had passed about two years before, but Luke's mom was still sucking air. She had gotten even more grumpy as the years had passed.

I figure she might live forever. The angriest ones always do. I could hear his mother's irritating voice in the hallway every once in a while: "Get me some tea and get me a tissue, Luke," and "Hasn't she got that kid out yet?" The kids had come to see their grandmother for who she was, and we all loved the parts of her we could.

"Mom!" Rae yelled in my face, looking slightly possessed. "Get the doctor. It's go time. Let's get this show on the road already."

What? Oh my God! I'm going to be a grandma, again!

I was so excited! "Okay, honey, be right back, but you need to let go of my hand, baby." I ran out of the room, rubbing my hand while asking for her doctor, and gave everyone a super quick update while breezing past, "Any minute now!"

An hour later, we were all there, surrounding Rae in her hospital bed, her brand-new perfect baby Ezra in her arms. Teo's toddler was fast asleep on his broad shoulder, and his wife held their five-year-old daughter's hand as she looked lovingly at her favorite auntie and newborn baby cousin.

Luke kissed Rae's cheek, and then Ezra's, and I heard him whisper "olive juice" before moving aside. His wife stepped in said some kind words to her with tears in her eyes, the kind of tears that wet every woman's face when they marvel at the miracle of a newborn. Grandma Smith was in the room with all of us, but had fallen asleep in a corner chair after having a peek at the baby and declaring, "All newborns look like Winston Churchill to me. Good luck with that one, kid!" At least grandma always kept it real.

My husband, Jack, stood behind me at Rae's bedside with arms wrapped around my ribcage. My daughter was exhausted and hypnotized by the little life she held in her arms. She looked up and locked eyes with me, "Thanks, Mom."

Her words startled me a bit. I stepped forward and brushed the hair to the side of her forehead. "For what?" I asked while stroking her head and staring at my new grandson.

"For everything, Mom. For being here, for always being here, for making sure that everyone can be here, right now, on this very important day. I know that you sacrificed a lot for us, and I know it was not easy for you after the divorce from Dad. But you always made everything easy and right. You taught us how to work things out and how to save ourselves in this life and rely on people who are worthy of our trust. I just hope that I can be as great of a mom to Ezra that you are to me."

Speechless, we shared a silent moment, where no words were necessary. Just more tears of joy and absolute awe between us.

"I would do it over a million times for you and your brother, honey. And now you know, all those times I said, 'I love you more,' that it's true. Look what you did, baby. Look at this precious little life. There is nothing quite like the way a parent loves their children." Rae pulled Ezra even closer and I touched his tiny foot.

Luke was suddenly standing by my side with his arm around my shoulder, and his eyes wet with tears, too. We smiled softly and victorious in the choices we had made over all these years, to co-parent with flexibility and grace and raise our children from two loving homes. We had both attended their birthday parties, school conferences, sports practices, games, dance recitals, music concerts, and high school graduations. Teo got his basketball scholarship, and we sat together at their college graduation ceremonies, helped plan their picturesque weddings, were at the birth of our first two grandchildren, and now Ezra's special day. I cannot imagine anything more a mom or dad could ask for.

"I'm one lucky lady," were my last words to Jack that night right before we drifted off to sleep. He snuggled in and whispered in my ear, "I love you, Vanessa."

And everyone lived happily ever after.

Well, you know, as much as any of us truly can. There had been the usual hiccups, speed bumps, and occasional Grand-Canyon-sized challenges, but we had each other's back. And that's what made the difference. At the end of the day, we were respectful and we were kind. We cared about one another and knew life was imperfectly perfect. And that seemed good enough to calm whatever titanic-sized shipwrecks showed up.

"Life is a marathon, not a sprint," my counselor had told me that year after the divorce as we were preparing to terminate services.

It takes time to run the race, indeed, and there are all kinds of hazards along the course. But, there's always been an answer, always a way through, when I've allowed compassion and grace to light the way.

Compassion, grace, kindness, and respect. These drive the best choices—choices to act, think, and conduct ourselves in a certain way with ourselves and with others in our life.

Choose well, my friends. Your children and their children's legacy are worth it. Of this, I am absolutely certain.

—Vanessa

Remember, a list of Hints, Hacks, and Hell-No's can be found at the back of the book for a quick reference.

To Go Down the Rabbit Hole

"To enter into a situation or begin a process or journey that is particularly strange, problematic, difficult, complex, or chaotic, especially one that becomes increasingly so as it develops or unfolds."

(An allusion to Alice's Adventures in Wonderland by Lewis Carroll)

Farlex Dictionary of Idioms.

HOW THE HECK DID WE END UP HERE?

MY HANDS GRIPPED the worn, wood-grain steering wheel of this new-to-me, beat-up, but totally rad 1965 Ford Mustang convertible, currently parked outside our local tavern. Satisfaction settled in as it hit me: *Vanessa has no idea what is about to go down.*

I picked up my phone and considered making one last call to her. It was harder than it should be, assembling enough courage to stand up for myself after she'd run over me for years.

Iggy's image caught my eye in the rearview mirror. My loyal four-legged pal was comfortably settled in the backseat—curled tightly in a blanket that smelled like my amazing daughter, Rae.

Since that first night sleeping on the couch at a buddy's house, this sweet new ride had doubled as our temporary home. It had been a week since I'd left Vanessa, and it was just me and Igg's while I got things worked out. Hopefully, this divorce would be over quickly.

"Nothing but props for yah," I said and instantly saw Iggy's slobber-wet jowls curve upwards in a smile. An image of him as a pup tore through my thoughts with some force—our family dog, running in the backyard, chasing my now middle-school-aged son, Teo.

Man, I miss my kids.

It seemed best for Teo and Rae to stay put with their mother in the house until I could establish a new place and have them with me 50% of the time. I took the cash out of our joint savings account to buy this new ride that I'd always dreamed of owning—the exact one Vanessa fought me on every time I brought it up. Plus, I needed cash for the deposit on an apartment, and to eat, and to forget about my failed marriage with the help of a few adult beverages.

All necessities, I told myself. *Well-deserved after working my tail off to pay the mortgage and house bills, car insurance, health insurance, everything for the kids, and even support Vanessa's careless spending habits.* I thought about all of her expensive designer shoes and purses piled up in our closet. *What a waste.*

While I worked outside the home day and night, climbing my way up in the company that employed me, Vanessa had stayed home with the kids. She'd promised to get a job and help out with bills after the kids were in school, but never followed through, on anything, ever. All she did was nag and complain about me and what I was doing, or not doing, or might be doing.

A wave of anger rolled through me, and I smacked the steering wheel with my open palm. *The woman is impossible to please!* She was absolutely suffocating with all her rules and demands. I could do no right, no matter how hard I tried, or what books I read, or what marriage therapists she dragged us to see. My blood really started to boil. *Nothing was ever good enough!*

After stuffing what had become raging venom all these years during our miserable marriage, I was ready to finally speak my mind, once and for all. I auto-dialed her number.

"What do you want, Luke?" she answered with the contempt I had become accustomed to over the last several years.

I know I screwed up, but why did you have to make me pay for it every day of our marriage? Why could you never just appreciate all my efforts?

With absolute conviction, I laid into her. "You and I are done. Finished! You hear me? There is nothing left of our marriage. I have been a doormat to your high heels far too long, a sponge for all that senseless complaining. You will not control me with your stupid rules and unreasonable demands one minute more! I'm going to find a woman who will appreciate me. No one else will ever put up with a c*#! like you!"

Click. I hung up the phone before she could respond.

Ha! I said it—I said the forbidden C word. I showed her—Ms. Nothing's Ever Good Enough. What a great prelude to the process server who should be arriving at her front door any minute now. He had better time his arrival exactly as instructed, after the kids are in bed. Teo and Rae don't need to see their mother losing her mind and acting a fool. She's got to be bipolar—those mood swings of hers were even worse after each of the kids were born.

Feeling proud about taking a piece of my manhood back, I turned around and gave Iggy a victory belly rub and a couple of dog biscuits to keep him busy. I got out of the car, pulled up the hoodie on my sweatshirt, and jogged through the wind and rain into the local bar where I promptly bellied up on the corner stool that I'd been comfortably perched on after work each evening for the last week.

"Thanks, Lloyd," I said when a cold beer was promptly placed in front of me. "Start me a tab, man. Might be a long one." My shoulders slumped over, and I exhaled. The adrenaline high from yelling at Vanessa had begun to fade, and I felt a little ashamed. Plenty of guys at work had been divorced over the years, and I had vowed to never act the way most of them did.

Smooth move, Luke. You gotta get it together, man. I just know Vanessa is going to fight me for the kids. She has always acted as if they are "h-e-r" kids. Why didn't I leave sooner? It's going to be so much better without her around—in my own place, able to parent the way I think is best.

Feeling a glimmer of hope about a own home with the kids and my newfound freedom, I started taking in the surroundings. I had not spent this much time in a bar since college, where Vanessa and I met when she was studying to be a teacher and I was working on general studies.

The bar was dimly lit with dark wood paneling. A few booths with ripped-up vinyl seats lined one wall, and six tables with mismatched chairs had been scattered throughout the front area of the establishment. There was a game area in the back with billiards, dart boards, and several old-time pinball machines. There were a few other middle-aged guys sitting around and, mercifully, a couple ladies in the back room shooting pool and moving to the beat of music playing on an old-fashioned jukebox.

Huh, I see why Rae loves this song so much. It suits me perfectly right now, "This is my fight song, take back my life song, prove I'm alright song…"

"Hanging in there, Luke?" Lloyd asked, startling me back to reality.

"I'm good," I replied, lying through my clenched teeth but appreciating the song that was filling me with courage to see this divorce through. A couple minutes later, my new theme song ended and some other sappier melody filled the space. Immediately, my courage was replaced with sadness and then anger. *Why do so many songs have to be about love? It causes poor young guys to believe it's real. 'Til death do us part—bunch of bologna!*

"Another one, Lloyd!" I said loudly.

Lloyd set down the beer and looked at me carefully before he started in, "Yah know, Luke, I know a guy."

I looked up and met his eyes but said nothing.

"You've been here every evening this week, and I see your Mustang parked all night in the back of the lot. Nice ride, dude." He offered a fist bump, and I bumped back before he continued, "You're going to need a good attorney, or she is going to take you to the cleaners—probably even come after your sweet new ride, your

401K, and the dog, too. Women see divorce as an opportunity to score cash and prizes, man. You need to lawyer up."

I leaned in, "Tell me everything you know about finding an attorney. I filed the divorce paperwork and asked for full custody of the kids using the do-it-yourself legal forms a guy at work directed me to. But I don't have an attorney yet. You really think I need one? How much does an attorney cost? I don't have a lot of liquid assets right now."

I'd heard horror stories about the cost of some divorces. So far, it was doable with the $300 filing fee and another $100 for the process server to deliver the lawsuit on Vanessa. *I wonder how that is going?* I wrung my hands in delight, with sweet revenge coursing through my veins.

Rapidly, the feeling of victory was replaced with confusion about what would happen next. With less enthusiasm, I asked, "Are you divorced, Lloyd? I don't know how this works."

Lloyd leaned down on the bar and lowered his voice. "Like I said, I know a guy. Everyone just calls him Bulldog. He is the best in town, and no one messes with him. He lives up to his nickname. Disorganized, but gets the job done in a courtroom. He'll make sure you don't lose everything, and that you get to see a lot of your kids. He'll also put your ex in her place when she takes the stand. Totally worth the price of admission." Lloyd's happy snort was laden with an evil undertone. He stood up and then sauntered down the bar to help another customer.

See a lot of my kids? What exactly does that mean? My brain hurt wondering what percentage was "a lot." I took a pull off the fresh pour in front of me. Everything had started to go numb, partly due to the booze but also at the thought of having to give Vanessa child support or spousal support, losing my hard-earned retirement, my new ride, the dog, and having anything less than 50% time with my kids. *Teo and Rae will live with me half-time, and I'm not paying her one red cent!*

Just as my anger resurfaced, readying me for a fight, Lloyd reappeared in front of me and scribbled an address on a napkin along with what looked like a secret password: "open sesame." He told me to go see Bulldog during daylight hours, seven days a week, but not before noon. "No need to call ahead. Just show up, knock twice, and use the password."

Weird, but it's not like I know any other attorneys, and Lloyd's been a buddy since grade school.

My corner barstool served its purpose for the night as I kept pace with the rest of the bar patrons and noticed the two ladies playing pool danced more provocatively with each cocktail. *Now, that's what I'm talking about.* Watching their fine rear-ends swinging to the beat was reason enough for me to hit the gym a little harder and return these middle-aged biceps and abs back to their former college glory. *This clean-cut, tough-but-charming guy is going to bring sexy back*, I thought while admiring myself in the reflection of the mirror behind the bar.

At bar close, I walked to my car/hotel/sweet new ride where Iggy was passed out in the driver's seat.

As I opened the door, a nauseating concoction of wet dog, garbage, and sweaty socks about knocked me over. "Dude, you're rotten," I admonished and fanned out as much foul air as possible while Iggy hit the bushes and then hopped right back in.

The next day's agenda began playing in my mind as I squeezed myself into the tiny backseat and curled up in Rae's blanket, the only good smelling thing around.

Buy some dog food. Check.

Find a place to live. Check, check.

Meet Bulldog—after 12:00 p.m., knock twice, and use the secret password. Got it!

With the all-important bar napkin containing Bulldog's info wadded up in my pocket, a satisfied smile crossed my face as I drifted off, imagining Vanessa's shock after being served with the divorce lawsuit and my demand for full custody of the kids.

It seemed like I had just fallen asleep when Iggy woke me up that next morning with his disgusting tongue, licking every inch of my face.

"Iggs, go on, man," I said, pushing him and his nasty breath off me. He immediately jumped back up and landed on my belly. "Okay, okay, let's go." He leapt out the door and I followed him into the bushes for some privacy.

While standing there and doing our business, I remembered the time Teo had whipped his pants down at the Fourth of July fireworks display and, in front of the entire town, used the closest tree for a urinal— completely unashamed.

Ha! God, I love that kid! I chuckled to myself. *The good old days. Man, time flies. I cannot believe he's a teenager already.*

I zipped up and when Iggy was done sniffing around, we loaded back into the car and headed to the nearest 7-11 where I picked up a bag of dog food, hot coffee, and a donut.

Iggy and I sat on the curb together, outside the convenience store, enjoying breakfast and some sunshine. "No work today, Igg. Daddy's gonna find us a place to live." I had called in sick to my job, which I never do, so I have plenty of time saved up for emergencies like this.

I opened the "for rent" brochure I'd pulled off the rack by the door on my way out and started scanning available properties. *Time to find a temporary place until I'm back in my own house—soon.* Quickly, I scanned through the pages and found a studio apartment close to my office and in a trendy area downtown that I was sure the kids would love. Seemed worth checking out.

Price is doable. Wow, a pretty good deal actually.

Me and Iggy hopped in the Mustang. I dialed the apartment number that was listed and a youthful female voice answered. She told me I was welcome to come have a look, and that I should hurry. She said the apartment would not last long at this steal of a price.

It was a quick fifteen-minute drive into the city from our family home without traffic, but it took three times longer during morning rush hour. I parked in the "reserved for new tenants" spot right outside the apartment building, left the windows down for Iggy, and walked toward the front doors. There was an intercom system on the wall to the right of the doors that looked like a TV. An exquisite young woman introduced herself as CoCo and then buzzed me in. She was so stunning and so kind that it took me a minute to get my bearings. Quickly, she escorted me to the sixth floor and into a small studio apartment numbered 666. I know, I know. It doesn't sound great, but it's cheap and temporary. Good thing, because it's really just one big room that we will all have to share while the kids are with me, no less than 50% of the time.

I'm sure they'll love the view of the city and being downtown, out of the suburbs. We can make forts like we did when they were little.

I signed the lease and CoCo handed me the keys. With newfound pep in my step, I exited the building and headed down the exterior walkway back to the Mustang. Iggy had his head sticking out the window and was barking like a maniac at a flock of pigeons on the sidewalk. *Crap! I didn't ask about having a dog here.* Tempted to go back in, but wanting to move on with my day and hopefully hire Bulldog as my attorney, I decided to get going and figure it out later.

I pulled the balled-up bar napkin Lloyd gave me with Bulldog's info out of my pocket and typed his office address into my phone, noticing that my company had done some restoration work on a few buildings nearby. *It is a sketchy neighborhood for sure.* Trusting Lloyd and his experience with Bulldog, I decided there was nothing to lose. After dropping the top on my Mustang, we drove from one end of the city to the other. *Never thought I'd be living downtown in the city.*

This was going to be a good opportunity for the kids to get out from under their manicured suburban life. *Ms. Nothing's Ever Good Enough worries about Every-Single-Thing. I bet she will flip about the kids living downtown, in the big-bad-scary city. With their dad. Ha!....and there's not a thing she can do about it!* A knowing feeling that everything was all going to work out washed over me. *It's going to be good for the kids to have time away from their mother. I'll finally be able to parent them the way I want to without her talking over me all the time, butting in, watching my every move, and just waiting to offer her two-cent criticisms.*

"Turn left on Washington Street. Turn right on Pine. Destination ahead one quarter of a mile."

Thank you, Waze Map Lady. This is a woman I can depend on.

"Looks like we've arrived at stop number two, Iggy. I think Bulldog's office is down that alley over there." I put the top up and when I couldn't find Iggy's collar and leash, I told him to follow me. Iggy has great manners off-leash. Vanessa used all those hours for her "girl time," out with her bestie Juls, while me and the kids did all the hard work in obedience class with our family pet. I hate that Vanessa always insisted on putting Iggy in a kennel out back. *Heartless, I swear the woman has no soul.*

Iggy stayed velcroed to my left side as we walked toward the alley. There was a rusty, white metal sign jutting out from above a door about one-quarter of the way down with sun-faded letters. Finally, I made out the words: "Attorney at Law."

This must be it, I thought, apprehensively approaching the door. Ignoring my gut, I reminded myself that I was there, on word of mouth from an old friend. *I also don't have another plan.*

I checked my watch. It was past noon, so I knocked twice and immediately heard the shuffling of feet and then a burly voice answered from the other side: "And?"

"Open sesame," I announced, feeling more than a little ridiculous.

"Anyone with you?" A peephole positioned mid-door clinked to the side and one big, brown, bloodshot eyeball stared me down.

"Just my dog, Sir." I pointed down, unsure if bringing him was the right decision.

The deadbolt was unlocked, and the door swung open enough for me to see a large man dressed in a cheap suit, with worn shoes, walking away from the door across the dimly lit office.

Without looking in my direction, he waved me in, and I assumed Iggy was welcome, too. The place was a mess of papers and files and filing cabinets everywhere. I saw two desks, one that the man who opened the door was headed towards and the other where a woman with a tight, low-cut shirt was sitting, her bare foot propped up on a stack of files atop her workstation so she could paint her toenails. She looked up, smiling at me, and stopped chewing her gum long enough to say, "Hey!" When she noticed Iggy, who was now hiding behind my leg like Rae used to do, she shrieked, dropped her little toenail paintbrush, and ran directly at us. "Oh my gosh, we don't get too many puppies in here. He is adorable! What's his name? How old is he? Is he a he or is he a she? Wolfgang, did you see this little fella?" she asked the burly man who was now seated in an overstuffed chair behind a desk piled high with files.

Wait, what? Wolfgang? Am I in the wrong place?

"Lola, leave the man alone. He's having a family crisis and needs my help."

"Awwwww, can I watch your pup while you and 'The Dog' are meeting, please? I'm great with animals and children—like cosmic connection great!"

The Dog? Does she mean Bulldog? She better mean Bulldog.

"Lola!" the man at the desk hollered, authority thick in his command.

"Sure," I said to the animated lady standing in front of me who was somehow completely unaffected by the man's curt tone. "His name is Iggy." Iggy looked up disapprovingly and then gave Lola a low warning-growl before she reached down, scooped him up, and effortlessly carried all forty-some pounds of him back to her desk.

"Come on over here, son," directed the heavy-set man at the desk with a quick wave of his hand. His tenor demanded attention and respect. It was evident why nobody messed with him. I walked to the man's desk and tried to hide my smile when I noticed a small wood burning stove in the corner and the words "filing system" hand-painted onto the side. The Dog noticed me noticing his paper-burning incinerator and laughed. "A gift from one of my favorite clients. I think you know him. Lloyd works at a little hometown tavern outside the city."

I nodded in response. "Yes, sir. Lloyd and me go way back to grade school. We've spent some extra time together this week. He said you're the best. I'm Luke Smith. Are you Bulldog?"

The man leaned back in his chair and ran one hand through his thick black hair. He looked me over. "Wolfgang Hornedcowdog. Most clients just call me Bulldog. How can I help?"

It took me a minute, but I got it. A horned cow is a bull. Add dog, and you get Bull-dog. *Clever, a real word-artist! I hear that the best attorneys always are.*

"Well," is all I could get out. There I sat, trying to compose an answer to his seemingly simple question, looking everywhere but at the man who I desperately needed on my side.

Bulldog snapped his chair forward, "Son, you're getting a divorce. It didn't work out. What do you most want to keep from your not-so-blessed union? Let's start there—the 'keep this' list."

Oh, well that's not too hard.

My new ride.

My 401K.

My La-Z-Boy.

My big screen TV.

My power tools.

My kids.

"My kids!" I blurted out. *Obviously, they are at the top of the list.*

I proceeded to rattle off the rest of my "must keep this list" as Bulldog scribbled everything I said onto a piece of paper.

"That's it? Your complete list?" he asked, sounding perplexed and a little disappointed. When I nodded, he continued, "You're still in the house with the kids, right?"

Sweat instantly beaded at my brow. "I moved out last week. Teo and Rae are with their mother in the house. I thought that would be best for them. Did I do something wrong?"

A totally expressionless "Umhum," was all I got in response.

Bulldog looked at me to continue, but what exactly he wanted to know I was not sure. "I have a place for them, for us. I have the keys and everything."

"Tell me more. Where? And what is this place like?" he asked nonchalantly.

"It's in the new trendy waterfront district downtown. A studio apartment. A bit on the small side, but we'll make it work."

"Make it work? Are you not making it work already? When did you last see your children?" His questions launched at me in rapid-fire fashion.

"I have not seen my kids in a week, since I left the house. I didn't take much with me except the essentials, one duffle bag, and the dog. I just wanted out. It was not possible to live with Ms. Nothing's Ever Good Enough for one more second. I filled out the divorce paperwork online with the help of a guy from work who split from his wife last year."

"Rookie mistakes. We can get those patched up." Again, with the nonchalant tone.

Patched up? I stared at Bulldog like a deer in the headlights, waiting for him to tell me what our first move would be to fix whatever I had apparently already made a mess of.

We were interrupted when Lola started giggling at an exceptionally high pitch. I looked over and saw Iggy sprawled across her lap, upside-down, tongue hanging out. And right on cue, he released his famous flatulence, serving to defuse the tension that had been building inside of me. I shook my head and laughed it off and noticed a smile on Bulldog's face, too.

Turning my attention fully back towards him, I asked, "What is our first move?"

Bulldog pulled a clean and neatly-stapled bundle of paper from his side desk drawer. It looked to be a contract with lots of legal mumble jumble. He pushed aside a stack of papers so he could lay the contract in front of me along with a pen.

"Take your time reading through it and then sign on the dotted line. Page twenty-five."

"Could you just break it down and give me the skinny?" I asked, hoping that I wouldn't have to spend my whole day in this dark room.

"Sure, kid." Bulldog went through page by page and he made it quick.

We arrived at page twenty-five where I placed my John Hancock as instructed. Reaching into the back pocket of my Levi's, I found my wallet and handed Bulldog the card with the largest credit limit. Bulldog assured me his hourly fee was far more reasonable than losing everything in court without his well-seasoned legal expertise.

'Nuf said, done deal. This guy is not losing anything.

After running my plastic through the square on his phone, Bulldog relaxed with his game face on. We talked through my financials first and finally got to the kids. He told me that Ms. Nothing's Ever Good Enough had obviously been the "primary parent," since she was a stay-at-home mom, and I had always been the breadwinner. He said I had some work cut out for me if I wanted to get sole legal custody of my kids and nothing less than 50% parenting time.

Bulldog straightened one thing out for me. He said that children nearly always spend time with both of their parents after a divorce. No one gets "full custody," he said, wherein a child is forbidden contact with one parent or the other, except in highly unusual circumstances, which mine were not. The court had an obligation, he further explained, to ensure Teo and Rae had reliable access to their mother and to me after we were divorced. It was their legal right.

Huh, wish I had known that before I filled out the online divorce paperwork.

Bulldog proceeded to tell me that I would need to "step it up" with regard to my "historical patterns of parenting." I needed to show more involvement in primary parenting areas of Teo and Rae's lives if there was any chance of me getting to have the kids half of the time. He laid out some possibilities for stepping up my involvement and said I had some choices to make. He would stall the legal process so there was adequate time for me to "demonstrate" my parenting strengths, desire, and capacity to be more involved than I had been throughout the marriage.

Our meeting ended with me holding onto the legal pad of notes Bulldog had made, on which he had written possible ways to step up my parenting over the next few months. I had decisions to make and looked forward to considering the best way to "bolster my legal standing" later that night in the comfort of my new apartment.

Bulldog mentioned a child custody evaluation at the very end of our time together, though didn't say much else about it. He said he wanted to see how things unfolded before offering too much more on the subject, but that I should definitely be prepared to go forward with a child custody evaluation before this whole process was over. We shook hands, and I looked over to Lola's workstation where she and Iggy were now snuggled up, enjoying an afternoon siesta together.

I spoke Igg's name and he stirred. "Iggy, come on, boy," I said a little louder. He looked up, licked Lola's cheek, hopped down from her lap, and met me by the door.

Lola lazily rocked forward in her chair and peeked over the piles of paper on her desk, "Bye-bye, my love," she mumbled sleepily to my dog, yawning and adjusting the low-cut top that had slid to one side. She waved as we walked out the door.

In the sunny alley outside, I noticed Iggy's toenails were painted bright purple and laughed, "You got yourself a new friend, Igg? She's a real looker, pal." Iggy strutted his stuff down the alley and we made it back to the Mustang, which thankfully, in this rough neighborhood, still had all four wheels. We hopped in and I decided to hit the drive-thru for a burger and fries.

Home sweet home, here I come.

The smoking hot apartment manager, CoCo, had assigned me an underground parking space earlier that day, and we pulled into the spot marked number 12—ironically Teo's lucky number, printed on all of his basketball jerseys since the first grade.

I was not sure what to do with Iggy since he was not exactly on the lease, but I decided it would be best to wrap him up in Rae's blanket and then instruct him to be quiet. I'm pretty sure Igg speaks English because he follows my directions to a T—like a good boy.

Now that I think of it, he was the only one in the house who ever listened to me.

We headed up to the sixth floor and found my new pad, apartment number 666. I sat Iggy down to unlock the door and when I did, he stepped out with his purple toenails on full display. I chuckled again as we walked into our new home together.

It was the same place but not quite as exciting without CoCo here. It was empty, really empty—a reminder that I needed to get over to the house and collect my stuff. All I had with me was dinner in a brown bag and Rae's blanket; down in the car there was a pillow, a duffle bag of clothes, my things for work, Iggy's bag of kibble with his water bowl, and nothing else.

Iggy curled up on the wooden floor by the bay of uncovered windows and dozed off with the city lights shining in. I sat down next to him, in my new place, with my burger and fries and the legal pad Bulldog had prepared for me. There were lots of notes about my case and my choices for moving forward with the divorce.

I guess he truly anticipated that at some point, we would be in front of a judge, and that I would be talking to a child custody evaluator because he wrote with emphasis in red sharpie:

"Do Not Do Anything, Say Anything, or Put Anything into Writing That Would Make You Look like an Ass in Front of an Evaluator or Judge."

Don't be an ass. Got it. No problemo. Can do!

He also commented that I should assume from here forward that every conversation I have with Vanessa in person, by phone, email, or text will be recorded. He suggested I do the same.

Now what exactly are my choices?

Below are three different ways Luke can choose to prepare for and navigate through the upcoming child custody evaluation.

Expose Vanessa's incompetence and step in as the primary parent.
Go to page page 271 to follow Luke's experience through this choice.

Become Super-Dad and inspire the kids to beg for more time with me.
Go to page 335 to follow Luke's experience through this choice.

Demonstrate why the kids would benefit from equal time with me.
Go to page 397 to follow Luke's experience through this choice.

"Fear is the path to the dark side.
Fear leads to anger.
Anger leads to hate.
Hate leads to suffering."

~Yoda~

PROVE SHE'S INSANE

Expose Vanessa's incompetence and step in as the primary parent for my children.

I BLINKED AT the words Bulldog had written down.

"Expose your ex for who she really is by provoking her into a physical altercation."

This must be a joke.

I'd mentioned to Bulldog that I knew a guy from work who had gotten a restraining order on his wife when they separated, which had really worked in his favor. Ms. Nothing's Ever Good Enough was a real pain in the rear, but she and I had never been in any sort of physical altercation, so I didn't really think this was going to be a route I could take in my divorce. Apparently, Bulldog decided to entertain the idea.

"Be sure that you suffer a visible injury and that she is not hurt. Not so much as one hair on her head is to be harmed. Period. After 'provoking' her, call the police, have her arrested, and then file the restraining order."

Wow. That's...

"This choice is pretty risky," Bulldog's instruction continued. "There is a lot of room for error, and it could backfire in court or with the kids. This choice will most likely launch your family into a child custody evaluation.

However, if you get it just right, and a judge signs the restraining order, it will be like winning the divorce lottery. You will get the house back, and Vanessa will not have access to the kids until the court determines it is safe for Teo and Rae to see her again. This will be enough time for you to win back their affections and run interference with any negative things she has told them since you left the house."

I'm sure she has been badmouthing me to the kids.

"It would be best to provoke her after she has been out for cocktails," was Bulldog's last note on the matter.

I looked out the window and grinned, remembering the days when Vanessa was loose and fun. *She could really throw down some cocktails back in the day and have a good time.* I caught my breath. *Damn it, Luke. She's not that gal anymore. Get serious about making her look like the horrible woman she's proven herself to be.*

I looked at the bottom of the first page and the note that Bulldog had written in red sharpie pen:

"Never Ever Admit to Anyone, Under Any Circumstance, That You Heard This Advice from Me. Doing so is a Violation of the Contract You Signed–Page 16 Paragraph 4 Subsection 12 items 1-52."

Secret passwords. Secret legal advice. This is like being in a movie. Again, my gut told me this was a bad choice, and terrible legal advice, but I quickly dismissed the foreboding feeling. This choice did feel satisfyingly vengeful. And although overly theatrical for me, it sounded like the outcome could be outstanding. Then, my gut spoke loud and clear. *I really want to expose her, but this is not a good idea. It seems very dramatic and borderline illegal.*

My gut kept churning, but the angry voice inside me reveled in the thought of crushing my ex. *It might do Ms. Nothing's Ever Good Enough some good to sit in jail for a night after treating me so terribly throughout our marriage. Plus, I'd be back in the house and have uninterrupted time with Teo and Rae. How risky could it be? It's not like anyone is actually going to get hurt, and people get restraining orders against each other all the time.*

My head began pounding from the internal turmoil that considering this choice had unleashed. I put the legal pad down and started flipping through Instagram on my phone. It had been a long day, and this was a lot to consider. I decided to curl up next to Iggy for warmth, with our one blanket, and fell fast asleep next to my dependable little buddy.

The next morning, I woke up for work and hustled out the door without a thought about my choices in the divorce. By midday, I was all-encompassed in my job again and trying to find a way to spend time with the kids and really show that I am an outstanding dad.

Days turned to weeks turned to months, with familiar routines blending together.

Several uneventful months had passed since Bulldog and I had first met at his office. True to his word, he had stalled the legal processes to give me the time I needed to step it up and really show my full parenting capacity, which Ms. Nothing's Ever Good Enough had muted all these years, because I work full time outside the home.

Bulldog hadn't given me a phone number to reach him or offered up an email address, but he had called me twice to check in and a few letters had been sent to my apartment address via snail-mail. One of these letters included Vanessa's response to my petition for full custody, which I now know means something entirely different than having the kids with me all the time and only allowing them to see their mother whenever I say they can.

Ms. Nothing's Ever Good Enough was being a real princess, demanding this, that, and everything else through her powerful Attorney of the Year.

Money, money, money—all she wants is cash and prizes. Lloyd had been spot-on about that. *Get a job already and make your own money for once, woman! When is this ever going to end? I'd like to move on with my life.* I looked around the tiny living space, frustrated that I hadn't yet been able to move back into the home I paid for and raise my children the way I thought best.

CoCo down in the rental office had my full attention, but was a real challenge. I had dropped by her office most days for a little chit-chat and even brought in flowers on Administrative Assistant Day. She had yet to accept my invitation for an evening cocktail up in the 666.

What is it with women and that stupid superstitious number, as if I am the devil himself for renting a space with 666 on the door?

Poor Rae thought it was "creepy," and it really seemed to scare her to be at my place, no matter how much I assured her there was nothing to be afraid of.

Daddy's got your back, girl—always!

With the help of our attorneys, Vanessa and I had established a parenting time schedule. Kids were with me every other weekend. It was not enough time, but Bulldog said having a regular parenting time schedule at this early stage is best, and better than not having a schedule at all. He said to agree temporarily, and we'd get more time added later. It really sucked. Even criminals see their kids more often than I am allowed to, and I'm a hardworking, dedicated, loving father who has always been there for my kids.

There is no justice in our broken legal system.

Ms. Nothing's Ever Good Enough told me the kids "hate" coming to the apartment, especially Rae who was certain it's haunted. Teo grumbled that it's boring, and he does not like being away from his friends, especially on the weekend. This was not the way I pictured things going when I left the house, which now seemed like a lifetime ago.

Something needs to give.

Sitting in my favorite La-Z-Boy chair that she had finally let me take from the house, I pulled out Bulldog's list of choices from our very first meeting—the list of possibilities for moving forward. So far, I had been unable to do much of anything beyond survive. It was hard making choices about how to move forward with dismantling your life and routines of the previous two decades. Everything was foreign and the excitement of starting over had long subsided. I reread Bulldog's advice—the "secret advice" about getting a restraining order against Vanessa.

"Like winning the divorce lottery..."

What do I got to lose? I thought to myself looking around the mostly-empty, pathetically-furnished, sardine-sized apartment that had become my home. CoCo had even kicked Iggy out in a rant about my lease and "no animals allowed on the property."

Poor guy is stuck back at the house with Ms. Nothing's Ever Good Enough and her stupid rules and his outdoor kennel! My anger had fully risen to the surface and was at a steady, rolling boil. *I want my house back, the kids back, and Iggy back without her around. If this is the easiest way to get all that, then I'm in. I'm going to make her pay!*

First, I called my lifetime best friend, Mike, to confirm that Vanessa and his wife, Juls, still went out for cocktails every week. He confirmed that Margarita Mondays was still a thing for the girls and asked why I wanted to know. I paused for too long and stumbled through a quick white lie, not wanting to give away my plan.

"Luke, what are you doing, man? You're not gonna do anything stupid, are you?" My friend sounded genuinely concerned, but his assumption just made me angrier and more determined. I quickly changed the subject to the possibility of meeting up to watch a game soon and then said goodbye. But not before he nosed into my business again, "Luke, I know you're pissed. Just don't do anything you are going to regret, okay, bro?" I told him I wouldn't and then ended our call.

Next Monday night is it.

Monday could not show up fast enough. Once I'd decided that getting a restraining order against Vanessa was the right thing to do, even Jesus, Buddha, Ghandi, the three of them together, or any other authority or divine power could not have talked me out of it.

The moment finally arrived, and I drove from my office to the suburb where I parked on the street outside my house. My plan was to catch her before she went into the house, so the kids did not see or hear anything. I figured the bruise already on my left arm would go a long way to support my story when I reported to the police that she had attacked me.

I could see her car was not there, but the sitter's SUV was in the driveway. Vanessa had started farming the kids out since I left so she could party in the evenings with her girlfriends. Apparently, it was fine for Teo and Rae to spend time with anyone and everyone else, except for their dad.

My heart raced as I saw headlights approaching in the distance. When I recognized her vehicle, my whole body started to hum with the anticipation of getting everything back—and Vanessa getting exactly what she deserved. I was not sure how I would explain all of this to the kids, but Rae had already heard my mother say a while back, "Your mother should be thrown in jail." When Rae asked me questions about why grandma said that, my only answer was a true one—Grandma was a little bit nutty.

At least the idea of their mother going to jail has already been introduced, and Rae will have confidence knowing one of her grammy's speaks the truth.

Ms. Nothing's Ever Good Enough pulled her vehicle into the driveway, and I set my cell phone to record, hoping a video would provide all the evidence needed. When she stumbled out of her car, clearly intoxicated, I quickly approached her like a hungry animal stalking its prey. "Hey, Vanessa," I growled seductively in the most provocative way I could.

Like the exorcist's twin, Vanessa whipped her head around, looking shocked as hell. "What do you want, Luke?" she seethed through clenched teeth.

I saw her hands ball up at her sides and kept walking slowly in her direction, but she did not back away. *Obviously. Because I have never, ever, in all these years harmed or threatened this woman, and she is not the least bit afraid of me.*

"What are you doing here, Luke? You don't live here anymore! You need to leave right now!" I could tell she was about to lose her shit.

Perfect!

I ramped up my efforts, "Come on, baby. It's been a long time. Can't we just spend one night together, for old time's sake? I need a little lovin' from my best girl."

That's all it took. She actually lunged in my direction, but a little to the left. Remembering Bulldog had said she must be "completely unharmed," I gently broke her fall before she hit the pavement and then stood her back upright.

The help I offered seemed to make her angrier. She was spitting, quite literally, all kinds of nasty names in my direction, while flailing her arms, pointing her finger in my face, and demanding that I leave "her" house immediately!

Your *house? We used inheritance money from* **my** *grandfather's passing for the down payment. I have made every single mortgage payment since, and still am, along with managing all the bills, even though I don't live here anymore, because the stupid temporary court order your attorney drafted says that I have to!*

I noticed the porch light had been flipped on and dogs had started barking all over the neighborhood. I did not need to call the police because someone else already had, and the Five-O came flying down the street with lights and sirens blazing.

Adrenaline kicked in. *This is even better than I could have planned it!*

As anticipated, the police saw my ex intoxicated and completely unharmed, and me with an ample size bruise on my left arm. Neighborhood witnesses reported hearing Vanessa screeching up a storm and disrupting the peace.

While I was making sure the police officer had my full statement, I heard Rae crying and yelling from the porch: "Don't take my mommy! Please don't take my mommy!" I looked up to see Teo and Rae standing on the front porch, in their pajamas, watching the scene unfold with the babysitter standing protectively between them. Teo looked super embarrassed and pissed, and just shook his head at me and his mother before walking back inside the house.

They'll get over it. In the end, they'll realize I'm doing what's best for them.

When the police asked if I wanted to press charges, I replied, "Yes."

They cuffed and carted Vanessa away in the back of a squad car. As the officer handed me his business card with the case number, I asked about filing a restraining order. He told me I had to do that at the courthouse the next day.

When the front yard was finally quiet, I entered the home I had left months before to find the sitter shell-shocked, sitting on the couch with Rae who was curled up in her lap and sobbing. Teo was nowhere to be seen, although I heard the beat of loud rap music coming from downstairs in his bedroom.

"Hi, Rae. Daddy's here. Everything is going to be okay now, honey."

My daughter looked up for a second with hatred in her eyes—something I had never seen before. She was clinging to the sitter for dear life. When I walked over to the couch and sat next to them, offering Rae to move into my lap, she refused. Using as soft a voice as I could muster, I assured her it would be okay and apologized for the scene. The visibly conflicted young woman decidedly took my daughter by the hand and walked Rae into her bedroom.

After Rae calmed down a bit, and was tucked safely in her bedroom, the sitter returned to the couch where I was beginning to crash as the adrenaline waned. Standing above me, she told me that she had noticed big changes in both of the children and was concerned about their welfare and well-being because of this divorce. Then she gave me her number and asked that I call anytime for help, as she really cared about Teo and Rae. She grabbed her purse and closed the door behind her as I just sat there, in my house, for the first time in months, and soaked it all in.

The plan actually worked! I was in the house, and Ms. Nothing's Ever Good Enough was out. I could hear Iggy out back in his kennel and walked outside to get him, "Hey, boy!" I opened the gate, and we had one heck of a happy reunion.

It was a long night for the kids and me. With Iggy's help, the three of us managed to talk it out over a super late-night pizza and arrived at a moment where the kids actually seemed happy that I was back home. We all fell asleep together in the living room around midnight, like we used to do when pretending to be on a campout.

Morning came too soon, and it was chaos trying to get out the door for school, but we did it. I thought about letting them stay home, but knew it would look better for my case if I managed their morning routine and delivered them to school on time.

Score one for Daddy!

I took the day off from work and went right from school drop-off to the courthouse and filed the restraining order. A judge granted it, temporarily awarding me the house and care of the kids. Ms. Nothing's Ever Good Enough could not come within 500 feet of me, the house, the kids, or their schools. She had the right to a contested hearing but, due to her violent outburst the night prior, ending in her arrest, she would not be able to see Teo and Rae until the court had heard all the evidence.

I drove immediately from the courthouse to Bulldog's office where I knocked twice and used the password. Seated across from him at his desk, I proceeded to tell Bulldog everything that had happened. He listened to every word and then told me to keep the apartment and enjoy the heck out of the next two weeks in my house with my kids. He was sure with Attorney of the Year on the other side, Ms. Nothing's Ever Good Enough would request a contested hearing and that the restraining order would probably be dismissed.

What? All that planning and drama was for nothing? I bet the court upholds restraining orders against men all the time. Such a biased system!

Bulldog was right. We went to the contested hearing less than two weeks later, and the judge dismissed the restraining order due to some crap evidence showing the bruise on my arm was too "old" to have happened the night of the incident. Vanessa played all sweet and innocent and looked like a victim standing behind her all-powerful Attorney of the Year. I had a hard time explaining why I was at the house that evening, "lurking," as her attorney kept saying, out in the street just waiting for Vanessa to return home.

The kids' counselor testified, along with some of their teachers and the sitter, about the negative impact my children have suffered since the split and especially after witnessing the police arrest their mother in their front yard. The subsequent two-week disruption in the relationship with their mother was untruthfully described as "traumatic," rather than the peaceful break and necessary time with their dad that it had actually been.

The kids did not even ask about their mother once— not at all.

In the end, the court signed a mutual no-contact order, so Vanessa and I were not allowed to be around each other. The judge ordered that Teo and Rae were to spend every other weekend with me again, and the balance of time with their mother. He gave my ex "exclusive use" of the house, and we were ordered to participate in mediation, a county-run parenting class, and a child custody evaluation, which the judge said was to help inform the court about the total dynamics of our family and our parenting capacities, and to help define the best interests of our children.

So basically, a stranger gets to decide what's best for my kids?

Bulldog had a hint of worry on his face as we parted ways in the courthouse parking lot. "Risky" was the understatement of the year to describe how hazardous this choice had turned out to be. My gut told me an evaluation on the heels of this cluster was not going to turn out very well for me—that I had royally messed up this time.

So much for not being an ass, I thought as I drove back to my studio apartment.

My place had been empty for two weeks while I was at the house. I checked the fridge and found a pack of moldy cheese, half a bottle of ketchup, a jar of olives, and two beers. I grabbed a beer and headed over to my La-Z-Boy where I plopped down in front of the television and fired up the PlayStation, needing some mindless time in my nothing-box to veg in front of the tube and play my son's favorite videogames.

I logged into NBA 2K20 and noticed Teo's gamertag, RimRocker12, was live. My ex must have picked up the kids right after court today.

I sent RimRocker12 a message:

"hey kid, are yah doing ok?"

Nothing. No response. Crickets. But, I could see he was still playing the game and that my message was delivered.

I tried again:

"hey buddy, I'm worried about you and your sister."

RimRocker12: "go to hell dad"

What?! Who is this kid? Teo does not speak this way to me, ever!

I tried to address it:

"Language, son. I know this is a rough time but we'll get through it. Sorry I had to leave, again. I'll get this worked out with your mother real soon."

RimRocker12: "you ruined our lives I hope you die"

What has his mother filled his head with now?

RimRocker12 logged off, and I was left alone in my cruddy apartment with two beers and twenty bucks to my name. At least the kids were due over to the apartment on Friday.

She better not try and keep them from me.

Thursday and Friday that week, I navigated on autopilot at work. Friday evening could not roll around fast enough. Vanessa and I met at a "neutral location," aka McDonalds parking lot, where the kids begrudgingly dragged themselves and their things from her car to mine. Neither kid spoke a word in the car. Teo's nose was in his phone and Rae sat cross-armed in the backseat, staring out the window. I tried to make conversation by asking about school, sports, and friends, but nothing. They would not breathe even one word in my direction.

Just like their mother's silent treatment. They must have learned this from her!

We pulled into the underground lot at the apartment and went upstairs. Rae immediately made herself a fort, and completely enclosed it like a tent, around my bed. She taped a "DO NOT ENTER" sign on the outside, went inside, and did not come out, except to use the bathroom. I made sure she had water and brought her food. Teo sat in front of the PlayStation and stayed there, in my La-Z-Boy, all weekend.

This was obviously the worst choice I could have made. Curse Bulldog for not shutting it down the moment I had mentioned it! How am I going to fix this?

I apologized over and over and begged the kids to speak to me, to look at me, to yell, to scream—anything but silence—but they were more stubborn than I remembered.

Sunday finally rolled around, and we packed up. I drove them to the suburb and dropped them "curbside" at the family home, which meant that I stayed in the car, as directed by the judge, until Teo and Rae were safely inside with their mother.

This house needs to be sold. I'm not paying her way, not one more bloody second.

Back at my apartment, I sat down in the La-Z-Boy, grabbed Teo's controller, and turned on the television. Resident Evil2 was running. The message box was open and the full chat history was visible. Teo had been jabbing with his best friend, Ethan, all weekend (gamertag: SeekNDestroy). I scrolled all the way to the top of a conversation they'd started on Friday night. What I saw shocked the life out of me.

RimRocker 12: "i hate my fing dad man im stuck here all weekend"

SeekNDestroy: "sorry dude wish I could help"

RimRocker12: "can you believe he had my mom arrested he should be the one in jail"

Shit, now my kid thinks I'm an asshole?

SeekNDestroy: "karma always wins man"

RimRocker12: "my mom is so pissed my life is ruined bc of my stupid parents divorce"

SeekNDestroy: "my mom says you and your sister can live with us"

RimRocker12: "bro that would be awesome"

He should be mad at her, not me, and to even consider switching families! My anger at Ms. Nothing's Ever Good Enough was matched only by the fear of losing my kids.

The dialogue went on and on about how awful our family was and how wonderful Ethan's family is. Ethan's parents are divorced, too, but they hadn't had as much divorce drama. I scrolled down to Saturday evening.

RimRocker12: "can you believe he is still holding us hostage over here there isn't even any decent food im starving"

SeekNDestroy: "i can ask my mom to order a pizza or send grubhub over with a burger"

RimRocker12: "thanks man that would be dope"

SeekNDestroy: "tomorrow your home right"

RimRocker12: "yah but who knows what will go down tomorrow my dad is dropping us off at the house and last time my parents were both there there was a huge deal with cops, and he had my mom thrown in jail and then we didn't see her for weeks remember"

I didn't have her thrown in jail. It was her behavior that got her arrested!

SeekNDestroy: "maybe he will let you bring me along the next weekend you have to go there like your wingman brotha I got your back"

RimRocker12: "yah cool maybe ill ask my mom"

SeekNDestroy: "remember to delete all of this so you dont get in trouble"

RimRocker12: "word"

With my heart sunk and stomach soured, I closed the chat box.

All I wanted to do was to get away from my suffocating ex, move on with my life, and spend time with my kids. It seemed so simple, I seethed as I grabbed my ATM card, favorite hoodie, and phone, and headed for the bar.

I bellied up on the corner stool. *At least this feels familiar, and people here will talk to me. My life is pathetic. I need this divorce to be over and put it all behind me.*

I took the first cool sip of my beer and felt the phone in my pocket buzz, alerting me that there was a new email. I opened it and winced when I saw a correspondence from the court-assigned evaluator who wanted to meet this coming week at her office.

I replied back, "Is tomorrow good? I could come in anytime." Thankfully, I still had a lot of paid time off stored up at work.

Best to get this over with. I wonder why she's working so late on a Sunday evening. Maybe she's working with a lot of families right now?

She had a 10:00 a.m. on Tuesday open on her calendar, and I took it. She told me to bring a form of payment, as there was a several thousand-dollar balance due in full at or before our first meeting. She also told me it would be helpful to look over her webpage beforehand, and think through a timeline of important family events. She assured me that I did not have to fill out any paperwork in advance—good thing since I hadn't been given any paperwork and the computer and printer were still at the house.

I planned on just being myself and letting this lady see the real me—an imperfect, but hardworking guy who loves his kids more than anything else and wants to be a big part of their lives forever. I pulled up the evaluator's website on my phone and clicked the tab that said "Pricing." A picture loaded at the top of the page showing a fortune cookie. The fortune read, "Marriage is grand. Divorce is one hundred grand."

Ain't that turning out to be the truth.

I read a little further and learned that a custody evaluation was often the way to a stipulated agree-ment—a way for families to avoid the financial and emotional hardship of a courtroom trial, which often costs each party ten to twenty thousand dollars or more. At the start of this, I had been looking forward to my day in court; but now, after the whole restraining order fiasco and being nearly bled dry financially, anything that promised to move our family toward an end and save me money sounded pretty good.

Tuesday morning, I arrived at the evaluator's office promptly at 10:00 a.m. without having had an opportunity to talk to Bulldog about what to say or not say. I would have to go this first meeting alone and stop in to see him afterwards.

When I opened the door to the evaluator's office, the lady at the front desk welcomed me and offered a mug of coffee or cup of water. I accepted the coffee, and she handed me a disclosure form to read, date, and sign. Once I had secured a copy for my own records and she had swiped my plastic, the evaluator walked in from another room and introduced herself with a firm handshake.

She seems like a genuine, people-person kind of gal, I thought as she led me into a back office where she motioned for us to sit in the two comfortable chairs by the window. *Hot coffee and a comfy chair. Not a bad start to the day.*

The evaluator was all business and welcomed me with a professional smile. She asked if I had any questions before she started in with her spiel about how the evaluation process works, wanting to make sure we were both on the same page. I did not have any questions, since I hardly knew anything about this, except that I'd just paid her a small fortune. So, I settled into the chair and listened to her talk.

"Well, Luke, most parents are a bit nervous meeting me for the first time, although usually feel much better by the end of our two hours together. I know it has been a long road leading up to today, and you're likely emotionally and financially exhausted."

Damn straight about that.

"Add to it the constant worry about your children, and a parent can really start to feel like they have been swept down the proverbial rabbit hole. Good news is that this evaluation is an opportunity to step back from the adversarial high conflict that litigation often creates between two parents, as we fully explore and concentrate on the needs of your children. We'll be discussing the strengths of each parent and both parents' concerns, and then put our big brains together to design the best plan for Teo and Rae." She gave me a settling smile, confident in her conviction to understand my family.

I was completely on board with combining our big brains on behalf of my children until she kept talking about working together as a "team"—her, me, and Ms. Nothing's Ever Good Enough, with whom I am currently court-prohibited from having any contact. That seemed important to share, but she was on a roll, so I let it go.

"I have never met a parent who didn't love their children. Mothers and fathers come to this process, both wanting what they believe is in their children's best interest. They both want their children to win the game but are working from different playbooks. My hope is to bring you and the children's mother 80% of the way toward the middle, and then provide enough guidance and direction that the two of you can finish off the final 20% by infusing the plan for Teo and Rae with specific details to meet the unique needs of your family. When both parents are invested in the final plan, when both parents feel heard and that they had a say in what's best, then the plan is far more likely to work versus a judgment imposed on your family by the court. Make sense?" Again, she flashed me that satisfied look, like she really intended the best for our family.

Cautious, but feeling hopeful, I nodded in agreement. "We have a no-contact order. Is that a problem? Are my ex and I supposed to be coming in here together at some point?"

The evaluator inhaled deeply through her nose and, with raised eyebrows, gave me a knowing look. "Ah, well that isn't too uncommon with parents moving through an evaluation process, unfortunately. You'll be able to share with me in a short while, the details about how the no-contact order came to be. You and the children's mother will not be attending any evaluation sessions together. There are four meetings with you and two of those meetings include the children—one here at the office and one at your home. All that I do with you, I will also do with the other parent. Eight family meetings total. Four with you and four with Mom—four total that include the children. You with me?"

I nodded my head again, feeling a little overwhelmed.

"So, Luke," the evaluator began moving us toward the starting line, "the goal of our time today is for you to educate me about the story of your family. How you got from point A (meeting the other parent) to point B (a custody litigant). Only a very small percentage of divorcing parents participate in an evaluation. I'm curious to learn all about why your family is here and begin to understand ways in which I can best assist your children and family moving forward." She paused before giving me further instruction. "It would be helpful if you could go down memory lane..."

With that, my brain suddenly transported me back to college and the first time I saw Vanessa, with her petite frame and firm behind, dancing with her friends inside our favorite campus bar. I felt a wave of joy rush through me, and then just as fast was pulled back to the moment, into the evaluator's chair, my joy replaced by a heavy feeling of being defeated and lost. It was the equivalent of emotional whiplash.

Crap, she's still talking—giving directions. I focused back on the evaluator's voice.

"Relay information in chronological order—paint a picture of the most significant events in your family's timeline. Throughout the story, please highlight the most important details of your children's lives (residential moves, school/academics, friendships, important relationships, activities/sports/music, health, religion, special needs, special services, successes, areas where they struggle and excel, etc.). You good?" she asked.

"Yep," I replied with more confidence than I felt.

She continued, "Secondary to learning about your children's lives is for me/us to understand patterns of conflict between you and the other parent. Patterns of conflict are important for us to identify because embedded within them are often your parenting concerns; and unless we make an effort to understand and mitigate the unhealthy patterns of conflict that exist now, those unhealthy patterns will continue on after the divorce and cause trouble for your family going forward. Repeated exposure to parental conflict is detrimental to Teo and Rae and will cause them irreparable harm over time."

With that, she gestured in my direction, as if she were offering me the floor to start talking.

Wait, what does she want me to say? I stared blankly, blinked a few times, and shifted uncomfortably in the chair. *The timeline. Important family events. She wants the story.*

I squared my shoulders and started in, "Well, I have a good job with a stable income that supports our family. My ex has been at home with the kids while I have been at work to provide for everyone. I've never been late on a bill and the kids have never gone without anything. All that I do is for them, and I really love my kids." From there, I told her everything. In two hours, I described the days each of the kids were born, and all the important moments of their life since. I explained the ways in which I had been an active and "primary" parent in their lives and how difficult Ms. Nothing's Ever Good Enough has made everything for me with her controlling, dictator-like ways, never letting me be a fully-involved parent. I shared about all my best qualities and all of Vanessa's worst and laid it on thick. I conveniently left out the whole botched restraining order ordeal, hoping she didn't know about it.

It was the first time someone had heard my life story, twenty years of it anyway, and just listened without offering any criticism or their two cents. By the end of our session, I felt a whole lot better and like a pretty good dad.

The evaluator hardly spoke a word after her introductory speech, but piped in when I had finished. "Luke, thank you for sharing about your children and family. We will plan to meet again soon, after I have talked with Teo and Rae's mother. I'll send you an email with some possible dates and times." She stood up and walked me out.

That's it? No feedback? No compliments on my parenting? I thought I slayed it?

I followed her to the door, thanked her for her time, left the office, and drove straight to Bulldog's. Once there, I followed the usual routine and was promptly seated across the desk from him. He did not have too much feedback either—said it sounded like things went well and told me to keep up the good work. He suggested I take notes at the next meeting, when the evaluator would share Vanessa's parenting concerns with me.

Can do!

The second evaluation meeting was scheduled about two weeks out, and it was business as usual until then. The kids spent time at the apartment the weekend in between meetings. Teo mostly played his video games, but walked down to check out some basketball courts on Saturday afternoon. Rae refused to join him, even for a walk, proclaiming that, "The city is dangerous!" No doubt her mother's crazy influence.

As soon as Teo was out of the space, Rae started talking. "Do you hate Mom?" she asked accusingly, looking me in the eye and quite assertively for such a small person.

My daughter was instantly in tears. I must have paused just a little too long before answering because she interpreted my silence as a "yes" before I could soften the blow, dance around the issue, or come up with a better though equally truthful adjective.

I'll never lie to my kids.

"Why do you hate Mommy? Why does Mommy hate you? Why can't everyone just be nice and get along?" She sobbed while I sat on the couch with her, rubbing her back, wondering what on earth to say until she found her own answer: "You and Mom need to be grounded, on restriction, sent to the principal's office, or sit in detention all day. I heard Mommy and Grandma talking, and they said you should be in jail, just like you and Grammy said right before Mommy went to jail. Is our whole family getting locked up and thrown into the 'hoosegow'? Will me and Teo become foster kids, like Annie, and have to suffer a Hard Knock Life?" Tears continued to pour out of her.

Where'd she hear the term hoosegow? Comforting my daughter was like trying to cuddle an angry gator. She was loud and dramatic, with a theatrical flair. Always had been. I loved my baby girl's stubborn feistiness and knew it would serve her well one day, but it was extremely uncomfortable. After an hour or more of Rae carrying on like her parents' divorce was the end of the world, all I could think to do was to assure her that I loved her, that her mother did the best she knew how, that her grandmothers were both nutty, and that it was all going to be okay. Just like with her mother, my words seemed only to make my daughter angrier.

I'll never understand women, even this little one I helped create. I gave Rae a hug, got her a grape Popsicle, and then suggested she rest in her tent for the rest of the afternoon. That would give me time to ponder ways to get back into her good graces.

As I sat in my La-Z-Boy listening to my daughter's slowly-abating sobs coming from inside the tent next to me, I shook my head quietly. *Kids go through divorce every day, thousands of them. I hadn't really thought about all the ways my leaving the house might make my kids feel. It was just time to get out of the house and away from Ms. Nothing's Ever Good Enough. I had no idea it would cause so many big feelings. I hope this evaluator can help straighten things out.*

The second evaluation meeting was different from the first. I was greeted in the same way, and then the evaluator and I went to the back office; but this time, once we were seated, the evaluator told me she had an agenda. Today would be more of a structured interview. There were lots of questions about my parenting style, discipline of the children, routines in my household, the kids' healthcare and dental care, extended family relationships, holiday traditions, activities, their friendships, and school. We walked through my ideas about the best parenting plan and why I thought it would work for Teo and Rae. That part was easy. 50-50 is what I wanted and what all kids needed after a divorce. Everything I'd read online confirmed this fact, and so had Bulldog.

Then it was time for the evaluator to share my ex's parenting concerns, so we could sort through some of the disagreements and she could hear both sides of the issues.

Bring it, lady. I put my game face on and asked for a notebook and pen to take notes.

It was not easy listening to and responding to all of Ms. Nothing's Ever Good Enough's complaints. When we finally made it through the litany of her BS,

I decided to tell the evaluator about my suspicion that my ex is bipolar. I saw her write that down and provided anecdotal stories about all of Ms. Nothing's Ever Good Enough's bat-shit crazy behavior. I needed her to know that my ex is the wacko, not me, especially after the less-than-favorable outcome of that incident between us in the driveway with the now-dismissed restraining order and all. After twenty minutes, I was finished, satisfied that I had crushed her as good as any sane-minded man possibly could.

The evaluator looked at me, concern now on her face and started in, "Sometimes during this process, there is a need for psychological testing. Different testing measures can help us get a better look at a person's true cognitive, emotional, and psychological functioning as it relates to their parenting capacity. Given the concerns you and your wife have shared about each other, I will be making a referral for testing as part of this process."

Sweet, she's sending my ex to a shrink!

"Remember," she continued, "whatever I do with one parent, I do with the other. Both you and the children's mother will need to participate in testing."

A lightning bolt of fear struck as her words sunk in. "So I need to get tested, too?" I nearly choked out the question.

She offered that a letter would be forthcoming, providing all the information we would need to contact a forensic psychologist and get set up with him.

"You don't do that part?" I asked, heart still racing.

"No, I am a social worker and do not administer testing," she answered. "Psychologists are trained in the area of testing. You will meet with the doctor for a clinical interview, and spend a few hours completing paper-pencil tests that will help us better understand if you or Vanessa suffer from emotional or personality disturbances, for which a form of treatment would be useful going forward. The goal is to identify any potential mental health problems now, during this unique window of opportunity, so everyone can get the help they need to be their best self. Teo and Rae need two healthy functioning parents to thrive. If Vanessa suffers from a bipolar disorder, this will help uncover it."

Disturbances, mental health problems, unique window of opportunity...

"I suppose that costs a pretty penny?" I couldn't hide my sarcasm.

The evaluator told me there was a separate and additional fee that I would pay directly to the psychologist according to his fee agreement.

Terrific, I'd better put in for some overtime, or get a second job!

We scheduled our third evaluation meeting—the parent-child interaction with Teo and Rae—for Friday afternoon, right after I picked them up from school. She suggested that in preparation, I tell the kids a little bit about her and her office and let them know that their mother and I have both been in to see her. I was not to "coach" them in any way about things they should or should not say. She promised the burden of all this was not theirs, and she was simply interested in getting to know them a little bit—wanting to hear whatever was on their minds. She was clear that we were not to talk about any adult issues during any of our upcoming meetings that included the children.

Guess I'll text Teo before Friday so he knows about the after-school meeting and can tell his sister about it, too.

I left the office feeling out-of-sorts and disoriented, knowing I had to come up with more money and that a shrink was going to have a look in my head. I was worried about what the kids might say to our evaluator at the meeting on Friday. Neither one of them was very happy with me. It seemed really important they said positive things about our relationship and that we looked happy together, or at least as if they liked me a little bit.

Think, Luke. Think.

On the drive home, the most brilliant answer came to me.

Teo loved basketball. He had big dreams of playing in college and I always told him that hard work beats talent. With grit and a can-do attitude, anything was possible. Basketball was his life, and anything to do with this sport pleased him, especially the latest and greatest pair of overpriced court shoes. I knew LeBron had a new limited edition shoe out that was all the rage.

"Siri, how much are the new LeBron's?" I asked my trusty know-it-all companion from my La-Z-Boy chair that afternoon.

Siri always had an answer for me, without any snark: "Here's what I found on the web for How Much Are the New LeBron's: $275 dollars US."

Christ! I took a deep breath and considered my options. *Well, a dad's gotta do what a dad's gotta do, I suppose. This divorce is costing me a fortune anyway, and I'll probably have to file for bankruptcy before it's over. I'll need to get Rae something special, too. She likes everything shiny but diamonds seem excessive. She likes art, but that seems too "normal." She loves Iggy... That's it! I'll get her a new puppy!*

But, no dogs allowed at the apartment. These were the rules, per CoCo. I could not risk getting tossed out. Maybe a fish. Nah, too boring. A hamster. They seem easy enough to take care of, but their nasty teeth gross me out. A guy at work has guinea pigs at his house. I could probably ask him for some pointers. They seem like a more substantial pet—something furry Rae could hold in her lap and snuggle when she's here with me.

I dialed up my buddy.

"Smith, what gives?" his voice answered on the other end.

"Hey brother, I need to ask about your guinea pigs."

He laughed, "You in the market for a pet, Luke? Need something alive to keep your feet warm at night, man? I heard about the divorce. Rough, dude," he offered.

"Things are fine with the divorce," I lied. "My daughter needs a pet to have at my place and I remembered your kids have guinea pigs. Can you tell me about them? Are they much work to care for? What do they eat? How much do they cost?"

His full-belly laugh put me on edge. "You want to get a guinea pig to keep at your place? Well, it's your lucky day, man. We just had another litter last night. They are social critters and need to live in pairs. Come and pick out whichever two you want."

Free I can afford!

My work buddy continued on, "I've got an extra cage, since there's way too many for a cage now at my place, and all the supplies they need. You can take all that stuff outta here, too. They eat pellets and lettuce— lots and lots of lettuce."

I can afford lettuce!

"Can I stop by later tonight? Are you sure I need to take two?" I questioned.

"Sure, man, stop by anytime. And yes, you need to take two," he replied.

We ended our call, and I immediately sent a text to Teo's phone:

"Teo, bud, I scored you the new LeBron's! You can get them this weekend when you're over here at the apartment with me."

Sending...Delivered and Read.

Next a text message to Rae: "Hi, baby girl. Daddy got you a new pet, well pets, for when you are here at my place. I know you really love animals and miss Iggy on the weekends."

I attached the cutest picture of a guinea pig I could find from the web.

Ding. Rae texted right back: "OMG! Really? I want to come and see them now! Can I come over and see them now?"

Her excitement made me smile.

Why didn't I think of this sooner?

"Today is Mommy's day with you, honey. I'll pick you up Friday after school. We are going to see a lady called an evaluator. As long as you behave at the office meeting, we'll come back to the apartment, and you can hang with the guinea pigs".

"Awesome! thanks daddy!"

"Anything for you, baby girl. I love you, honey."

Teo took his sweet-ass time replying but finally said: "What gives, Dad? You trying to buy our love now? Rae's running around here yelling about guinea pigs."

"Hi, bud. This has been such a hard time for you guys. Can't a dad just do something nice for his kids?"

Nothing. I tried a few more times.

"Teo. You there, kid?"

"Teo, did you want a different pair instead?"

"Teo, you want to meet up on PlayStation later?"

Ghosted by my own kid.

He'll come around, I hoped quietly to myself.

On Friday afternoon, I picked the kids up from their schools for our 3:30 p.m. meeting at the evaluator's office—the "parent-child interaction," she had called it. Rae was already disappointed. She had thought maybe I would bring the guinea pigs along in the car, which I had not. Teo was easy to read. Still ticked off at me.

When we walked into her office, the evaluator was ready for us. "Hi there!" she welcomed, extra cheerfully.

After exchanging a few words with Teo and Rae, she invited all of us into the back office. It was obvious they had been here already. Rae was happy to see this lady and gave her a hug. Teo even talked openly with her, in a polite and mature way. *I wished he talked to me that way.* Nevertheless, pride swelled for the young man I knew Teo was becoming.

This time, in the space where we had met before, there was a large white piece of paper sitting on the little table and colored pencils, markers, crayons, watercolor paints, and stickers sitting out. "Teo, grab that bigger chair again." He gave her a crooked smile, and plunked his rear-end into the comfortable chair while I pulled a child-sized wooden chair up next to Rae. "Here's what I'd love for you to do first. I want you to create a family picture together—a memory you'll never forget or vacation, a holiday or anything you wish—where everyone in the picture is doing something."

All three of us nodded as the evaluator backed out of our space. Music started playing in the background, which helped to lighten the mood. On cue, my theme song started to play and I decided to sing along, "This is my fight song, I'll be alright song..."

Rae shook her head shamefully, and Teo gave me a look like I had gone mad.

Fine, you stuck-in-the-muds, I'll sing a little louder. They always laughed about it when I "embarrassed" them publicly in that lovable kind of way that only a dad can.

After fifteen minutes or so, the evaluator asked how we were doing and if it would be okay for her to come over and see what we had created.

Both kids agreed she should see their work. When they sat up, I laid eyes on their drawings. I was confused at first with all the black and red coloring, thick lines, and... uh oh... angry people, police cars, and a picture of the devil with "666" above his head.

"Wow, there is a lot going on here," our evaluator commented. "You two are great artists," she said to Teo and Rae. She looked over to my area of the paper where I had drawn a sketch of Iggy and me, driving in my Mustang. "I see Dad's got some mad art skills, too. Who do you suppose those two are in the car?"

Rae piped up, "That's my dog Iggy that I told you about last time—the one my dad stole when he ran away from home and left mommy."

"Oh, honey, we've been over this. Daddy has apologized over and over about Iggy and I didn't run away from home—not from you and your brother," I assured my daughter.

Rae shot eyeball lasers in my direction.

She's got her mother's temper, that's for sure.

Teo sat silently with a satisfied smirk on his face.

I should have brought those darn guinea pigs and the receipt for proof of Teo's shoes, too. Buttered 'em up more before we came in here.

"Kids, would it be okay for Dad to sit out on the comfy couch for a while, so the three of us could talk a little bit and maybe play a game of UNO™?" The evaluator broke the awkwardness of the last couple minutes with her gentle voice.

"Great," I said, rising from my little wooden chair, eager to get the heck out of there. Without waiting for the kids to answer the question, I collected my things and headed for the door, shutting it behind me as I walked toward the safety of the comfy couch.

Could this get any worse?

There was a magazine rack in the waiting area and a *PDX Parent* subscription with the words Choose Your Own Adventure written across the front cover. It showed a snow-capped mountain in the background. I grabbed a copy and sat down, considering the adventure I had been on since leaving home and filing for divorce. From the couch, I tried to listen in, but there was music playing in both rooms and a loud white noise machine whooshing beside me. I could not make out anything concrete, except for my daughter crying again and the baritone of Teo's voice once in a while.

I hope the kids at least mention the cool new stuff they know I have for them.

Panic struck. I didn't actually have Teo's shoes for him at the apartment as promised, because the stupid shipping was delayed. Apparently, plenty of people could afford $275 for a new pair of shoes and LeBron couldn't keep up to satisfy the orders.

When the evaluator and kids emerged from the back office, thirty minutes or so later, my children looked at peace, and Teo was even smiling. Rae gave the evaluator another big hug before she sent both of them to a treasure box and said, "I'll see you Sunday at the apartment. Have fun with those guinea pigs you haven't met yet, Rae. Maybe they'll have names by Sunday." I thought I saw her look sideways at me, disapprovingly.

Geez, am I getting paranoid now?

She continued, "And Teo, those LeBron's? My son would be so jealous!"

Uh oh.

"I'll be excited to meet Iggy at home with Mom next week, too, guys!" she concluded.

I cringed when she mentioned their mother, and I saw the kids avoid the topic, too. We quickly left her office and headed to the car. Rae yapped a million miles a minute, excited to meet her new pets, while all I could think about were Teo's shoes that I did not yet have.

Back at the apartment, we ordered our usual Friday night pizza. Teo had practice, which I drove him to and from, and Rae brought the guinea pigs along in my duffle bag.

All Teo said when I explained about the shoes was, "Figures," and then a few minutes later followed up with, "You really are a total disappointment, Dad."

They pick up on everything their mother says!

The evaluator was due at the studio on Sunday morning at 10:00 a.m., so we spent Saturday cleaning up, which took all of ten minutes in my tiny little place, and much of the day setting up the guinea pig habitat.

Rae would not let me call it a cage. Teo went to the outside courts again and played hours of video games from my La-Z-Boy.

As I dozed off Saturday night, my last thought was of the impending home visit, and relief that this process was almost over. Finally, the last evaluation meeting had arrived.

Come hell or high water, at least we'll be done.

The evaluator knocked on the door at 10:00 a.m., and Rae let her in with one hand while she held one of her guinea pigs in the other.

"Good morning, Rae. Who is this little fella?" the evaluator queried while petting his fluffy head.

Rae was in full theater mode, a natural actress, and said, "Welcome to our humble home! What you see is what you get. Seriously, there's no more." She grabbed the evaluator's hand and led our court-appointed professional toward her makeshift fort/bed/guinea pig habitat. The "keep out" sign was still up, but she invited her in and the evaluator obliged.

Teo was only half-awake, still reclined in the La-Z-Boy. I told him to get up and brush his teeth, and he sauntered off at the speed of a sloth, to the bathroom, just ten steps away.

Rae popped her head out and asked me for some privacy. The evaluator peeked her head out next, right beside Rae's, and asked if I minded stepping into the hallway for five or so quick minutes so Rae and her could talk. Teo too, when he got back from the bathroom.

Par for course, kicked out of my own place.

"Sure, you got it," I answered with my most charming smile and cooperative tone.

After more like ten or fifteen not-so-quick minutes, the evaluator opened my apartment door. She said goodbye to Rae and the guinea pigs and told Teo, "I hope those LeBron's get here soon, before the start of your next season." She closed the door behind her and made eye contact with me. "Alright, Luke. You have a cozy home here. Are you scheduled with the psychologist for testing?"

"Yes, my appointment is on Tuesday."

"As soon as we have the testing data back, I will be calling your personal references, as well as the kids' teachers and their counselor. With that, I can wrap up the evaluation report for Teo and Rae and help get your family moving forward. I'll be in touch." She collected some paperwork from me, shook my hand, and left.

Pleased to have the evaluation meetings complete, I walked back into the apartment, and both kids told me they wanted to go "home." Rae wanted to take her new pets, but I told her those stayed with me. Since I really needed some downtime to process all this drama, I agreed to drop them off early. I told Teo to check in with his mother to be sure she was at home, and he let me know that he already had. I drove them back to the suburb, six hours ahead of schedule, and dropped them off curbside at Ms. Nothing's Ever Good Enough's new apartment. Bulldog had forced a sale of the house to stop the financial hemorrhaging. The only victory I had scored so far.

The meeting with the psychologist was brutal. Hours of pencil and paper tests after spending too much time telling my life story to another professional. The test questions were weird. He told me there were no right and wrong answers, and I did my best.

I left the psychologist's office with a massive headache, a cramp in my hand, and barely in time for dinner. So, I headed to Lloyd's bar. It was a familiar place, and Lloyd was the best listener I knew. A few cold ones and plate of food while we talked sounded great.

Bellied up on my corner stool, I felt much better. Lloyd was at the ready, with a beer and the best burger in town. He assured me that the end to all this misery was close, and no matter what the testing or evaluator said about me, what mattered most was an end to this divorce and the pain it caused. "You gotta move on. Move forward. Reclaim your life."

I could not agree more. This has been going on way too long.

There was a trial date on the court docket two months after my testing appointment. Bulldog mentioned the evaluator had sent word that she would have her report out well in advance of the trial date. "Well in advance" turned out to be a subjective term.

Less than three weeks before court, Bulldog called me during the workday and said he had received the evaluation report and I should stop by the office so we could go over it.

I quickly finished up what I was doing and then headed right down.

Bulldog held the report in his hand and matter-of-factly stated, "It could be worse."

He said some of the evaluator's conclusions, apparently supported by the testing data, had described me as "insensitive, manipulative, self-promoting, ego-centric, and someone with limited insight into the children's need for a home base with their primary parent."

This overly wordy and expensive report had better not cause too much of a problem for me. Some of the things Bulldog read in it were unbelievable and made me seem like a completely uncaring and incapable father to the two children I love more than life. I shook my head as he read through all the services and therapies and educational courses recommended to improve communication and parenting insights.

Who has time or money for all that?

Then I heard the parenting time recommendation: "The children should enjoy two long weekends a month with their father from after school Thursday (or 3:00 p.m.) until Monday morning at the start of the school day (or 9:00 a.m.). Once father has established a residence with bedrooms for the children and he participates in services as described below, the children's parenting time in father's care should be expanded to include a Thursday overnight during the alternate weeks and 50% of summer vacation."

Bulldog closed the report and sighed. "The evaluator had a lot of concerns that are supported by examples of your behavior and the psychological testing profile. These will not be favorable to our position at trial. It would be best to try and settle along the lines of the evaluator's recommendation."

I sat quietly, paralyzed by the flood of emotions. Anger. Confusion. Disbelief. Regret. Anger. Anger. Anger.

Though at my boiling point, I managed to articulate a question: "That means I don't get Teo and Rae 50% of the time right now, or ever, throughout the school year? Only during summer break, sometime in the future, and only if I get a bigger place to live and do therapy? That's not okay! I want my day in court, Bulldog! This is total bullshit!"

I saw Lola walking toward me with a bottle of whisky and two glasses.

"You got it, kid," Bulldog said. Lola set the glasses on the desk and poured each of us a shot. "You'll need to replenish your trust account with fifteen thousand dollars today, so I can get started preparing for trial— gather documents, prepare a memo, and send out subpoenas to potential witnesses," Bulldog continued. "It's going to be an uphill battle, but I've seen the court order something different than this evaluator's recommendations before, and there is nothing I love more than cross-examination with a worthy opponent."

This cannot be happening. How can this be happening? I took a long deep breath to calm myself down and handed Bulldog my one last credit card that was not maxed out before I stomped out of his office. I seethed all the way home and stomped again up to the 666, where I promptly turned on the PlayStation and started snooping through Teo's chats.

Wow, so much chatting with Ethan.

One text communication stood out amongst the sea of others.

RimRocker12: "the evaluator came over to the apartment today"

SeekNDestroy: "is she cool"

RimRocker12: "yah shes alright I showed her my dads stash of beer"

SeekNDestroy: "is he on the sauce all the time or what bro"

RimRocker12: "nah but I figured it might make him look worse than he is so we don't have to come over here half the time like he wants us to

SeekNDestroy: half the time like every other week or something like that dork seventh grader at school does hes such a moron"

RimRocker12: "yah he wanted me and Rae to tell the evaluator that we wanted fifty percent he got Rae new pets and said he got those LeBron's for me which I have never even seen hes probably lying and too cheap to actually buy me something that awesome"

SeekNDestroy: "fifty percent of what"

RimRocker 12: "time"

SeekNDestroy: "like half your time home and half there"

RimRocker 12: "yep"

SeekNDestroy: "why"

RimRocker 12: "cuz hes an ass"

SeekNDestroy: "well yah but why would he not want you to live at home with your mom where you have always lived does he want to take Rae away from your mom"

SeekNDestroy: "poor Rae would cry her eyes out away from your mom"

RimRocker 12: "yep she already does"

Enough! I shut it down. *Stupid kids don't know what's best anyway.*

There was nothing to do now but wait for a judge to hear our case and make a decision about what the future held for my kids.

Months followed by months of high conflict had consumed my life with a restraining order, a no-contact order, changes, loss, upset, selling our home, attorneys, bills-bills-bills, and what I was sure would be bankruptcy after the added cost of this trial.

The day of trial I entered the courthouse in my best clothes and hoped Bulldog was already there. No sign of him, so I headed up to our assigned courtroom and stopped short when I saw the impressive group of people assembled: the evaluator (who smiled and waved to me as if we were on speaking terms) and everyone who testified at the restraining order hearing, including the babysitter, the kids' counselor, a few of their teachers, Ms. Nothing's Ever Good Enough's bestie, Juls, and.....

Lord Almighty!

There was CoCo, from my apartment rental office, sitting right beside and chatting ever-so-casually with my ex and her all-powerful Attorney of the Year, who was dressed to the nines. In fact, it looked like they had all been to the spa together this morning. Because of the no-contact order, I had not actually seen my ex in a long time.

Damn, she looks good.

I hoped I was not violating the no-contact order by walking past her to get into the courtroom. There was no way to keep a 200-foot buffer between us, so I took my chances, seeking shelter away from the group of hungry vultures. No such luck. I entered the courtroom and immediately saw my mother-in-law who sneered and said to no one in particular, "Oh great! Father of the Year decided to show up."

I checked my watch. *The usual fifteen minutes early.*

Bulldog was seated at a table in front of the judge's bench. There were papers scattered everywhere, and he was wearing the same cheap suit I'd met him in. I hadn't thought to bring anyone along and hoped Bulldog had subpoenaed someone to testify on my behalf.

"Hello, son," Bulldog offered as he pulled out the chair next to him.

Within a few minutes, Ms. Nothing's Ever Good Enough and her attorney were seated at the table, too, and a clerk in front of the judge's bench authoritatively instructed: "All rise." Bulldog and I stood up at the same time.

The judge entered his courtroom and recited our family name, and the case number, and made record of who was in attendance.

I watched person after person parade in front of me, up to the witness stand, and talk about what a Ms. wonderful mother Ms. Nothing's Ever Good Enough is and always has been, the less active parenting role I have played, and how I've been an insensitive jerk when it comes to Teo and Rae's feelings and their emotional well-being in this divorce.

Even though Bulldog scored lots of points on cross-examination, things did not seem to be going in my favor. He spent the most time grilling our evaluator, and his manner with her put even me on edge. Once, the judge admonished Bulldog's "unnecessary tone" when he was yelling and turning purple. But the evaluator seemed unrattled. She beamed with positive accolades when speaking about the children, and then became more serious and critical when describing both the strengths and concerns about me and my ex.

I was called to the stand to testify, where Attorney of the Year was aggressive and downright mean and didn't speak a lick of the truth. We took a break for lunch and then were right back at it afterwards. Ms. Nothing's Ever Good Enough testified last. She should have been an actress with her Oscar-worthy performance. By 4:30 p.m. I hardly knew my own name. This had been the most exhausting and expensive day of my life. It was surreal to be here, doing battle with the woman I'd slept next to half my life.

The mother of my children.

I had no idea what the judge was going to do—what choices he was going to make based on the information that was presented in the exhibits and testimony. Teo's and Rae's lives had been strategically laid out in this court of law by the legal spin-doctor Vanessa had hired, who seemed superior to Bulldog in every way. Everything now rested within the purview of a man who had never met my kids—the family law judge charged with deciding Teo and Rae's future.

After Ms. Nothing's Ever Good Enough left the stand, the judge asked if there were any additional witnesses. There were none. He heard closing statements from each of our lawyers, and I was grateful for the job Bulldog did describing all of my best traits as a loving father. When closing arguments ended, the judge leaned back in his chair, crossed his arms over his round belly, took a deep breath, and looked somewhat distressed.

Silently, he removed his glasses, rubbed his eyes, put the glasses back on, and then sat forward and made eye contact—first with me and then with Vanessa, who was sitting to my right. Tension in the air was palpable as he began to speak, "I have been sitting on this bench the last twenty-three years, listening to disputes and gripes between divorcing parents about the very children each of them says they are here in this courtroom to protect. Reality is folks, being here and fighting with each other, tearing each other down in a court of law, does not offer any amount of protection to your children.

"I have not heard one shred of evidence today that convinces me either of you is a physical threat to your children's safety. Both of you have made some terrible choices along the way. Your choice (he looked at me) back when I saw your family at the time of the restraining order—well, choices don't get much worse than that, Mr. Smith. Your behavior then, and at times since, according to the people who testified today, has often been foolish, ill-advised, and most notably hurtful to Teo and Rae.

"While I am relatively certain the two of you will meet your children's basic daily needs, evidence presented today gives rise for particular concern, Mr. Smith, about your parenting capacity to nurture their emotional health. Given the mutual decisions that you and your wife made during the marriage, mom at home and you at work, the children have always spent more time in their mother's care. After their parents' divorce, children need consistency and continuity of what has been their normal. Stripping children away from the parent who they have historically relied on is harmful.

They are not accustomed to spending fifty percent of their time away from mother and with you, sir."

He took a deep breath and let out a huge sigh before continuing with his decision.

"Mr. Smith, it would be best if you started attending the children's counseling sessions, at their counselor's recommendation, of course. Perhaps a child-centered professional can help you gain more sophisticated insight about what Teo and Rae need moving between two homes. I can assure you it is far more than pets and the promise of expensive shoes."

Another pause and then, "The evaluator provided a roadmap for educational and reparative services that mother and father are hereby ordered to participate in, including individual therapy for both of you, a high-conflict parenting course, co-parent training, and use of the online communication platform Our Family Wizard."

After that, he gave each of us a hardened look and asked, "I believe that both of you, Mom and Dad, would jump in front of a bus for your children. Am I right?"

Vanessa and me both nodded in a rare moment of agreement.

"You love Teo and Rae so much that it would not even be a second thought to jump right out in front of a moving bus. Hear me now when I tell you that *you are the bus*. Mr. and Ms. Smith, you are the biggest threat to your children. The conflict between you harms them more than anything else. The acts of bitterness and name-calling, finger-pointing, blaming, blame-shifting, and gaslighting will ruin your children. I cannot stop you from doing those things. Only you have the authority to choose differently. Only you can protect Teo and Rae, through the myriad of daily choices you make about your own thinking, behavior, and conduct and especially your attitudes toward one another. If you want your children to be okay, to do better than okay, you have to take care of their parents. You have to take better care of each other, no longer as a spouse, but as the single most valuable asset in your children's lives. The two of you are the foundation that anchors the potential for everything else Teo and Rae will aim to achieve."

He looked satisfied. "My ruling is that mother will have sole legal and primary physical custody of the children; Teo and Rae will enjoy parenting time with their father according to the schedule recommended by the evaluator." The judge acknowledged our evaluator, seated in the back of the courtroom and thanked her for a thorough job, well done.

And that was it. The scolding was finished. The judge started telling Bulldog, as the moving party (the petitioner), to prepare the order, but then changed his mind and asked Attorney of the Year to take care of it. Apparently, he had more confidence in her ability to follow through and get things done with precision. Bulldog seemed fine with this.

As the courtroom emptied out, there was happy chatter and hugs all around for my ex from her tribe, and my mother-in-law actually stuck her tongue out when I walked past.

My ex... The judge's verbal reprimand during his ruling about this term lingered as I made my way, all alone, to the parking garage.

The judge had expressed great concern about the undercurrent of my anger toward the children's mother, what the children saw as "hatred" and he had told me, with no uncertain terms, that referring to her as "Ms. Nothing's Ever Good Enough" or "my ex" was hurtful and harmful to the kids—"our" kids. They were not "my" kids, or Vanessa's kids. They were human beings, not possessions. It was not "her time" or "my time"; the judge said that all time belonged to Teo and Rae. They were young people, with developing hearts and minds, and it was our job to protect them, according to him, from ourselves.

The outcome was not at all what I had envisioned for my big day in court. This did not feel like justice, but was definitely a legal and binding court order, our dissolution judgment, and the final say about how we would move forward with our children.

On my way out of the courthouse, I cursed all of it. Judges. Attorneys. Evaluators. Marriage. Divorce. Best friends whose wives testify against you. Smokin' hot lease agents. Bad legal advice. Guinea pig habitats built under blanket tents. And expensive basketball shoes that were never delivered.

I cursed all of it and left for home, in my Mustang, which was about all I had left, or so it seemed, on this awful and miserable day.

Below are two choices Luke can make at this point.

 Follow the judge's orders.
Turn to page 324 to find out what happens when Luke makes this choice.

 FIght for my children.
Turn to page 329 to find out what happens when Luke makes this choice.

⊚⊚ Two Years after Luke
Followed the Judge's Orders

We had just finished Rae's sixth grade parent teacher conference when Vanessa and I walked out into the cool evening air, leaves crisp and crunching beneath our feet. Of course, her teacher loved her, but not as much as we did.

She's quite the kid, that one, I thought as I remembered the birthday wish list she had handed me the previous weekend.

"Did she give you her birthday wish list?" I asked Vanessa as we walked toward our cars parked next to each other in the back of the school lot.

It had been about twenty-four months—two whole life cycles through the calendar year since our judgment—and things were beginning to feel "normal" again. We had done our best to follow the court-ordered plan. I'd talked to a financial consultant who came highly-recommended and avoided what had seemed like certain bankruptcy. Vanessa and I each started our new lives, as the judge had instructed, helping Teo and Rae transition smoothly between their two homes without witnessing any more conflict, arguments, or bad attitudes between their mom and me.

Teo was driving, and Rae was off to middle school. Time was moving fast, and we knew their childhoods were fleeting, so we were working hard to establish new traditions and make positive memories. Since the no-contact order was dropped when the dissolution judgment was signed, Vanessa and I were able to communicate again and with the help of some pretty awesome people, we had learned all new ways of doing that. In fact, we were talking better than we had during the last few years of our marriage. We sat together at Teo's basketball games and Rae's choir concerts and dance recitals.

Thanks to what the judge had said, and what the evaluator had talked about in her report, I'd worked hard to resolve my anger toward Vanessa and gained insight into the way that my thinking, behavior, and conduct negatively impacted Teo and Rae. The less angry I became, the happier *our* kids were. I could see it in everything they did.

They were both thriving at school, in their relationships, and with their activities. They loved their mom, and they loved me. As instructed by multiple professionals, we gave our children permission to love and be loved by everyone, including both of their opinionated grandmothers. Iggy even traveled with the kids now, between their two homes. I had moved from the city apartment into a nice house, not far from Vanessa's new place and near the kids' schools and their friends. It was not the life I signed up for when I asked Vanessa to marry me, but it was turning out alright.

"Yep!" Vanessa chuckled out loud.

"LEGOs are easy enough," I said. "I'll get her the big set she asked for—you think she's ready to build the entire Death Star?"

"Oh yeah, she can handle it. I'll get the few items of clothes and fancy high heels she wants." Vanessa glanced over and saw my eyebrows pull together in concern. "Don't worry, overprotective Daddy, they're not that high."

As we stopped short of our cars, I reached out and placed my hand gently on Vanessa's shoulder before asking the question that had inspired this conversation. "She wants a family birthday party, with both of us, her big brother, and her grandmothers—my mother and yours. Lord help us, do you think our mothers are ready?" Fearing the day already, I tilted my head back and looked up at the starry sky.

Then I grinned, remembering Rae's words, the #1wish that she had written in bubble letters, and colored bright pink with glitter sprinkled over the top for full effect. I was sure Vanessa gulped back a wave of anxiety, too.

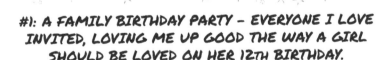

#1: A FAMILY BIRTHDAY PARTY - EVERYONE I LOVE INVITED, LOVING ME UP GOOD THE WAY A GIRL SHOULD BE LOVED ON HER 12TH BIRTHDAY.

I returned my gaze from the heavens toward Vanessa and smiled. "That kid—she's really something. Smarter than any of us. Our girl is gonna rule the world one day." I saw the same pride beaming from her mother's eyes.

That was a real moment for us—unexpected and powerful.

"Yes," Vanessa agreed. "And I'm sure that she will handle her grandmothers' behavior with all of that cleverness and grace."

"Yah, yah, I'm sure it will be fine—better than fine. Well, good night." I smiled and jumped into my Mustang and left.

As I drove home, I thought about how far we had all come. I absolutely hated this woman just two years ago; but today, I knew the truth: I still loved Vanessa. I loved her as the mother of our children, a co-parent, sharing the very most important work of our lifetimes—raising Teo and Rae up to be good and happy human beings.

For them, I was certain Vanessa and I would do anything, including manage our difficult mothers, so Rae could enjoy the best family birthday party ever.

Teo had really come around too and would appreciate this family-focused time. He had told me recently that he was "proud" of us—his mom and me—for finally sitting together at basketball games and being kind to each other. We had all learned through our counseling that being nice was a subjective term, but kindness and respect—these were the standards which our family agreed to value and uphold. Teo was tearing up the floor on his high school basketball team, had amazing friends, and he was getting decent grades. Our son was really growing into a wonderful young man. It took time, hard work, and skilled professionals who earned every cent we paid them to help us heal our family.

An image of the evaluator with her happy smile and wave at the courthouse popped into my mind's eye, and I even felt some gratitude for her and her compassionate and spot-on recommendations, even though I didn't understand them at the time. And the way she treated all of us with warmth and compassion through the most difficult time in our lives.

She is the one who gave us the road map to arrive here—right now—when our baby girl is about to turn twelve and wants all of us there at her party.

I turned into my driveway, pulled into the garage, hopped out, and went into my house. There were the guinea pigs in their hallway habitat, right outside the kitchen, where Rae said I would always remember to feed them when she was not there. "Hey, little dudes." I reached in and petted each of their heads. "Hungry?" I poured some pellets and then grabbed two leaves of lettuce from the fridge and a bottle of soda for me.

Home sweet home. This it truly was, with a separate bedroom for everyone.

I settled in for the night, feet propped up on the stool of my La-Z-Boy, ready to enjoy the big game. Mike would be over soon, and I was looking forward to the evening.

Thank God for enduring friendships and football— and my kids!

Man, I love those two knuckleheads.

Two Years after Luke Disregarded the Judge's Orders

"Can you believe that teacher?" I asked Vanessa as we walked toward our cars parked in the dark school lot. We had just finished Rae's sixth-grade parent teacher conferences and walked out into the cool evening air, fallen leaves crisp beneath our feet. It was the first time we had attended conferences together in years, and it was awful. Middle school did not permit separate times, like elementary school always did.

It was about twenty-four months—two whole life cycles through the calendar year—since our judgment. Things had continued to be strained between Vanessa and me. Even worse, I think, since she had gotten custody of the kids and wielded it over me like a weapon. We had decided we did not have the time or money to participate in all those court-ordered services the judge said we needed, and our kids were having problems.

Teo had gotten into trouble after a fight at school. When he was arrested, the cops found weed in his pocket and now he has a juvenile counselor and community service hours. He was unable to get his driver's license as a result of his delinquency. And Rae was off to middle school, apparently failing all of her classes, according to the teachers we had just met. She hardly ate at all and, while thin was in, her PE teacher just told us she was worried that maybe Rae had taken it too far and had an actual eating disorder.

I was starting to worry about both of them. Time was moving fast. I knew their childhoods were fleeting, and their futures were not looking so bright at the moment.

Teo had stopped playing sports in favor of video games and smoking weed. He had a whole new crowd of friends in high school and could not pass a class to save his life. Maybe if he actually attended class... At this rate, he was headed to be a dropout. Rae had become the class clown and was totally boy crazy. I'd caught her sneaking a boy into my place one weekend not so long ago.

Poor sap got what was coming to him.

I was mad as hell all the time—at work, at the kids, at Vanessa, at her mother, at my mother. The kids moved between houses when we told them to, and they despised it. Rae kept running away, and Teo preferred his friends' couches to my or his mom's place. My heartless ex re-homed Iggy and broke Rae's heart. The guinea pigs "disappeared" when I decided to release them—in the forest. Those little buggers were a lot of work, and Rae was not around enough to take care of them.

"Yah, a real peach," Vanessa responded, "saying Rae has problems. The only problem Rae has is having to spend weekends with *you.* She's miserable at your place, Luke. The kids were just fine until you up and left and turned their worlds upside-down. You destroyed all of our lives. You're such a selfish asshole."

"Whatever, woman," I provoked. "It's all my fault, huh? Ms. Nothing's Ever Good Enough—right, Ms. High and Mighty?"

I wasn't surprised when Vanessa shoved me with all of her might. I stumbled backwards a bit, but I outweighed her by a good fifty or more pounds and was completely fine. Always on-guard around her, I already had my phone turned on with the audio and video recording, and I dialed 9-1-1. I figured that eventually I'd have enough evidence stored up to file a modification with the court, and win custody of the kids from her.

I knew just what to say so that the police cars came screaming into the school lot as other parents leaving their child's conferences looked on. We had gotten to be on a first name basis with most of the local police force over the past three years, as they responded to our "domestic disputes" with regularity and had become familiar with Teo and Rae, too. I showed them the video of Vanessa shoving me a few minutes before. The officers gave us another stern talking to and instructed us to part ways immediately. The kids were at Vanessa's house that night—at least they were supposed to be. They pretty much came and went as they pleased, not minding any of the rules either of us tried to set. I know if they were with me a lot more of the time, and away from their mother, I could get them back on track.

I drove home as instructed, frustrated again that the law always favored women. If I had shoved Vanessa the same way she'd just shoved me, we all know where I'd be right now.

Suddenly, the words of the evaluator's report rang in my ears:

We know that children exposed to ongoing conflict and negative information about their parents, *always* have long-term emotional problems. Children who are exposed to ongoing parental conflict and unstable home lives *will* have adjustment problems in their preadolescent and teen years that most commonly manifest in extreme defiance and anger, delinquent behavior, substance abuse, teen pregnancy, eating disorders, suicide attempts, failing grades, and high dropout rates at school. It is one of the only certainties in the professional literature and surely not the legacy these parents wish for Teo and Rae.

Bunch of bologna. We're all doing fine—just fine!

"Bad decisions, made with good intentions, are still bad decisions."

~James C. Collins~

BE AWESOME

Become Super-Dad and inspire the kids to beg for more time with me.

BULLDOG'S NOTES READ, "Be more awesome than you have ever been before. Show up at everything to do with the kids, including doctor, dental, and counseling appointments. Request a full and complete copy of Teo and Rae's written medical and counseling records, start going to school events and all extracurricular activities, sign up for teacher conferences and be sure you are listed as "primary" on all school and activity forms, invite the kids' friends over to your new place, and start socializing with their friends' parents so they can serve as character witnesses if need be. Plan the most amazing birthday parties for them this year, and go all out celebrating the upcoming holiday. Outdo their mother in everything by showering the kids with love, affection, and gifts. Kids love 'stuff.' Start volunteering in Rae's classroom, go on field trips, and help out more often with Teo's basketball team and Rae's dance company, too."

Not sure how I'll look in a tutu, but if Bulldog says I need to do it to win this custody battle and crush my ex, I will. I chuckled at the thought and kept reading.

"This choice could be somewhat controversial," Bulldog's notes continued. "Suddenly inserting yourself into these areas of the children's lives needs to be done with measured tact. If done thoughtfully, and with diligence not to upset the kids' normal routines, there is little to no way that a judge can deny you equal parenting rights and time because you will have successfully demonstrated a high capacity for primary parenting responsibilities and evaluators are likely to assess the same. Mothers tend to 'wig out' during a divorce when their children's father starts showing a more concerted interest in areas of a child's life that the mother has always controlled.☺"

I shook my head at the happy face he drew—it was an all-knowing, slightly-wicked happy face, right there at the end of the last sentence. *Yeah, she does love the control. She really does have dark lord energy. Oh shoot, I still haven't changed her profile picture.*

A picture of Darth Vader had popped up when Ms. Nothing's Ever Good Enough called me during my first meeting with Bulldog, along with Vader's classic theme music, which was now Vanessa's assigned ringtone, "da da da dota da dota da." Bulldog had chuckled and complimented my creativity, but then advised that I change the picture and the ringtone since judges and evaluators do not look kindly upon this type of humor: "It would be seen as detrimental to the children, should they see or hear the reference to their mother as one of the greatest villains and symbols of evil known in pop culture."

I don't know. I think the kids will think it's hilarious. I'll show them next weekend. If they don't like it, we'll figure out something different together.

I turned my attention back to Bulldog's notes. "Under no circumstances are you to date the single, or married, mothers of Teo and Rae's friends—even the hot ones. This means no fraternizing with friends' mothers after dark, no sharing of alcoholic beverages or other mood-altering substances, and no kissing, hugging or... any sexual contact."

This seems like a no-brainer, I thought as I finished my cup of coffee. *Fear not, kids. Super-Dad and his super-suit to the rescue!* I chuckled as I hustled to get ready for work and planned my first few appearances as the new and improved version of me.

Several uneventful months had passed since Bulldog and I first met. He hadn't given me a phone number to reach him or offered up an email address, but he had called me twice to check in and sent a few letters to my apartment address via snail-mail. One of these letters included Vanessa's official response to my petition for full custody, which I now know means something entirely different than having the kids with me full-time and them only getting to see their mother whenever I say they can.

I should have Googled "full custody" when this all started, so I didn't sound like such an ass. Bulldog specifically told me not to be an ass. I'll do better now that I know.

All the years of our marriage, and certainly since the separation, Ms. Nothing's Ever Good Enough had never shared when the kids were scheduled to see the doctor or dentist, and I had no information about who their teachers were this year or even so much as their counselor's first name. So, I had to start doing some good detective work. I'd called my mother to see if she knew any of these key people in my kids' lives and also reached out to my best man and best friend, Mike, to see if he could get any of this information out of his wife, Juls, who was still Vanessa's BFF.

Between my mother and third-hand information from Mike, I had quickly acquired the names of some of the professionals who knew Teo and Rae. I had also figured out how to request their medical records, which were super-handy because they also contained names and phone numbers for their counselor and dentist and Teo's orthodontist.

I'd also started the process of obtaining the full written record from the kids' counselor, but it wasn't easy. She seemed suspicious when I called and had asked that I come in and meet with her. So, we set up a day and time, but I had to cancel because something important came up at work and I could not get away. Plus, Ms. Nothing's Ever Good Enough's attorney kept objecting, saying it was a violation of the kids "sacred space" and that releasing the records "jeopardized the therapeutic relationship." This only made me more curious to see what was actually in those written records, so we kept pushing back and became locked in an unproductive legal dance of fancy-schmancy words—really expensive words—between attorneys.

In the meantime, Ms. Nothing's Ever Good Enough's attorney had motioned for a custody evaluation and suggested several professionals, who Bulldog had promptly advised against. We ended up having a hearing with the judge, who then appointed the evaluator. Bulldog assured me a child custody evaluator would have access to the kids' counseling records and would also speak with the counselor directly. So, if the counselor was going to continue giving me a hard time, I should let it go for the moment. We had our proof that I had tried and that the counselor was uncooperative.

After the court hearing, I understood that an evaluator was a trained professional who would meet with both parents and the kids. She would talk to personal character witnesses for me and my ex, and also to professionals who were involved with our family. The process was expensive, although it sounded cost-productive in the grand scheme of things. The evaluator's calendar was full, and we could not get started for two months, so I decided to keep establishing myself as a more actively involved father in those areas of Teo and Rae's life, that Vanessa always controlled.

After I figured out who their pediatrician was, I was able to set up an online portal account, which gave me access to the kids' medical history, immunization record, medications, upcoming appointments, and after-visit summaries. It was even easy to email their doctor directly, so I started a conversation and introduced myself, providing her a full synopsis of this ugly divorce. When I logged in and saw that Teo and Rae both had well-child exams scheduled, I marked my calendar to attend.

Ms. Nothing's Ever Good Enough had always monopolized the kids' medical and dental appointments. She purposefully scheduled them while I was at work, and never had the common courtesy to invite me to attend. Unless the kids were bloody, broken, or bruised, I knew nothing about the healthcare Teo or Rae received.

On the day of the appointment, I arrived to the medical building early and was sitting in the waiting room when Vanessa and the kids walked in. Rae spotted me first and looked surprised, since she'd never seen me at the doctor's office before. She waved a little hesitantly with a crooked, one-cheek smile, then hid behind her mother. Teo was on his phone and oblivious to his surroundings—his modus operandi. Ms. Nothing is Ever Good Enough went straight to the front desk to check in without noticing me.

When she turned around, I flashed her my million-dollar smile and waved hello from my seat near the fish tank and bookshelf filled with Dr. Seuss stories. Her face went pale, and she nudged Rae toward her big brother before marching over to me. Standing front and center, hands on her hips, Ms. Nothing's Ever Good Enough laid into me, right there, in the doctor's office waiting room, surrounded by other parents and their children. "You..."

After having all of my buttons pushed by this woman who knows them so well, I stood up and went right back at her with the same amount of intensity. Our fingers in each other's faces, and our voices raised, I could feel everyone else's eyes focused on the two of us. It didn't take long before several nurses and one big dude in a security uniform surrounded us. Once we stopped yelling, the only sound in the room was a soft sobbing cry, coming from someplace by the front desk. It was my sweet Rae wrapped up tight in her big brother's arms, crying her little eyes out. Teo looked protective and pissed.

"See what you did!" Ms. Nothing's Ever Good Enough got in the last jab before hustling over to the kids and ushering them promptly out the door. I was left standing alone like the jackass everyone assumed I was.

All I wanted was to be a part, to feel involved and informed about my children's healthcare. That didn't seem like so much to ask. At least I can say that I tried, and she interfered with my parenting rights.

I asked the security guy for his name and phone number in case my attorney needed a statement about what went down in the waiting room. He happily obliged—told me he had been through a nasty divorce too and that I should keep fighting for my kids. Although not quite like I envisioned, the day was not a total loss.

I had a witness now—a person from the medical office who would vouch for my good intentions as a dad.

Back at work that afternoon, I saw on Rae's school website that teacher conferences were the following week and that it was easy to sign up online. I pulled up the online form and saw my ex had already chosen a day and time.

Seems like a giant waste for the teacher to have to talk about the same kid twice. Surely, we can sit in the same room and focus on Rae. I mean, we are adults!

I placed my name beside hers on the same day and at the same time and made a note in the calendar on my phone.

The morning of Rae's conference, I took some extra care in my little bathroom, making sure I looked and smelled great. I wanted to leave a good impression. Nothing spoke Super-Dad to a young teacher quite like a prompt and caring soon-to-be divorced dad.

When I arrived outside Rae's classroom, another family was still in the room with the teacher. I figured Mrs. Snyder was running a few minutes behind, so I took a seat in the hallway. While sitting there, another couple arrived, and my ex was nowhere to be found. When the classroom door opened, I went right in before the couple in the hall could get up from their chairs and introduced myself as Rae's dad. The teacher furrowed her brow in apparent confusion and checked a piece of paper that was taped to her desk—apparently the day's schedule. Mrs. Snyder met my anxious gaze and apologized, "Mr. Smith, I assume? Your wife changed the original meeting time. She bumped it back a day. Rae's conference took place yesterday. I'm terribly sorry, but Mr. and Mrs. Johnson are scheduled in the time slot right now for their child's conference."

I begged for just one minute of her time to talk about my awesome daughter, and she flat-out denied me. Thwarted and upset, I stormed out of the school while mumbling nothing too nice under my breath. My grandmother always said, "If you don't have anything nice to say, do not say anything at all." This golden rule had obviously skipped a generation with my mother, but I tried to heed grandma's advice. Some days, it was not possible.

That wasn't the first impression I wanted to make on Rae's teacher, I brooded while making my way back to the Mustang. *Maybe I can still volunteer or go on a field trip.*

Driving home, I decided that sports were a more natural arena for me, and I'd continue to step up my efforts there with Teo and Rae.

Since making the decision to become Super-Dad, I'd sat in the front row at almost all of Rae's dance competitions—hooted, hollered, yelled her name, and applauded loudly with a standing ovation every time she took a bow. That seemed to go well and without incident, except Rae complained that I was "too loud" and "embarrassing," which I was certain all the girls' her age said about their parents. I assured Rae that other audience members only saw a proud dad—and that I thought she was absolutely the best and was so glad she was okay with me coming to her events. Rae's eye-rolls were getting worse—an annoying habit she learned from her mother. There were also a few run-ins with my ex in the parking lot after Rae's dance competitions. She kept saying that Rae did not want me there, but I knew better. Kids always wanted their parents' support. The more I attended, the more I regretted not coming to these competitions all along.

I had also contacted Teo's basketball coach to see about helping with the team. He said parents were not allowed to coach at the private club where Teo played, but suggested that I spend time coaching my son during open gym. That would have been an excellent suggestion, except that I didn't have parenting time with the kids on weekdays during open gym time. So, I decided that coaching from the sideline during Teo's games would be good enough to show any future evaluator or judge that I, in fact, am an active participant in all of my children's extracurricular activities.

At Teo's next game, I sat midcourt and on the front row of the bleachers. I encouraged Teo's every move and put those stupid referees in their place after bad calls, which turned out to be most of the game. When I realized the high school kid running the scoreboard could not put his phone down long enough to keep up, I really let him have it every time earned points were not reflected on the scoreboard. At half-time, Teo's coach came over and said that while he appreciated my enthusiasm, he would like me to tone it down a bit.

He's so over reactive. I'm just supporting my son and cheering him on.

The half-time pep talk from Teo's coach left me feeling agitated. So, a couple minutes into the second half, the ref made another terrible call and I lost it. A technical foul was given to the team based on my outburst, and some big guy in a security uniform escorted me out of the facility while a bunch of parents clapped, including Ms. Nothing's Ever Good Enough and her gaggle of snickering friends. I looked over at the team as I was pushed through the doors and saw Teo slumped over on the bench, his face buried in his hands.

"Sorry, buddy. I'm so sorry," was all I could mutter on my way out, just before I heard the faint sound of my daughter crying—again.

Geez, what is wrong with me? I'm usually a put-together guy, an upstanding citizen, and hardworking parent! My life is unraveling!

I drove right home and sat down in front of my big screen to think. As my blood pressure lowered, I decided that being outside the apartment other than for work and an occasional happy hour at the bar down the block was just too much pressure at the moment. Staying in for the rest of the day and night seemed best. I opened Uber Eats and ordered food, then sent a quick text apology to Teo and asked that he give his sister a hug from me. I did not expect a response and never got one.

On my best behavior from here on out.

While dozing off that evening, I remembered Bulldog had suggested I invite the kids' friends over to the apartment and get to know their parents better.

The following day, I sent each of my kids a text message asking which of their friends they would like to invite for the weekend. Teo replied fairly quickly with Ethan's name—the obvious choice and his best buddy since preschool. Rae rarely answered my text messages, calls, or FaceTime attempts. Ms. Nothing's Ever Good Enough told me that our daughter didn't want to visit my "haunted house" at all. Of course, that made me wonder what filth she had been filling Rae's head with, causing our sweet daughter to not even want to visit her loving daddy anymore.

My heart was heavy. Rae and I had always been super close. Daddy's little girl from the start. Being the good guy I am, it seemed best to acquiesce. So, I sent Rae a text saying she could stay with her mom this weekend, I loved her, and I would see her soon. The text message showed it was "read," the same with all my other recent text messages, so hopefully Rae was actually reading them and would stop ghosting me in the near future.

For now, Teo, his buddy, and I would have fun together this weekend. Teo took the lead and arranged a ride with Ethan's mother from the suburb to my downtown studio apartment. I told him to be sure and invite Ethan's mother for dinner, although I was a little concerned about seating since there was only the La-Z-Boy, a small couch, and my twin-sized bed for furniture.

Friday night rolled around and they arrived at 6:00 p.m. Ethan's mom, Susie, decided to walk the boys upstairs and seemed a little unsure when she entered my place, making a smart remark about the number 666 on my door. The boys got comfortable in front of the big screen and made plans for a PlayStation marathon. I asked if they were hungry and, in perfect unison, they requested pizza.

I looked at Ethan's mom, Susie, and asked if she was hungry and wanted to get dinner. Without any words, she gestured with a scrunched-up face, lift of her shoulders, and upturned hands—the universal sign for, "Whatever." I suggested we could walk down the block to a little bar that had a great menu since the boys were old enough to stay alone for an hour or two. I ordered and paid for the pizza online, ran through the basic instructions of staying home alone, and then left with Susie. Bulldog said I needed character references, and I planned to make the best impression on Ethan's mom, quietly hoping she had not heard anything about my recent displays of questionable public behavior.

It was a nice evening, and the sun was starting to set. I remembered Bulldog had said not to stay out past dark with any of the friends' mothers. Not much chance of that given the time of day, although our circumstances seemed innocent enough. As we walked, we reminisced about the boys growing up so fast and how crazy it is that they are already teenagers. The bar was more crowded than usual, and I didn't see any open tables, but there were two stools at the end of the bar, so we bellied up.

Susie ordered a Rum and Coke and I asked for a tall beer. We talked and laughed and laughed some more with each drink. Before either of us knew it, we had completely lost track of time and the fact that we had intended to eat. I checked my phone, and it was 10:30 p.m.—way past dark! I texted Teo, and she texted Ethan just to make sure they were still alive and well back at the apartment. Neither of the boys seemed to notice the passing of time. They said they were fine, had eaten all the pizza, and were still hooked up to their game. So, we stayed until the bartender said it was last call.

Susie is way more fun, and hot, than I remember, I thought as I followed her out of the bar. We started making our way toward my apartment, both of us enjoying a good buzz. Instinctively, I reached for her hand while the city lights twinkled all around us. I'd not felt this connected to anyone in a long time, and she told me she hadn't either.

Nearing the apartment garage, I asked if she wanted to see my cool ride, and she replied, "Heck yah!" Of course, she was super impressed by my '65 Mustang Convertible and asked if she could sit inside. I obliged by opening the door and motioning for her to hop in. Then I followed her. One thing led to another and before long…

Boy, I am going to be in deep with Bulldog, but at least she'll be a good character reference. It was the last thought I remember before the windows fogged over.

After that night, Susie and I continued to see each other from time to time as "friends with benefits," and I found renewed hope in my heroic quest as Super-Dad.

Teo had a kickass birthday party that I arranged in November, at Topgolf, with twenty-five of his buddies from sports and school. Rae, who was now talking to me sometimes, wanted a pony for her birthday, so we rounded up every student from Mrs. Snyder's fourth grade class and rented an entire barn of ponies at a small farm about twenty miles outside the suburb. Since it was a considerable distance from the suburb, I arranged a party bus to pick up each guest at their home and deliver them back afterwards. These birthday parties cost me a fortune, and then some, but totally showed up their mother's at-home sleepover parties with a movie, cupcakes, and microwave popcorn. I could practically see my Dad of the Year framed award hanging on the wall.

Susie gave me the rad idea of taking the kids shopping for their own Christmas presents this year, so they could pick out exactly what they wanted. I set no limit on their spending; so when one credit card maxed out, I simply pulled another from my wallet and had even applied for two new back-up cards to ensure the kids had the best and most memorable of all birthdays and major holidays this year. I needed to be absolutely certain they both had good things to say about their dad when the custody evaluation got rolling, right after the first of the year. It seemed like forever since the judge had ordered it.

On Sunday night, after an amazing Christmas celebration weekend with the kids, I decided to do a little cleaning. Rae always made a blanket tent over the bed when she slept at my place, and I decided to start there. While picking up all the snack wrappers, I found a balled-up piece of notebook paper with her handwriting all over it. At the top it, she'd written, "Dear Dad," My stomach did a flip-flop as I decided whether or not I should continue reading. I mean, she balled it up and didn't actually give it to me, so...

Read it, you sap! This is a chance to understand your daughter. Don't be such a coward!

I took a deep breath, smoothed out the paper, sat down on the bed, atop all of Rae's fort blankets, and started reading.

Dear dad why did you have to ruin our family. Why are you so mad at mom and have to fight with her all the time. She didn't do anything wrong. It is ~~embarising~~ imbarising to me when you yell loud at dance and that time at Teo's basketball game when you got arrested out of the gym. Where did you go. I'm always worried about you getting in trouble and going to jail because you act so naughty now. Like at the doctor office OMG!!!!!!!!!!!!!!!!!!!!!!!!!!!!!!!!!!!!! !!! I love you and hate you for being mean to mom and leaving us. The birthday party with ponys was awesome but I heard kids moms at school saying you are buying me and Teo's love. I do not know what that means but the group of moms were not happy about it. Why are you making this so hard for me. I never see Miss Laura my special talking person any more because well I do not know why but mom says its your fault. Miss Laura and me used to make slime during counseling and she is amazing and this haunted house you moved to sucks and I hate the city. Don't ever think about taking Iggy away from me again, and get your own blankets, these are mine and its weird when you smell them. Just stop it already.

I felt sick as I crumpled the paper up and shoved it in my blue jean pocket. *I just wanted to divorce Ms. Nothing's Ever Good Enough and move on with my kids and a fresh start. I never wanted to hurt Teo and Rae. This divorce has nothing to do with them.*

There were a lot of blankets that I folded up, somewhat in a daze. I was stuck on Rae's comment about her mother saying it was all my fault.

How is any of this my fault? I moved out, got a nice place for the kids, continue to pay for everything, am following my attorney's advice and trying to be a more involved dad.

After folding the last of the blankets and stashing them under the twin bed for the next time Rae came over, I dropped into my La-Z-Boy and flipped on the TV to relax. That's when I noticed the PlayStation was still running and the chat box was up on the screen.

Did Teo purposefully leave this up for me to read?

RimRocker12: "another weekend at dads at least he is going all out to buy us whatever we want I mean anything at all he must feel guilty about stuff or whatever"

SeekNDestroy: "dude hes sleeping with my mother!!!!!!!!!!!!!!!!!"

Oh for the love of all that is holy! How on God's green earth do the boys know about that? We are always so careful.

RimRocker12: "its just gross but if it means hell buy me whatever I want then whatever"

SeekNDestroy: "what if they get married we would be like real brothers"

RimRocker12: "word!"

SeekNDestroy: "that would be sweet dude"

SeekNDestroy: "you could move here to our big house cuz I aint moving into that rat hole your dad rents downtown in the city"

No respect!

RimRocker12: "word!"

Pipsqueak: "im comin too anything to get out of this haunted house"

Who is Pipsqu......OMG its Rae!

SeekNDestroy: "hi little sis you ok over there"

Pipsqueak: "yah dad fell asleep early and is snoring like a train"

SeekNDestroy: "he is the loudest snorer ever"

Pipsqueak: "gota go Teo is being a butt"

SeekNDestroy: "later little sis"

RimRocker12: "dont encourage her man she is so annoying"

SeekNDestroy: "i love Rae bro"

RimRocker12: "yah she can be cool sometimes the divorce is really hard on her"

SeekNDestroy: "my parents divorce sucked but didn't take as long as yours"

RimRocker12: "what is my parents problem"

SeekNDestroy: "who knows man hang in there back to the game"

Pipsqueak? I had no idea Rae had a gamertag and chatted online. She better not know about me and Ethan's mom or anything about anything to do with any of that yet! I'm gonna tear her brother a new one next time I see that kid if he has said one word to his sister and polluted her innocence with his dirty teenage mind.

I went back to the bed and grabbed one of Rae's blankets from underneath because sleeping with it was comforting and made everything hurt less. Covering myself up, I closed my eyes and tried to rest.

This divorce is awful and my family needs help. Thankfully, the custody evaluation starts tomorrow and we can get some answers to move us forward. What a mess our family has become—like the circus on steroids. Hopefully, this evaluator can sort it all out.

I didn't have anything special prepared for the first evaluation meeting, but planned on being myself and letting my goodwill shine through. Let this lady see the real Luke—the hardworking guy who loves his kids more than anything else, who is making every effort to do his best, and who plans on being a big part of their lives forever.

I pulled my phone out of my pocket and found the evaluator's website and clicked the tab that said "Pricing." A picture loaded at the top of the page showing a fortune cookie. The fortune read, "Marriage is grand. Divorce is one hundred grand."

Ain't that turning out to be the truth.

I read a little further and learned that a custody evaluation was often the way to a stipulated agreement—a way for families to avoid the financial and emotional hardship of a courtroom trial, which often costs each party ten to twenty thousand dollars or more.

She has my attention.

At the start of all this, I had been looking forward to my day in court; but now, being nearly bled dry financially, anything that promised to move our family toward an end that's best for my kids and save me money sounded pretty good.

I finally dropped off to sleep, hopeful that things would turn around soon.

The next morning, I arrived at the evaluator's office promptly at 10:00 a.m., opened the door, and the lady at the front desk welcomed me and offered a mug of coffee or cup of cold water. I accepted the coffee, and she handed me a disclosure form to read over, date, and sign. Once I had secured a copy for my own records, and she had swiped my plastic, the evaluator walked in from another room and introduced herself with a firm handshake.

She seems all right. I decided to proceed with optimistic caution as she led me into a back office, and motioned for us to sit in two comfortable chairs by the window. *Hot coffee and a comfy chair. Not a bad start to the day.*

The evaluator was all business and welcomed me with a professional smile. She asked if I had any questions before she started in with her spiel about how the evaluation process works, wanting to make sure we were both on the same page. I did not have any questions yet, so I settled into the chair, sipped my coffee, and listened to her talk.

"Well, Luke, most parents are a bit nervous meeting me for the first time, although usually feel much better by the end of our two hours together. I know it has been a long road leading up to today, and you're likely emotionally and financially exhausted."

Damn straight about that.

"Add to it the constant worry about your children, and a parent can really start to feel like they have been swept down the proverbial rabbit hole. Good news is that this evaluation is an opportunity to step back from the adversarial high conflict that litigation often creates between two parents, as we fully explore and concentrate on the needs of your children. We'll be discussing the strengths of each parent and both parents' concerns, and then put our big brains together to design the best plan for Teo and Rae." She gave me a settling smile, confident in her conviction to do what's right for the kids.

I was on board with us combining our big brains to create solutions for my kids until she kept talking about working together as a "team"— her, me, and Ms. Nothing's Ever Good Enough, with whom I am not even on speaking terms.

The evaluator continued, "I have never met a parent who didn't love their children. Mothers and fathers come to this process, both wanting what they believe is in their children's best interest. They both want their children to win the game but are working from different playbooks. My hope is to bring you and the children's mother 80% of the way toward the middle, and then provide enough guidance that the two of you can finish off the final 20% by infusing the plan for Teo and Rae with specific details to meet the unique needs of your family. When both parents are invested in the final plan, and both parents feel heard and that they had a say in what's best, the plan is far more likely to work versus a judgment imposed on your family by the court. Make sense?" Again, she flashed me that satisfied look, like she really intended the best for our family.

Still cautious, but feeling hopeful, I nodded in agreement.

"You and Ms. Smith will not be attending sessions together. There are four meetings with you, and two of those meetings include the children—one here at the office and one at your home. All that I do with you, I will also do with the children's mother. Eight family meetings total. Four with you and four with Mom. You with me?" she queried.

I nodded my head again, feeling a little overwhelmed.

"So, Luke," the evaluator began moving us toward the starting line, "the goal of our time today is for you to educate me about the story of your family. How you got from point A (meeting the children's mother) to point B (a custody litigant). Only a small percentage of divorcing parents ever participate in an evaluation. I'm curious to learn all about why your family is here and begin to understand ways in which I can best assist your children and family moving forward." She paused before giving me further instruction. "It would be helpful if you could go down memory lane..."

With that, my brain suddenly transported me back to college and the first time I saw Ms. Nothing's Ever good Enough, with her petite frame and firm behind, dancing with her friends inside our favorite campus bar. I felt a wave of joy rush through me, and then just as fast was pulled back to the moment, into the evaluator's chair, joy replaced by a heavy feeling of being defeated and lost. It was the equivalent of emotional whiplash.

Crap, she's still talking—giving directions. I focused back on the evaluator's voice.

"Relay information in chronological order—paint a picture of the most significant events in your family's timeline. Throughout the story, please highlight the most important details of your children's lives (residential moves, school/academics, friendships, important relationships, activities/sports/music, health, religion, special needs, special services, successes, areas where they struggle and excel, etc.). You good?" she asked.

"Yep," I replied with more confidence than I felt.

She continued on, "Secondary to learning about your children's lives is for me/us to understand patterns of conflict between you and the other parent. Patterns of conflict are important for us to identify because embedded within them are often your parenting concerns; and unless we make an effort to understand and mitigate the unhealthy patterns of conflict that exist now, those unhealthy patterns will continue on after the divorce and cause trouble for your family going forward. Repeated exposure to parental conflict is detrimental to Teo and Rae and will cause them irreparable harm over time."

With that, she gestured in my direction, as if offering me the floor to start talking.

Wait, what does she want me to say? I stared blankly, blinked a few times, and shifted uncomfortably in the chair. *The timeline. Important family events. She wants the story.*

My confusion was interrupted by, "Da da da dota da dota da ...." I looked down and saw Darth Vader's ugly mug, theme song and all, and Ms. Nothing's Ever Good Enough displayed across the top of the phone that I had carelessly laid face up on the table between us. I silenced that sucker in record time and pretended like it didn't happen, hoping the evaluator didn't catch any of that. No such luck.

"Maybe best to change the picture and music, Luke," she said with a quick wink and then brought me back to the task at hand. "Let's hear it."

I started in, "Well, I'm a hard-working guy who has always made supporting my family a priority, along with caring for my children in every other possible way." From there, I told her everything. In two hours, I described the days each of the kids were born, and all the important moments of their lives since. I explained the ways in which I had been an active parent in their lives and how difficult Ms. Nothing's Ever Good Enough had made things for me with her dictator-like ways. I shared about all my best qualities and all of my ex's worst and laid it all on thick.

It was the first time someone had heard my life story, twenty years of it anyway, and just listened without offering their two cents. By the end, I felt better and like a great dad.

The evaluator hardly spoke a word after her introductory speech "Luke, thank you for sharing about your children and family. We will plan to meet again soon, after I have talked with Teo and Rae's mother. I'll send you an email with some possible dates and times." She stood up and walked me out.

That's it? No feedback? No compliments on my parenting or pat on the back?

I followed her to the door, thanked her for her time, left the office, and drove straight to Bulldog's. Once there, I followed the usual routine and was promptly seated across the desk from him. He did not have much feedback either—said it sounded like things went well and told me to keep up the good work. He suggested I take notes at the next meeting, when the evaluator would share Vanessa's parenting concerns with me.

The second evaluation meeting was scheduled about two weeks later, and it was business as usual until then. The kids spent time at the apartment the weekend in between meetings, and Rae remade her fort. Teo mostly played his video games, but walked down the block to check out some basketball courts. He wanted me to come along and shoot hoops "like the good old days," but Rae refused to go out, even for a quick walk, proclaiming that, "The city is dangerous—no place for a little girl to be wandering around." No doubt her mother's influence and probably her exact words.

As soon as Teo was out of the apartment, Rae started talking. "Do you hate Mom?" she asked accusingly, looking me in the eye and quite assertively for such a small person.

My daughter was instantly in tears. I must have paused just a little too long before answering because she interpreted my answer as a "yes" before I could soften the blow, dance around the issue, or come up with a better though equally truthful adjective.

I'll never lie to my kids.

"Why do you and Mommy have to fight? Why can't everyone just be nice and get along?" She sobbed quietly while I sat on the couch rubbing her back, wondering what on earth to say. Rae continued before I could speak, "You and Mom need to be grounded, on restriction, sent to the principal's office, or sit in detention all day."

She has no idea I'm already here.

Rae brought up things from years ago in addition to the conflict she had witnessed more recently. Her mind was like a steel trap. The kid remembered everything, especially the bad stuff, and she was completely inconsolable; comforting her was like trying to cuddle an angry gator. She was loud and dramatic, with a theatrical flair. Always had been.

After an hour or more of Rae carrying on like her parents' divorce was the end of the world, all I could think to do was assure her that I loved her, that her mother did the best she knew how, and that we would get everything worked out. My words were of little comfort to Rae and, just like with her mother, they seemed to make her angrier.

I'll never understand women, even this little one I helped to create. I gave Rae a hug, got her a grape Popsicle, and then suggested she rest in her tent for the afternoon.

As I sat in my La-Z-Boy, listening to the slowly-abating sobs coming from my daughter inside the tent next to me, and I shook my head quietly. *Sheesh, kids go through divorce every day, thousands of them. I hadn't really thought about all the ways leaving the house might make my kids feel. I was just trying to get away from Ms. Nothing's Ever Good Enough and had no idea my leaving would affect them so much. I hope the evaluator can give me some pointers.*

The second evaluation meeting was different from the first. Once we were seated, the evaluator told me today would be more of a structured interview. She asked about my parenting style, daily routines, and discipline of the children.

These are not things I think about too often, but I answered the best I could. "My style is a balance of firm and loving. Routines have changed since moving out of the house and our weekends are mostly unstructured, fun time. And, my kids need very little discipline; they are quite amazing and never have to be punished."

"Discipline and punishment are very different things, Luke," she began. "Punishment is punitive, and makes children feel small and insignificant. The root word of discipline is 'disciple' and that word means 'to teach.' This approach to behavior modification empowers children by guiding and helping to shape them into solid human beings."

Why do I feel like I blew that question?

When she asked about the kids' healthcare and dental care, I mentioned attending their well-child visits and the scene Ms. Nothing is Ever Good Enough had made at the medical office. I shared about the security guard who gave his contact information as a witness and handed her the business card he had given me, but she seemed unimpressed.

When the evaluator asked about their schools and whether or not I participated there as a volunteer or had attended conferences with Teo and Rae's teachers over the years, I briefly touched on my experience with Mrs. Snyder and moved on.

Next, she asked me about our holiday traditions and that's when I really got to shine. We talked about what the kids look forward to each year and I really talked up their recent extravagant birthday parties and the amazing no-holds-barred Christmas just past.

She asked who my "go-to" people were—the support system that I relied upon for help with the kids when needed. I told her I did not need much help, but had dependable co-workers at the office, my mother, and Susie who was always ready to lend a hand.

When she asked me about any new relationships, anyone significant in my life who had been introduced to the kids, I was suspicious she might know something about me and Susie but played it off and denied spending time with anyone significant at this time.

I'm not getting serious with anyone ever again anyways.

Then it was time for the evaluator to share Vanessa's parenting concerns, so we could sort through some of the disagreements and she could hear both sides of the issues.

It was not easy listening to and responding to all of my ex's complaints. When we finally made it through the litany of Ms. Nothing's Ever Good Enough's BS, I was ready to get the heck out of there. It was more of the same—my soon-to-be ex saying I should have and could have and if only I would have...

If I don't show up, I'm in the wrong. If I do show up, I'm in the wrong. She always wanted me to plan a birthday party and when I did, it was apparently wrong, too.

The evaluator said she was looking forward to talking with my personal references about their observations of my relationship with Teo and Rae. She also said she would be contacting other professionals who know our family to get their observations as well.

We scheduled our third evaluation meeting, the one with Teo and Rae, for Friday afternoon, right after I picked them up from school. She suggested that in preparation I tell Teo and Rae a little bit about her role with our family and describe her office and let them know that their mother and I have both been in and talked with her. I was not to "coach" them in any way about things they should or should not say. She promised the burden of all this was not theirs, and she was simply interested in getting to know them a little bit better—wanting to hear whatever was on their minds.

Guess I'll text the kids before Friday so they know about the after-school meeting.

I left the office feeling pretty good about how things were shaking out. I was a little uncertain what other people might say—all those references. Professionals, like the counselor they apparently no longer saw, according to Rae, probably did not think too highly of me. And their pediatrician might not be too complimentary since my contact there has been minimal. Whatever Mrs. Snyder was going to say scared me the most.

Water under the bridge, I convinced myself. *Water under the bridge.*

On Friday afternoon, as I was driving to pick the kids up from their schools for our 3:30 p.m. meeting at the evaluator's office—the "parent-child interaction," she had called it—I was feeling confident about how I had prepared myself and everyone else.

I had suggested to Teo that he tell the evaluator about the good times he was having in the city. He was spending a lot of time down at the basketball courts and had met some of the local ballers and even won a little cash playing one-on-one.

I'd called my mother to get her up to speed. She was one of my three personal references and I wanted to make sure she would do a good job. I told her to focus on all my strengths and best assets as a dad. She'd assured me that would not be difficult, as I had always been her favorite son. My mother hated Vanessa and I asked her to keep that in check—to only share a couple examples of her rotten parenting and then move on.

My second and third personal references were a guy from work I had known over ten years, and Susie, who I figured could do her magic. She had gotten to know the kids and me pretty well. And of course, I told her to keep our "relationship" on the down low.

I picked Teo up first. "Sup" was the big hello he had for me after almost two weeks with no contact. We proceeded to shoot-the-breeze on our way to get Rae— Teo never saying more than a few words per sentence, but saying everything necessary with his expression and tone. The kid was obviously not happy with me.

Frustrated with Teo's attitude, I glanced down at the guinea pigs on the back seat as I pulled up to Rae's school. After CoCo had kicked Iggy out, I'd gotten Rae a pair of guinea pigs from a guy in my office. They were cool little pets—something furry Rae could hold in her lap and snuggle when she's at the apartment with me. They seemed to help lessen Rae's fear of my haunted house, as she liked to call it. Of course, I specifically asked that she not refer to our home as haunted when she talked with the evaluator. I'd decided to bring the little fellas in hopes that the evaluator would be impressed with the big smile on my daughter's face, because she could not not smile around the rodents.

"Oh, Daddy, you brought them!" Rae was so excited when she hopped into the back seat and saw her pets. "Is it okay to bring them to the meeting with the lady?" she asked. "I'm sure it's fine, honey," and hoped that it was.

When we walked into her office, the evaluator was ready for us.

"Hi there!" she welcomed, extra cheerful today. After meeting the guinea pigs, Sebastian and Renegade, and exchanging a few kind words with Teo and Rae, she invited us into the back office. It was obvious they had been there already. Rae was happy to see our evaluator and gave her a hug. Teo talked openly with her, in a polite and mature way.

Wow, he knows how to be a gentleman. Impressive. My chest swelled with pride.

In the space where we had met before, there was a large white piece of paper sitting on the little table and colored pencils, markers, crayons, watercolor paints, and stickers sitting out. "Teo, grab that bigger chair again," the evaluator directed. He gave her a crooked smile, and plunked his rear-end into the comfortable chair while I pulled a child-sized wooden chair up next to Rae. "Here's what I'd love for you to do first. I want you to create a family picture together—a memory you'll never forget, a vacation, a holiday or anything you wish—where everyone in the picture is doing something."

Rae had "the pigs" in their travel carrier up on the table with us, and she'd opened the zipper end, "so they can see us better," she'd said.

All three of us nodded as the evaluator backed out of our space so we could get started. Music began playing in the background, which helped to lighten the mood.

The kids and I discussed a couple of ideas that we could draw as a group, and then decided to each work on our picture memories separately.

After fifteen minutes or so, the evaluator asked how we were doing and if it would be okay for her to come over to see what we had created.

Both kids agreed she should see their work. When they sat up and I laid eyes on their drawings, I was confused as my brain attempted to register what was on the paper. Teo had drawn himself in a reclining chair playing video games. That much made sense, but then there was a second kid, a boy next to him playing videogames, and a huge speech bubble above both their heads that read: "Brothers Forever." Beside the speech bubble was a lady and man, making out, tongues and all, labeled: "Dad and Susie."

OMG!

My eyes darted to Rae's drawing next. It was Darth Vader, holding a cell phone that read "MOM" across the top. And if the universe was not already a cruel place, my damn cell starting ringing in my pocket, right on cue—"da da da dota da dota da." I silenced it quickly but not before the evaluator shot me a disapproving look.

She turned her attention from me toward the kids. "Wow, there is a lot going on here. You two are great artists," she said to Teo and Rae. She looked over to my area of the paper where I had drawn a sketch of Top Golf next to a whole herd of ponies. "What do you suppose Dad drew over there?"

Rae piped up, "Oh that's me and Teo's birthday parties. Dad never planned parties before. Sometimes he even had to work and couldn't be there. But this year, he went all out! We cannot wait until next year to see what Dad comes up with."

Those parties were once in a lifetime, baby girl. Daddy's wallet cannot do that twice.

The evaluator peeked into Rae's travel carrier and said, "Don't you have two guinea pigs?"

Rae peeked in next and immediately freaked out! "Oh no, Renegade is missing! Daddy, where is he? Did he get out?" Rae squealed. Chaos quickly overwhelmed the room as all of us began searching for Rae's loose rodent, except for Teo who was in his cozy chair smirking, with his cell in hand set to record, for his Instagram feed later no doubt. Renegade was on the move.

Thankfully, the evaluator spotted him in short order and scooped him up. Rae comforted Renegade and put him back in the carrier with Sebastian.

"Guys, would it be okay for Dad to sit out on the comfy couch for a while, so the three of us can talk and play a game of UNO™?" the evaluator asked in her gentle voice.

"Great," I said, rising from my little wooden chair, eager to get the heck out of there. Without waiting for the kids to answer the question, I collected my things and headed for the door, shutting it behind me as I walked toward the safety of the comfy couch.

Could this get any worse? I took my place on the comfy couch. There was music playing in both rooms and a loud white noise machine whooshing beside me. I could not make out anything concrete, except for my daughter crying again and the baritone of Teo's voice once in a while.

When the evaluator and kids emerged from the back office, thirty minutes or so later, my children looked at peace and Teo was even smiling. Rae gave the evaluator another big hug before she sent both of them to a treasure box and the evaluator said, "I'll see you Sunday at the apartment. Keep close track of those guinea pigs, Rae. And Teo, don't be betting too much of your money down at the courts."

What is she talking about? He's only won a couple rounds of one-on-one.

"I'll be excited to meet Iggy at home with Mom next week, too, guys!" she concluded.

I cringed when she mentioned their mother, and I saw the kids avoid the topic, too. We left her office and headed to the car without too many words between the three of us.

Back at the apartment, we ordered Friday night pizza and then Teo had practice, which I drove him to and from. Rae brought the guinea pigs along since they pretty much went everywhere with us—her "emotional support animals," I teased.

Rae set up her tent, hung a "keep out" sign, and played with her pets. She was texting her mom a lot, which I asked her to stop doing, because this was my time, not her mother's time, and I didn't get very much of it. Their mother saw them almost every day, and I was protective over every second I got to spend with Teo and Rae. There was no need for Ms. Nothing's Ever Good Enough's interference.

The evaluator was due at the studio on Sunday morning at 10:00 a.m., so we spent Saturday cleaning up, which took all of ten minutes in my tiny little place.

As I dozed off Saturday night, my last thought was of the impending home visit, and that this process was almost over. Finally, the last evaluation meeting had arrived. *Come hell or high water, at least we'll be done. Finally, this has been going on way too long.*

The evaluator knocked on the apartment door promptly at 10:00 a.m., and Rae let her in with one hand while she held one of her guinea pigs in the other.

"Good morning, Rae. Which piggy is this?" the evaluator queried while petting Renegade's head.

Rae was in full theater mode, a natural actress. "This is Renegade! Welcome to our humble home! What you see is what you get. Seriously, there is no more." She grabbed the evaluator's hand and led our court-appointed professional toward her fort/bed/ guinea pig habitat. The "keep out" sign was still up, but she invited her in and the evaluator obliged.

Teo was only half-awake, still reclined in the La-Z-Boy. I told him to get up and brush his teeth, and he sauntered off at the speed of a sloth, to the bathroom, ten steps away.

Rae popped her head out of the tent and asked me for some privacy. Then the evaluator peeked her head out, right beside Rae's, and asked if I minded stepping into the hallway for five or so quick minutes so she and Rae could talk. Teo too, when he got back from the bathroom.

"Sure, you got it," I replied with my most charming smile and cooperative tone.

After more like ten or fifteen not-so-quick minutes, the evaluator opened my apartment door. She said goodbye to Rae and encouraged Teo that she'd be watching for him in the NBA one day. The evaluator closed the door behind her and made eye contact with me. "Alright, Luke. You have a cozy home here. I'll finish calling personal and professional references and can then wrap up the evaluation report for Teo and Rae. I'll be in touch." She collected some paperwork from me, shook my hand, and left.

When I walked back into the apartment, the kids were both in a good mood. We enjoyed the rest of our Sunday afternoon per the usual routine, and I drove them back to the suburb at 6:00 p.m., right on time, and dropped them at their mother's new apartment. With Bulldog pushing hard on the issue, the family home had finally been listed and sold.

Things are looking up.

We had a trial date on the court docket just two months after the home visit. Bulldog said the evaluator had sent word to him and Attorney of the Year that she planned to have her report out well in advance of the trial date. "Well in advance" turned out to be a subjective term. Less than three weeks before our hearing, Bulldog called me during the workday, said he had the evaluation report, and told me to come down to his office.

I finished up what I was doing and then headed right down.

Bulldog held the report in his hand and stated matter-of-factly, "It could be worse."

He said some of the evaluator's conclusions had described me as "disingenuous, insensitive, over-the-top, to the emotional impact on the children, and Disneyland Dad." She actually used that ridiculous, over-used cliche: "Disneyland Dad."

This wordy and expensive evaluation report better not cause too much of a problem for me. Some of the things in it were unbelievable and made me seem like a completely uncaring and incapable father to the two children I love more than life. I shook my head as he read through all the services and therapies and educational courses recommended to improve communication and parenting insights.

Who has time or money for all that? I just want to spend time with my kids.

Bulldog told me, "The evaluator has a lot of concerns that are supported by firsthand examples of your behavior. Why didn't you change that ringtone like I advised early on? Sounds like it caused trouble. None of this will be favorable to our position at trial. It would be best to try and settle along the lines of the evaluator's recommendation."

I sat quietly, paralyzed by the flood of emotions. Anger. Confusion. Disbelief. Regret.

"Tell me what yah want to do, kid." Bulldog broke the silence as Lola set two glasses on the desk and poured each of us some really good whisky.

"Can we make an offer, asking for more parenting time than what the evaluator recommended?" I asked. "That seems better than settling on this or going to trial."

"You got it, I'll send an offer to opposing counsel this afternoon and see where it goes," Bulldog started. "Either they accept our offer, offer something else and we split hairs about that, or we all go to trial and let a judge decide." He paused and then continued, "If we cannot settle, you'll need another fifteen grand deposited into your trust account for trial. I've seen the court order something other than this evaluator's recommendations before, and there is nothing I love more than cross-examination with a worthy opponent."

This can't be happening. How can this be happening?

I seethed all the way home and stomped again up to the 666, where I promptly turned on the PlayStation and started snooping through Teo's chats.

One text communication stood out amongst the sea of others.

RimRocker12: "the evaluator came over to the apartment today"

SeekNDestroy: "is she cool"

RimRocker12: "yah shes alright I showed her my gambling wins from the basketball courts here in the city almost $2000 now bro"

SeekNDestroy: "your dad has no idea about the betting right"

RimRocker12: "nah but I figured the lady might take an interest"

SeekNDestroy: "what did she say"

RimRocker12: "she asked if my dad ever came along to the courts"

SeekNDestroy: "did you tell her he is too busy making out with my mom"

RimRocker12: "actually"

SeekNDestroy: "dude no way you ratted out your dad and my mom"

RimRocker12: "yep"

SeekNDestroy: "why"

RimRocker12: "cuz hes been an ass since he left my mom"

SeekNDestroy: "well yah but why would you involve my mom shes not an ass does Rae know"

RimRocker12: "yep she knows and thinks it will be cool to live with you guys"

Enough! I shut it down. *Teo's gambling? Rae knows? Where did this all go wrong?*

Just then, my phone let me know there was a voicemail. It was from Bulldog: "No dice, son. They rejected our offer and their counteroffer was trash. We're headed into trial. Stop by when you can and get me the retainer to start preparing our case. We don't have a lot of time to get our ducks in a row so we can win this thing the hard way."

Damn it. Completely defeated, I realized there was nothing left to do but pay Bulldog more money and wait for a judge to make the very important decision about what the future held Teo, Rae, and me.

Months and months had passed since I'd left the house, consumed by high conflict, arguments, public displays of ugliness, changes, loss, upset, attorneys, bills-bills-bills, and what I was sure would be bankruptcy after the added cost of this trial.

I entered the courthouse in my best clothes and looked for Bulldog. No sign of him, so I headed up to our assigned courtroom but stopped short when I saw the impressive group of people assembled. I recognized the evaluator who smiled and waved to me as if we were on speaking terms. Next to her was Mrs. Snyder, Rae's teacher. A couple people I did not recognize were in the group, and I figured one must be the kids' counselor that I'd never met. Teo's basketball coach was there and some ladies I recognized from Rae's dance competitions. Ms. Nothing's Ever Good Enough's bestie, Juls, shot me a nasty look. Next to her was a man I sort of recognized but could not place.

Ah ha! It was the security guard from the doctor's office. I made eye contact and he walked toward me. "Hey man, thanks for coming," I said and offered a handshake.

He went a little pale and then apologized, "Sorry, bro. Your wife's attorney subpoenaed me before yours did, so I am technically her witness." He shrugged and returned to the group that was carrying on like this was some sort of casual social event.

Is that CoCo? The gorgeous woman from the rental office was sitting right beside and chatting ever-so-casually with my ex, both of them dressed to the nines. It looked like they had been to the spa together this morning.

Damn, my ex looks so good. I really hated myself for thinking so.

I needed to find Bulldog and decided to check inside the courtroom. As I walked in, I saw my mother-in-law who sneered and said to no one in particular, "Oh great! Father of the Year decided to show up."

I checked my watch. *The usual fifteen minutes early.*

Bulldog was seated at a table in front of the judge's bench. There were papers scattered everywhere, and he was wearing the same cheap suit I'd first met him in. I hadn't thought to bring anyone along and hoped Bulldog had subpoenaed someone, in a timely manner, that was able to testify on my behalf.

"Hello, son," Bulldog offered as he pulled out the chair next to him so I could sit. Bulldog let me know that Susie was running late but was under subpoena and would be here for me, and that my buddy Mike, who he thought would make a terrific witness, checked in and then went down to use the restroom. We had agreed my mother would do more harm than good so Bulldog had made no effort to call her. And, even though Vanessa's attorney had subpoenaed the medical office security guard, Bulldog assured me he would still prove useful to our case.

Within a few minutes, Ms. Nothing's Ever Good Enough and her attorney were seated at the table, too, and a clerk in front of the judge's bench authoritatively instructed: "All rise." Bulldog nudged me and I followed his lead.

The judge entered the courtroom and recited our family name and the case number, and made record of who was in attendance.

I watched person after person parade in front of me, up to the witness stand, and talk about what a wonderful mother Ms. Nothing's Ever Good Enough is and has always been and then about the less active parenting role I have traditionally played, notwithstanding my more recent efforts to show up everywhere "like a bull in a china shop." They agreed that I was responsible for "causing conflict after conflict in front of the kids since their parents split."

Even though Bulldog scored lots of points on cross-examination, things did not seem to be going in my favor. He spent the most time grilling our evaluator and his manner with her put even me on edge. Once, the judge admonished Bulldog's "unnecessary tone" when he was yelling and turning purple. But, the evaluator handled him like a pro. She beamed with positive accolades when speaking about Teo and Rae, and then became far more serious when describing both the strengths and concerns about me and my ex.

I was called to the stand to testify, and Attorney of the Year was aggressive and downright mean and didn't speak a lick of truth. We took a break for lunch and then were right back at it afterwards. Ms. Nothing's Ever Good Enough testified last. She should have been an actress with her Oscar-worthy performance. By 4:30 p.m., I hardly knew my own name. This had been the most exhausting and expensive day of my life. It was surreal to be there, doing battle with the woman I'd slept next to half my life.

The mother of my children.

I had no idea what the judge was going to do—what choices he was going to make based on the information that was presented in the exhibits and testimony. Teo's and Rae's lives had been strategically laid out in this court of law by the legal spin-doctor my ex had hired. Everything now rested within the purview of a man who had never met my kids—the judge deciding their future.

After Ms. Nothing's Ever Good Enough finished, the judge asked if there were any additional witnesses. There were none. He heard closing statements from each of our lawyers, and I was grateful for the job Bulldog did describing all of my best traits as a loving father. When closing arguments ended, the judge leaned back in his chair, crossed his arms over his round belly, and took a deep breath, looking somewhat distressed.

Silently, he removed his glasses, rubbed his eyes, put the glasses back on, and then sat forward and made eye contact—first with me and then with Ms. Nothing's Ever Good Enough, who was sitting to my right. Tension in the air was palpable as he began to speak, "I have been sitting on this bench the last twenty-three years, listening to disputes and gripes between divorcing parents about the very children each of them says they are here in this courtroom to protect. Reality is folks, being here and fighting with each other, tearing each other down in a court of law, does not offer any protection to your children.

"I have not heard one shred of evidence today that convinces me either of you is a physical threat to your children's safety. While I am relatively certain the two of you will meet your children's basic daily needs, the evidence gives rise for particular concern about your capacities to understand and nurture Teo and Rae's emotional health. Given the mutual decisions made during the marriage, mom at home and dad at work, the children have always spent more time in their mother's care. After their parents' divorce, children need consistency and continuity of what has been their normal. Stripping children away from the parent who they have historically relied on is harmful. They are not accustomed to spending fifty percent of their time away from mother and with you, sir. Over many years, mother has established positive working relationships with the professionals who serve your children's best interests—their doctor, dentist, orthodontist, and teachers."

He took a deep breath and let out a huge sigh before continuing with his decision.

"Mr. Smith, neither you nor Ms. Smith is more important to the children. They need the best of what both of you have to offer. However, early childhood bonds are formed between the ages of zero to five, a time when Teo and Rae spent the majority with their mother and you reliably worked to financially support the household. That's very honorable, sir. By virtue of the way you and your wife set up household during the marriage, she is the primary parent, the CEO of the home, and conductor of the children's lives. You cannot simply show up now, everywhere you have not been before, and expect that to feel comfortable and natural to the children. Participation is terrific, and encouraged, though the way you have gone about it leaves something to be desired. It is important that you deepen your understanding about what children need after divorce."

He picked up the evaluation report. "The evaluator provided a roadmap for educational and reparative services that mother and father are hereby ordered to participate in, including individual therapy for both of you, a high-conflict parenting course, co-parent training, and use of the online communication platform Our Family Wizard."

After that, he gave each of us a hardened look and asked, "I believe that both of you, Mom and Dad, would jump in front of a bus for your children. Am I right?"

Vanessa and I both nodded in a rare moment of agreement.

"You love Teo and Rae so much that it would not even be a second thought to jump right out in front of a moving bus. Hear me now when I tell you that *you are the bus*. Mr. and Ms. Smith, you are the biggest threat to your children. Their exposure to the conflict between you harms them more than anything else. The acts of bitterness and name-calling, finger-pointing, blaming, blame-shifting, and gaslighting will ruin your children.

I can't stop you from doing those things. Only you have the authority to choose differently. Only you can protect Teo and Rae, through the myriad of daily choices you make about your own thinking, behavior, and conduct and especially your attitudes toward one another. If you want your children to be okay, to do better than okay, you have to take care of their parents. You have to take better care of each other, no longer as a spouse, but as the single most valuable asset in your children's lives. The two of you are Teo and Rae's insurance policies— the very foundation that anchors their potential for all the wonderful things they will achieve. Without that foundation, they are left to flounder, and we know children who flounder do not actualize their potential."

He looked satisfied, recited his findings, and then announced, "Mother will have legal and primary physical custody of the children, and Teo and Rae will enjoy parenting time with their father according to the schedule proposed by the court-appointed evaluator." The judge acknowledged our evaluator, seated in the back of the courtroom and thanked her for a thorough job, well done.

That was it. The scolding was finished. The judge started telling Bulldog, as the moving party (the petitioner), to prepare the order, but then changed his mind and asked Attorney of The Year to take care of it. Apparently, he had more confidence in her ability to follow through and get things done with precision. Bulldog seemed fine with this.

As the courtroom emptied out, there was happy chatter and hugs all around for my ex from her tribe, and my mother-in-law actually stuck her tongue out when I walked past.

My ex...

The judge's verbal reprimand during his ruling about this term lingered as I made my way from the courthouse, all alone, to the parking garage. He had expressed great concern about the undercurrent of my anger toward the children's mother, what the children saw as "hatred"; and he'd told me, with no uncertain terms, that referring to her as "Ms. Nothing's Ever Good Enough" or "my ex" and having Darth Vader represent her likeness on my cell phone was hurtful and harmful to the children—"our" children. They were not "my" kids or "your" kids. It was not "her time" or "my time." The judge said that all time belonged to Teo and Rae. They were not possessions. They were young people, with developing hearts and minds, and it was our job to protect them, mostly it seemed, from ourselves.

The outcome was not what I had envisioned for my big day in court. This did not feel like justice at all, but was definitely a legal and binding court order, our dissolution judgment, and the final say about how we would move forward with our children.

On my way out of the courthouse, I cursed all of it.

Judges. Attorneys. Evaluators. Marriage. Divorce. Best friends whose wives testify against you. Smokin' hot lease agents. Bad legal advice. Guinea pig habitats built under blanket tents. Mean fourth grade teachers.

Security guards. Darth Vader. And illegal courtside betting that teenagers hid from their parents.

I cursed it all and left for home, in my Mustang, which was about all I had left, or so it seemed, on this awful and miserable day.

Below are two choices Luke can make at this point.

Follow the judge's orders.
Turn to page 386 to find out what happens when Luke makes this choice.

Fight for my children.
Turn to page 391 to find out what happens when Luke makes this choice.

Two Years after Luke Followed the Judge's Orders

We had just finished Rae's sixth-grade parent-teacher conferences, and Vanessa and I walked out into the cool evening air, leaves crisp and crunching beneath our feet. Of course, her teachers loved her, but not as much as we did.

She's quite the kid, that one, I thought to myself as I remembered the birthday wish list she had handed me the previous weekend.

"Did she give you her birthday wish list?" I asked Vanessa as we walked toward our cars parked next to each other in the back of the school lot.

It had been about twenty-four months—two whole life cycles through the calendar year since our judgment—and things were beginning to feel "normal" again. We'd done our best to follow the court-ordered plan. I'd talked to a financial consultant who came highly-recommended and avoided bankruptcy. Vanessa and I had both started our new lives. As the judge had instructed, we helped Teo and Rae transition smoothly between two homes without them witnessing any more conflict, arguments, or bad attitudes.

Teo was driving, and Rae was off to middle school. Time was moving fast, and we knew their childhoods were fleeting, so we were working hard to establish new traditions and make positive memories. Vanessa and I were communicating better than ever with the help of some pretty awesome people who made sure we learned all new ways of doing that. We even sat together at Teo's basketball games and Rae's choir concerts and dance recitals.

Thanks to what the judge had said, and what the evaluator had talked about in her report, I worked hard to value my traditional role with Teo and Rae and resolved my anger toward Vanessa. Eventually, I gained insight into the way that my thinking, behavior, and conduct impacted Teo and Rae. The less angry I became, and the more negativity I released, the happier *our* kids were. I could see it in everything they did.

They were both thriving at school, in their relationships, and with their activities. They loved their mom, and they loved me. As instructed by multiple professionals, we gave our children permission to love and be loved by everyone, including their opinionated grandmothers. Iggy even traveled with the kids now, between their two homes. Rae left the guinea pigs with me, "for company" she said, while she and Teo were spending time at their other home. I had moved from the city apartment and into a nice house, not far from Vanessa's new place and near the kids' schools and their friends. It was not the life I signed up for when I asked Vanessa to marry me, but it was turning out alright.

"Yep!" Vanessa chuckled out loud.

"LEGOs are easy enough," I said. "I'll get her the big set she asked for—you think she's ready to build the entire Death Star?"

"Oh yeah, she can handle it." We both chuckled as Vanessa did the "da da da dota da dota da." Then she continued on, "I'll get the few items of clothes and fancy high heels she wants." Vanessa glanced over and saw my eyebrows pull together in concern. "Don't worry, overprotective Daddy, they're not that high."

As we stopped short of our cars, I reached out and placed my hand gently on Vanessa's shoulder before asking the question that had inspired this conversation. "She wants a family birthday party, with both of us, her big brother, and her grandmothers—my mother and yours. Lord help us, do you think our mothers are ready?"

Fearing the day already, I tilted my head back and looked up at the starry sky. Then I grinned, remembering Rae's words, the #1 wish that she had written in bubble letters, and colored bright pink with glitter sprinkled over the top for full effect. I was sure as Vanessa gulped back a wave of anxiety, too:

#1: A FAMILY BIRTHDAY PARTY – EVERYONE I LOVE INVITED, LOVING ME UP GOOD THE WAY A GIRL SHOULD BE LOVED ON HER 12TH BIRTHDAY.

I returned my gaze to Vanessa and smiled. "That kid—she's really something. Smarter than any of us. Our girl is well on her way to ruling the world, if that's what she wants." I saw the same pride beaming in her mother's eyes.

That was a real moment for us—unexpected and powerful.

"Yes," Vanessa agreed. "And I'm sure that she will handle her grandmothers' behavior with all of that cleverness and grace."

"Yah, yah, I'm sure it will be fine—better than fine. Well, good night." I smiled, jumped into my Mustang, and left.

As I drove home, I thought about how far we had all come. I had absolutely hated this woman just two years ago; but today, I knew the truth: I still loved Vanessa. I loved her as the mother of our children, a co-parent, sharing the very most important work of our lifetimes—raising Teo and Rae up to be good and happy human beings.

For them, I was certain Vanessa and I would do anything, including manage our difficult mothers so Rae could enjoy the best family birthday party ever. Teo had really come around too and would appreciate this family-focused time. He'd told me recently that he was "proud" of us—his mom and me—for finally sitting together at basketball games and being kind to each other. We had all learned through our counseling that being nice was a subjective term but kindness and respect—these were the standards, which our family agreed to value and uphold. Teo was tearing up the floor on his high school basketball team, had amazing friends, and was getting decent grades. Our son was really growing into a wonderful young man. It took time, hard work, and skilled professionals who earned every cent we paid them to help us heal our family.

Teo and Rae's family.

An image of the evaluator with her happy smile and wave at the courthouse popped into my mind's eye, and I even felt gratitude for her and her compassionate, spot-on recommendations, even though I didn't understand them at the time. And the way she treated all of us with warmth and kindness through the most difficult time in our lives.

She is the one who gave us the road map to arrive here—right now—when our baby girl is about to turn twelve and wants all of us there at her party.

I turned into my driveway, pulled into the garage, hopped out, and went into my house. There was Sebastian and his pal Renegade in their hallway habitat, right outside the kitchen where Rae said I would always remember to feed them when she was not there. "Hey, little dudes." I reached in and petted each of their heads. "Hungry?" I poured some pellets and then grabbed two leaves of lettuce from the fridge and a bottle of soda for me.

Home sweet home. This it truly was, with a separate bedroom for everyone.

I settled in for the night, feet propped up on the stool of my La-Z-Boy, ready to enjoy the big game. Mike would be over soon, and I was looking forward to the evening.

Thank God for enduring friendships and football—and my kids!

Man, I love those two knuckleheads.

Two Years after Luke Disregarded the Judge's Orders

"Can you believe that teacher?" I asked Vanessa as we walked toward our cars parked in dark school lot. We had just finished Rae's sixth grade parent teacher conferences and walked into the cool evening air, fallen leaves crisp beneath our feet. It was the first time we had attended conferences together, and it was awful. Middle school did not permit separate times, like elementary school had.

It was about twenty-four months—two whole life cycles through the calendar year—since our judgment. Things had continued to be strained between Vanessa and me. Even worse, I think, since she had gotten custody of the kids and wielded it over me like a weapon. We had decided we did not have the time or money to participate in all those court-ordered services the judge said we needed, and our kids were having problems.

I had stopped showing up to everything, since nothing I did seemed to pan out quite right. This only mattered for a short while anyway since the kids no longer participated in the things they used to enjoy. Rae even quit dancing. I assumed Vanessa took them to the doctor if they needed to go, and the dentist, too. She was harping on me to pay for half of their braces, but no way was I funding that when I wasn't even allowed at appointments.

Teo had gotten into trouble after a fistfight at the basketball courts. When the cops showed up, he had weed in his pocket and a gigantic wad of cash from the ongoing illegal betting that I had told him to quit as soon as I had found out about it.

The kid never listens.

Now Teo had a juvenile record, a court-assigned counselor, and community service hours. He was unable to get his driver's license at sixteen as a result of his delinquency.

And Rae was off to middle school, apparently failing all of her classes, according to the teachers we had just met. She hardly ate at all and, while thin was in, her PE teacher just told us she was worried that maybe Rae had taken it too far and had an actual problem.

I was seriously starting to worry about both of them. Time was moving fast. I knew their childhoods were fleeting, and their futures were not looking so bright at the moment.

Teo had stopped playing all organized sports in favor of video games and smoking weed. He had a whole new crowd of friends in high school and could not pass a class to save his life. *Maybe if he actually attended class...* At this rate, he was headed toward becoming a dropout. Rae had become the class clown, and was totally boy crazy. I'd even caught her with a boy down in the parking garage one weekend.

Poor sap got what was coming to him.

I was mad as hell all the time—at work, at the kids, at Vanessa, at her mother, at my mother. Susie wanted nothing to do with me. The kids moved between houses when we told them to, and they despised it. Rae kept running away, and Teo preferred his friends' couches to my or his mom's place. My heartless ex re-homed Iggy, which broke Rae's heart. The guinea pigs "disappeared" when I released them—in the forest. Those little buggers were a lot of work, and Rae was not around enough to take care of them.

"Yah, she's a real peach," Vanessa responded, "saying Rae has problems. The only problem Rae has is having to spend weekends with *you*. She's miserable at your place, Luke. The kids were just fine until you up and left and turned their worlds upside-down. You destroyed all of our lives, Luke. You really need to move out of that tiny apartment."

"Whatever, woman! It's all my fault, huh? Nothing's ever good enough—right, Ms. High and Mighty?"

There in the parking lot, as we approached our vehicles, Vanessa felt compelled to remind me of what the evaluator had written in her report "on page 18," she said. She looked puzzled when she noticed that I had absolutely no idea what she was referring to.

"Oh I'll email it to you, again, Luke. Please read it this time," she scoffed disappointedly and got into her car and left.

I sighed heavily and wondered, *What happened to our life?*

After parking my car in spot #12, I made my way up to the 666. While the studio was meant to be temporary, it was really all I could afford after the money I'd had to dish out for the divorce. I had filed an appeal but none of that had made a bit of difference, except in my bank account, and keeping me locked in conflict with Vanessa for an extra two years.

She really hates me now.

I plopped down in my favorite chair and opened the email from Vanessa that had arrived on my phone. The woman never wastes time when she has something to throw in my face. It was page 18 from the evaluator's report, and it read:

> We know that children exposed to ongoing conflict and negative information about their parents, *always* have long-term emotional problems. Children who are exposed to ongoing parental conflict and unstable home lives *will* have adjustment problems in their preadolescent and teen years that most commonly manifest in extreme defiance and anger, delinquent behavior, substance abuse, teen pregnancy, eating disorders, suicide attempts, failing grades, and high dropout rates at school. It is one of the only certainties in the professional literature and surely not the legacy these parents wish for Teo and Rae.

Bunch of bologna. We're all doing fine—just fine!

"It's not whether you get knocked down, it's whether you get up."

~Vince Lombardi~

CHOICE 3

GET A DIFFERENT LAWYER

**Time to play a different game—
one that I'm proud of.**

THE LAST NOTE Bulldog had written down for my consideration was: "Your third choice is a rare and unique one for the parents I represent. In fact, I advise against it, but it is my due diligence and ethical responsibility to present a full range of options. If you are interested in pursuing this path, you'll need a different kind of attorney. I'm not your guy."

Really? Wonder how many kinds of attorneys there are?

Curious what in the world Bulldog was talking about, and not really wanting to have to find and pay another retainer for a new attorney, I proceeded to read a typed page that was stapled to all the rest. At the top of this page, it read:

**Gold Star Co-Parenting
Family Law Annual Conference 2018**

This looked like a handout from a professional organization, not Bulldog's original stuff.

Developing an Effective
Co-Parenting Relationship 101

1. At a speed manageable for the children, begin to involve yourself more actively in their daily lives. Respectfully notify the other parent with enough time for her/him to digest that you now plan to attend school events, teacher conferences, and extracurricular activities. Be cautious with the other parent, as she/he is likely to feel suspicious of your motives at first. It is your burden to show her/him and your children that you are genuine in your desire to be more actively involved. You need to help your former spouse and children feel safe, to rebuild trust.

2. Respect her/his boundaries. Schedule separate times for conferences if she/he requests that you do so and sit a distance away from her/him at sports and activities. Schedule private consultations with the children's pediatrician and counselor to introduce yourself and sign up for all online medical, dental, and mental health portals so you have direct access to information in these areas. It will take time and consistency to establish collaborative relationships with professionals who know your children. Be present, be positive, be polite, be respectful, and always mindful of how your newly established presence in these areas impacts the children. Everyone's sense of safety is paramount. This

cannot be stressed enough. Unless everyone first feels safe, this will not work.

3. It is exceptionally important not to engage in adult conversation with the other parent at any time during which the children are present, especially during transitions and at their sports and activities. Actively minimize all opportunity for conflict with the other parent. A child's exposure to verbal (yelling and name calling) and non-verbal (anger, tension, hand gestures, and body language) is detrimental to them and erodes their sense of self-worth. Do not attempt to discuss any sensitive topic with the other parent (the parenting time schedule, grades, medication or health, etc.) when the children are present, even if they are 200 feet away from you on the soccer field. They'll know. They'll be distracted. They'll feel anxious and embarrassed and angry. Each time this happens, they will pull further away from you which leaves them vulnerable and at risk.

These things seem like total common sense. Why would I do anything else?

4. Don't compete with the other parent to win your children's favor at special times of the year, like their birthdays or major holidays, by giving them extraordinary gifts or once-in-a-lifetime experiences such as a brand-new car for their sweet-sixteen or a trip to Disneyland with their

entire class from school. The same is true for
pets. It is unwise to buy your children a puppy
(as a bribe for them to spend time with you),
or any kind of animal, until you are settled in a
permanent residence and the children have had
time to properly adjust.

Oh, come on! A puppy? No one does that. I shook my
head and kept reading.

5. Create new traditions and celebrations with
   your children now that they have a separate
   home with you. Some parents agree to have one
   birthday party for their child and one Christmas
   morning, all together, after the divorce. This
   can be especially challenging after parents re-
   partner, but it can be done. When children sense
   a bridge between their two homes (by seeing
   and experiencing healthy and cooperative
   adult relationships), they receive unspoken
   permission to ebb and flow between their two
   homes in an emotionally comfortable way. This
   is essential to a child's overall health and sense
   of well-being.

*I don't see why we couldn't figure that out sometime in
the future—after all this legal garbage is settled.*

6. Most importantly, demonstrate *flexibility* in
   general, and especially with holidays and
   celebrations, so that special times of the year
   do not become a source of tension and upset
   for your children. Emotional anniversaries

(the yearly experience of emotional trauma) can result when tension, conflict, and upset erupt at otherwise joyful times in a child's life. How parents behave post-dissolution not only impacts their child, but future generations in the family bloodline. What you say and do, and how you behave now, will have an impact on your grand and great-grandchildren in positive or negative ways. Whether it is positive or negative impact is up to you and the choices you make daily.

Wow, my choices have that much power—to impact great-grandchildren?

7. Mediate, Don't Litigate. Get into mediation as soon as possible with the other parent and co-create a parenting time schedule that is best for your children. "Best for your children" may not equate to exactly 50% of their time. It is best that a child's post-dissolution life closely resembles his/her pre-dissolution life. Continuity of care allows a child to properly adjust after this significant disruption in the family system. Quality of time, not quantity, is most vital to the child's comfort, psychological health, and greater sense of well-being. All time belongs to the children—parenting time is the legal right of a child, not his/her parents.

My stomach flip-flopped. Spending any less than half the time with my kids made my heart and everything else hurt.

Kids need their mom and dad equally, and parents should been seen as equally important, influential, and valuable to their children, right? Maybe time does not justify those variables? Maybe my choices do—the way I choose to spend time with Teo and Rae, and what they receive from it? I'll have to chew on that a bit more.

The last bullet point read:

- Be nice to your mother-in-law because the kids love their grandma regardless of how nutty she is and how poorly and unfairly she treats you.

Are you kidding me? I draw the line at being nice to Vanessa's mother. That woman is a total kook and has treated me like the enemy from day one. I have limits.

When I flipped the paper over, there was a whole page of resources: books to read, parenting classes to attend, support groups, communication platforms, and coaches.

In Bulldog's handwriting at the end of the list, it read, "I'll admit that if you do all of this, and Vanessa still asks for a custody evaluation, you are likely to come out on top—to crush your ex by reliably demonstrating all of this child-focused thinking and behavior."

"Kill 'em with kindness," as my own grandmother used to say. I took a deep breath, leaned my head back, and closed my eyes, knowing this was the right path forward.

An uneventful month or two had passed since Bulldog and I had first met. He hadn't given me a phone number to reach him or offered up an email address, but had called me twice to check in, and a few letters had been sent to my apartment address via snail-mail. One of these letters included Vanessa's response to my petition for full custody, which I now know means something entirely different than having the kids live with me full-time and only seeing their mother when I said they could.

Now that I know better, I can do better.

Vanessa and her attorney had more-or-less responded with, "Hell no! The kids are mine, you loser." She'd countered for the same things I had asked for with the do-it-myself, cheap get-divorced online forms. And, she'd asked for a whole lot more with regard to money. Vanessa seemed to understand that custody was about major decision-making, and parenting time was about the time kids spend in each home.

She's always been such a show-off and an over-achiever.

I feared I may have kicked the beehive a little too aggressively and acted in haste right out of the gate, not knowing any better back then. Vanessa's attorney was fierce, and sometimes Bulldog seemed only to be making things more adversarial.

After the last "billing statement" detailing thousands of dollars accrued simply by the attorneys emailing and arguing with each other, with nothing to show for it, I had decided it was time to find a new attorney. I knew that getting this whole mess settled outside of an ugly courtroom trial would be best for all of us, especially Teo and Rae.

After seeking word-of-mouth recommendations for quality attorneys from people I know well and whose opinion I trust, I retained a less expensive though equally experienced legal professional who was focused on helping me salvage my relationship with my children, saving me time and money, and working amicably with Vanessa's attorney. My attitude and outlook seemed far better matched with Paul, my new attorney of record, than it had with Bulldog. I was always in a better mood after talking with Paul, felt hopeful about my family's future, and things seemed to be picking up speed.

Immediately after coming onboard, Paul and Vanessa's attorney agreed that I could go to the house and get my stuff. Vanessa even packed up half of the kitchen so the kids and I would have utensils, cups, and plates to use at the apartment without the unnecessary expense of buying everything new. In fact, she actually gave me everything else I asked for from the house, without a big fight, including my big screen, my grandmother's silverware, and the extra PlayStation with some games. She also offered up some other random things too—mostly the kids' stuff so they could make the apartment feel more like home. This was a really big help for Rae, especially, to have some of her own things. When I asked for it, Vanessa even gave me a flash drive of all our family pictures from the computer. First, I made a picture book for Rae of our best family photos and left it near the bed. Then I printed our best family picture—all of us together with Iggy—and gave a copy to both kids. Teo didn't say much, but I know he carries it in his wallet.

It was strange, but Vanessa and I seem to be getting along better now since I switched attorneys. There have not been any fights or arguments when we transition the kids or see each other at sports and events. We are not exactly on talking terms, and she still pisses me off, but I have learned to walk away when I feel the anger surface, especially when the kids are around. We seem to be on the same page about protecting them from the ugly feelings between us and from all adult matters having to do with the divorce.

I started going to the gym after work and was now attending a men's group that my new attorney had directed me to join. There are some really angry dudes in the group, and some cool-headed guys like me. The group has taught me as much about what not to do, as it has about doing things in the best ways possible to optimize the outcome for Teo and Rae. For example, one guy in the group proclaimed that he had actually filed a motion to settle his divorce case with a sword fight against his soon-to-be ex-wife. "Trial by combat," he told us, "has never been banned or restricted in the United States." He seemed quite serious and did not understand why the rest of us had a good chuckle and then moved on.

My new attorney helped me set my sights on becoming the best divorced-dad possible. He referred me to a "divorce coach" who is like a counselor, only less touchy-feely, and knows a lot about child development and what kids need through their parents' divorce. I took the mandatory parenting class and then a few more online, including Parenting Beyond Conflict, and was surprised by how much I enjoyed them. "A gold star student," one of my teachers had said. I made sure she wrote that down on a piece of her official letterhead just in case I'd need this important observation later for an evaluator, or court, or whatever. I also read some of the suggested books. My favorites were *Joint Custody with a Jerk, People Can't Drive You Crazy if You Don't Give Them the Keys,* and *Loving Your Children More Than You Hate Each Other.* All this fit comfortably into my days as it seemed there was just more free time available since the split.

Vanessa and I attended mediation together and met with a professional gentleman that treated us well. Over several sessions, we worked out the temporary parenting time schedule, which I'm not altogether pleased with, but we follow it for now. We have also managed to create a holiday and special occasion plan for Teo and Rae, too.

The kids' birthdays came and went. We weren't ready for "family" togetherness yet, so we each had separate celebrations with the kids. Teo and Rae didn't seem to mind at all—celebrating their special day twice. Christmas went okay. The kids and I cut down our own tree, and Rae decorated the studio with lights and homemade snowflakes that she taped all over the floor-to-ceiling windows. That was a fun night, with Rae up on my shoulders to reach the top of the tree and Teo in my La-Z-Boy, barking directions, "Little to the left. No, no back to the right."

A couple of comedians, those two.

I was glad they seemed happy most of the time, aside from the usual ups and downs. They moved seamlessly between their two homes and were doing well in most areas of their lives, except Teo could hit the books a little harder. He complained about being distracted in class, thinking about the divorce, and sometimes just feeling sad. Rae was thriving, it seemed. The girl spoke her mind and expressed her feelings as they rolled through. Rae was the rare kind of person who could actually pull herself up by the bootstraps. She loved her counselor, who seemed to help a lot. The two kids sometimes went to counseling sessions together, and other times individually. Vanessa and I were both involved with the therapist, who was a neutral advocate for the kids.

The studio apartment was a great find in many ways, but caused a problem on Monday morning with the heavy traffic out of the city and back to the suburb where Teo and Rae attended school. The kids had been late to school a couple of times, so we started leaving my place at 7:00 a.m. They did not like getting up that early, so most weekends I dropped them off with their mom on Sunday night instead of at school on Monday morning. Our small space was also tricky, since Rae did not have much privacy, which turns out to be a massively big deal for a young girl her age!

Teo seemed to like our new pad alright, although both of them complain about the city and not being around their friends. Each have brought a friend over once or twice, but said it was "weird" and I didn't push. CoCo had kicked Iggy out of the apartment complex as soon as she discovered him—in her office, up on her desk, eating a sandwich she had left there while she was down the hall using the restroom. She said no animals were allowed, per the terms of my lease. So, the Iggster went back to live with the kids and their mom, which made Rae super happy. It had never really occurred to me when I left the house, how upset she had been about me taking the dog. I have since apologized to her a million times, although she keeps bringing it up, "But why, Daddy? Why did you steal Iggy? Why did you take my dog and my favorite blanket? Don't ever do that again."

Guess I'll just keep apologizing until she believes me.

I realized that to spend more time with the kids, I needed to move out of the city and back to the suburb where I could better meet their needs. Even though living closer to work has been great for me, their comfort is my priority. I planned to find a house back in our neighborhood and close to their schools.

I felt like we needed to get this divorce over and done. We had to figure out the final pieces so all of us could move on with our lives. I'd not met anyone new yet. Well, besides CoCo down in the leasing office, who was smoking hot but seemed somewhat uncertain about this middle-aged, well-meaning, almost-divorced man.

I wanted to step up my efforts with Coco, as she never stayed out of my mind for long. I didn't want to grow old alone and, at this rate, it seemed I would reach retirement before we were legally divorced. Guys in the men's group and people in the parenting classes all said to wait on a new relationship until the divorce was final, and the kids were ready for new people to be introduced into their lives, especially if the new someone also had children. I had learned that children whose parents split needed ample time to adjust to all the family change and the layers of grief and loss they experienced. So, I waited, for a lot of things beyond just this divorce process to move forward.

In mediation, Vanessa and I agreed, for now, that Teo and Rae would be with me three weekends in a row. I also saw them every Wednesday night for dinner in the suburb and attend all of their sports and activities throughout the week. We got a lot accomplished in mediation, but were stuck about who would have legal decision-making authority, and I wanted more parenting time with the kids than just three weekends per month. We found ourselves at an impasse. After the fifth session, our mediator told us he could not help any further and suggested we see a custody evaluator to decide about legal custody and the best parenting time schedule for Teo and Rae. He complimented us on our efforts and agreeing to as much as we did and then sent us on our way.

Off to the evaluation, I guess. Wish we could have avoided it.

I pulled out my cell and called the law firm that now represented me. My attorney was tied up with something else, so his paralegal took the call. We talked about what a custody evaluation involved. She mentioned a few different professionals with whom their firm was familiar and encouraged me to do some research on my own and see who felt like a good fit for our family. She told me to call back after I took time to look over the different evaluators' webpages and then to talk directly with Paul.

How can a guy know who is a "good fit" from looking at a webpage?

Online reviews for evaluators seemed bad when I Googled them, which didn't sit well with me. One of the evaluators on the recommended list had a tab on her webpage that addressed the negative reviews. This was helpful and made me feel a little better about things. She also had a comprehensive site with all sorts of valuable information, including her pricing and lots of divorce resources, and I could tell she was child-focused in her work with families. Everything was geared toward the children. There was even an office tour and "what to tell your children" page. She had even written a book!

I called the firm, certain in my decision about the professional I wanted to conduct our family evaluation. Paul told me that was good news, because the other side had requested the same evaluator. He explained that a stipulated order would be prepared, appointing this evaluator to work with our family, then the court would sign the order and we would be on our way.

The evaluation process was less intense than I had imagined, and the evaluator was great. It took about twelve weeks from start to finish, and I was feeling confident in the parent I had always been to Teo and Rae but particularly proud of how I had handled things since I'd met Paul and taken all of his advice. My relationship with the kids was better and stronger than ever.

I'd put together a little notebook for the evaluator with photos of the kids, their report cards, and some cool stuff they had made over the years including notes from Rae.

Love you daddy XOXOXOXXOXO

You are the best daddy ever daddy (HEART HEART HEART)

Olive juice daddy!!!!!!!!!!!!!!!

That last one was our little thing—the way "I love you" came out when Rae was little and learning to talk. It had stuck. *I imagine we'll say it forever.*

The evaluator gave me big kudos for all the personal work I had done since the split. She recommended that since Vanessa had been the stay-at-home, primary parent all along and had made major decisions for the children throughout our marriage, it simply made the most sense that she continued in this role. Our evaluator made it clear that one parent was not "better" than the other and that children needed the balance of what their mom and dad could offer. She emphasized that neither mother nor father were winners in this process. Teo and Rae were the only ones afforded the right to win, and would do just that, if Vanessa and I stayed on the positive trajectory we had already established.

Just after the evaluation got started, my lease ran its course, and I moved from the city and my tiny studio apartment back to the suburb where I rented a house just down the street from our family home—where Teo and Rae still live with their mom. Both of us were only two miles away from Teo and Rae's school, and the kids could walk or bike or eventually drive between their two homes. We practiced lots of flexibility and grace with one another and understood that it was not my time or her time—all time belonged to our children. The kids had keys to both of their homes and were welcome anytime. We followed the golden rules of *respect* and *kindness*, and everything else seemed to flow more easily as a result.

Let me be absolutely clear—this did not mean that Vanessa and I always liked one another or that we agreed on everything.

That would require a magic wand.

But we did the very best we could with what we had and continued to learn more so we could always keep doing better and make the best decisions possible for our kids.

Rae brought Iggy with her when she transitioned between homes, which seemed to make everything better for her. Because we lived close to one another, were communicating amicably, were both involved with their education, health, and counseling in supportive ways, and behaved at public events like sports and activities, the evaluator recommended a 50-50 parenting time schedule. Teo and Rae were going to live one week with me and then one week with their mother year-round. I could not be more thrilled.

Finally a voice of reason! This felt like justice for our kids!

The evaluator's recommendations were then incorporated into a stipulated dissolution judgment, with which the two attorneys took their sweet time arguing over every little word, for what seemed like an eternity, until they sent it off to the court for a judge's approval and signature. We never actually saw a judge or had to go through a courtroom trial, having worked it out with our initial efforts in mediation and then with the evaluator's recommendations and our attorneys' seasoned legal skills.

It was a triumphant feeling knowing Vanessa's opinion of me has shifted from being a "total disappointment" to a damn good co-parent. I had better insight to the man I was and had become to our children and, most profoundly, my part in the problems that had developed within the marriage. I had vowed to not repeat any of the old patterns and have lots of new resources and supportive people to inform my choices going forward.

While Vanessa still had her share of shortcomings and knew how to get under my skin, I rested easy knowing she is a great mom, and the kids are best served by having both of us in their lives. I was okay with their mother orchestrating all of their appointments and such. She was more organized than me and always on that laptop computer, doing her research, scheduling stuff, and signing up for this that and the other thing. The woman loves calendars and sticky notes and reminder messages and bleach!

She can have all that—it just leaves more time for the kids and me to have fun.

And, I am even cordial with Vanessa's mother, at least whenever I see her in person. For my kids, even climbing the equivalent of Mt. Everest is possible.

It seems like Teo and Rae adjusted to the divorce more quickly than Vanessa or I did. Rae wrote a note inside a Christmas card right before our dissolution was final. It read:

Dear dad you are the BEST daddy ever, and I love love love you to the moon and back. Thank you for moving out of the city and making my new bedroom so cool. Having Iggy with me all the time is the best gift and he likes the parenting time schedule too. It is awesome you come to my dance competitions now and gave me flowers last time. I liked the field trip we did together right before xmas. My teacher thinks you're the coolest dad ever and the kids like you too.

xoxoxoxoxoxoxoxox Olive juice—your best girl Rae.

That kid brings a grown man to his knees. I could not be more proud of her!

Teo was keeping A's and B's in school, and he mostly had all good friends. There were a couple of shady teenagers in the group, but Teo has a good head on his shoulders. He was becoming a more skilled basketball player all the time, and I took him to specialized clinics and skills training at his private club. He had a personal trainer and lifts weights with me at the gym, and we've got a hoop out in the driveway. In fact, I made him a bet: As soon as he could beat me, one-on-one, I would pay him $100. The kid got his cash last summer. He was more determined than ever to get a college scholarship.

During the weeks at his mom's house, Teo logs on and plays NBA 2K20 with me. He usually beats me, but anytime with my son was time well spent. Our last chat went like this:

RimRocker12: "hey dad wanna play"

KewlestDad: "yah bud give me a sec"

RimRocker 12: "ill be at the open court"

KewlestDad: "meet yah there"

RimRocker 12: "whats taking so long"

KewlestDad: "geez hang on ok I'm ready now"

RimRocker 12: "did mom tell you"

KewlestDad: "tell me what is everything ok"

RimRocker 12: "won an award at school for being the best ambassador"

KewlestDad: "what does that mean"

RimRocker 12: "like the best leadership award in the whole middle school theres a ceremony on friday in the auditorium are you coming"

KewlestDad: "YES im coming I would not miss it son I'm so proud of you and I see a text here about it from your mom ill be there for sure, cannot wait!"

RimRocker 12: "thanks dad moms calling me for dinner play later"

KewlestDad: "anytime kid, anything you need im right here for you"

Twenty Years Later

I could hear Rae screaming her head off in the adjacent birthing room at a pitch like I'd never heard any first-time mother sing before. It seemed best to keep my distance for the moment, so I waited out in the hallway with everyone else who was there to welcome my new grandson into the world. I decided to grab a coffee from the vending machine and got one for Jack, Vanessa's husband, who had become a good friend over the years. Vanessa was with Rae on the other side of the door, along with Rae's husband.

Teo and his wife and two kids were milling around, the kids bored, tired, and hungry. My son was an awesome dad, and he married the sweetest gal. They appeared to have it all together—their little family of four. He'd ended up playing college ball, and met his wife on campus. My mother sat in a chair with the rest of us in the waiting area, directing traffic and bossing everyone around in that curt tone of hers that had gotten worse over the years. Vanessa's mom had passed two years before, and Rae had given the eulogy at her funeral. I was glad for the close bond they had been able to share.

Suddenly, I heard Rae's voice yell out, "Get the doctor, Mom! It's go time. Let's get this show on the road already!" My spicy Rae knew how to make people move.

Vanessa ran out of the birthing room, yelling for the doctor, and offered an update to those of us standing around, "Any minute now!"

A grandpa again! Number three is on his way!

An hour later, we were all standing around Rae's hospital bed, gazing at perfect baby Ezra snuggled up in her arms. Teo's toddler was fast asleep on his daddy's shoulder, and his wife held their five-year-old daughter's hand as she looked lovingly up at her favorite auntie and new infant cousin.

I kissed Rae's cheek and then baby Ezra's. "Olive juice, baby girl," I whispered to Rae. She mouthed the same back to me, overcome with hormones and emotions and lots of tears. I moved aside so CoCo could step in and offer her blessings. Yup, the same CoCo that played hard to get—the smoking hot leasing agent from my first little studio apartment downtown. Turns out she was married when we first met but we reconnected years later and fell madly in love. We celebrated our fifteen-year anniversary just a week before. Though she doesn't have children of her own, she has been the best stepmom and "Greba" to our grandkids—the name Teo's oldest gave her, and it stuck.

Waterworks for everyone today. I wiped tears of joy and gratitude from my own face.

My mother had fallen asleep in a corner chair after having a quick peek at the baby and declaring, "All newborns look like Winston Churchill to me. Good luck with that one, kid!" At least Mom always kept it real.

I saw Rae was having a moment with Vanessa, and Jack was there, too; so, I kept my distance and marveled at all the love in this one room. Vanessa could not have chosen a better husband to help raise our children. He was an honorable, hardworking man, and had one son who the kids had grown to love. He was away at college but would be arriving in a few days to meet the newest member of our family.

Teo noticed I was emotional and leaned in for a hug. "Love you, Dad," he offered. "Look what you and Mom did—all of this, all of us, here together like we should be, one big happy family. I mean we're a little different from some, I suppose, but we're all happy and thriving and we made it work."

Sure did, kid. We sure did. I squeezed him and choked back more tears.

With that, I instinctively walked over to Vanessa and put my arm around her shoulder. We stood side-by-side, smiling softly and victorious, fulfilled by the choices we had made over all these years to co-parent with flexibility and grace and raise our children in two loving and stable homes. We had both attended birthday parties and holidays, just like Bulldog had told me only an elite few divorced parents ever choose to do.

We went to school conferences together, and chatted at practices, basketball games, dance recitals, choir concerts, band concerts, and their high school graduations. We were both invited to Teo and Rae's college graduation ceremonies, their weddings, the birth of our first two grandchildren, and now Ezra's big day. I cannot imagine there was any more a dad and a mom could ask or want for their family.

Soon, it was obvious that Rae needed to sleep. She and her husband needed time alone without all of us hovering. CoCo and I collected our things, including my mother. We gave a round of hugs and kisses and headed for home.

That night, CoCo was very busy cleaning and organizing—a favorite pastime for my wife. I heard her messing around in a back closet, shuffling boxes or something.

"Babe, come in here and watch a show with me. The game is over," I called out from the living room couch. Iggy III was sound asleep and snoring like a champ at my feet. Rae had asked that we take care of him while she and her family were at the hospital.

Love me some Iggy time!

Coco appeared in front of me, wearing a pair of plaid pajama pants and one of my old t-shirts that hung just right on her sexy frame. She was still every bit of a looker, a goddess like none else I had ever seen.

"Luke, look what I found." She handed me a piece of paper, worn and torn at the edges.

Before I finished unfolding the paper, I knew exactly what it was and paused, not sure I was ready to shed any more tears today.

"Oh, go on, you big baby. Just open it already!" she encouraged me.

This was a note, more than a note really—this was a declaration from Teo and Rae. It was written with the help of their counselor as they prepared to terminate services a year after our divorce was final. CoCo sat down beside me and snuggled in.

I took a deep breath, knowing these words would hit hard as they had before, without fail.

I opened the letter they wrote to us all those years ago—affirmation that through the chaos and all the uncertainties of divorce, our good choices and positive attitudes made all the difference for our family, for our children to be able to thrive.

Dear Mom and Dad:

We think you guys need to hear a few things from us and we hope not to get ourselves into trouble by sharing too much, right from our hearts. We do not plan to sugarcoat this, so buckle up, buttercups! Our feelings are bigger than us, probably even bigger than you two, and they matter in this mess you guys created and call a divorce. We know we are just kids and don't have adult rights and all that blah blah blah. But stay with us and hear this out. Here it goes......

We (your children, Teo and Rae—well I'm the one writing all this of course, but Teo's here with me and the counselor too). I'll start again. We really wish your marriage had worked out and sometimes think you might get back together, but also know that without a magic wand, that is not going to happen. We don't have a magic wand, so we're stuck. We get it. This is our new life. We know kids don't get to decide where they live and that you're the parents and we need to do what you say. And we are glad that you ask us what we think and we are even more glad that you never ask us to choose. We love both of you and could never choose between you. Thank you for finding our counselor, she has taught us all this stuff!

Kids are loving humans by nature. This is a known fact. Ask Siri if you must, or Google it. We want to love others and feel loved by others all the time, every day. It's really that simple. Love is super-duper important during our kidhoods. Please don't ever tell us who we are supposed to love or not love or be loved by or not loved by. Please stop saying bad things about the people we love and who love us, even our grandmas, who we think rock! And, especially nothing bad or awful about each other!!! When you do, we take it personally and end up feeling bad about ourselves. If there is one thing to change, this is it. Just stop! Just be kind! Or say nothing!

What's "fair" to us and what's fair to you are probably very different things, but when everyone is using this word all the time, it kinda starts to seem important. So we tell you what you want to hear because we love you and don't want to hurt your feelings. In fact we don't want to hurt anyone's feelings or rock the boat even a little bit, so we just tell everyone what they want to hear, even when it's not what we actually think or want, and usually at the expense of our own happiness a lot of the time. Life is not fair. You two taught us that, and it's time to take your own good advice.

We feel best, safest, and most secure when you make decisions together about us. We don't want to hear about judges or attorneys ever again. The evaluation lady you took us to see was ~~kick-ass~~. Oops Teo says I cannot write that word because he wants the word "amazeballs" instead to describe her. Okay, whatever. She was cool but still, we never want to see her again. It's so super simple you two just be kind and act right like the adults you are supposed to be.

We love stuff, that's the total truth. But don't buy our love. We already love you, especially when you are being kind and respectful to us, and to each other, and to everyone else. We are smart kids, smarter than you realize, and will milk you for every penny you've got if you start in with the whole Disneyland Dad and

Mastercard Mom thing. We Googled it. We know what goes on out there.

This divorce stuff really sucks. We feel sad and mad mostly, but other big emotions come and go, too. We need to know that you will not leave us, never—ever—ever, even when we act like the little turkeys our grandmas say we are. Teo says not to write that and get our grandmas into trouble but whatever, both of them say it, all the time. The point is, we need time to deal with so much change, and we might act out and get ourselves in a little trouble at home or at school. We need you on our team, both of you, and need our schools to stay a safe place where you two act cool and don't tell everyone about your stupid divorce. School is off limits for all bad behavior, and so are basketball games and dance recitals, too. Just don't mention the divorce—no gossiping, okay? Let's just still be a family the best we can now, even though we look totally different.

On to the subject of dating. Eewwwwh gross! We do not want to see either of you kissing or holding hands with anyone else, at least not yet. We need time to work through having two homes and do not want to share either home

or either of you with anyone new. Especially
if they have kids who will get into our things.
Please just focus your attention on us, your
kids, for a while anyway, before we have to
share you. We want both of you to be happy
again, even if that means stepparents down
the road WAY down the road, pretty please
with sugar on top and a cherry, and sprinkles
for mom!

Well we guess that's about it for now. Good
talk. We love you to the moon.

Love, Teo and Rae

XOXOXOXOXOX

"Compassion, grace, kindness, and respect," CoCo whispered while running her fingers through my hair. "The foundation that supported the choices you and Vanessa made all these years, even though it was hard—choices to act, think, and conduct yourselves in a thoughtful way even when you didn't want to. You two made it so easy for me and Jack to integrate into the compassionate culture your choices created."

I realized that was it—the simple summary of why a day like today was possible. Everything hinged on choices, mine and Vanessa.

Choose well, friends. Take the high road, even when it seems impossible. Compassion, grace, kindness, and respect are not always our first instinct. It takes training, time, repetition, and an intention to develop these winning ingredients that are key to coming out on top in everything you do, especially as a parent. Your children and their children's legacies are worth it. Of this, and maybe only this one thing, I am absolutely certain.

Luke

Remember, a list of Hints, Hacks, and Hell-No's can be found at the back of the book for a quick reference.

"Authenticity is a collection of choices that we have to make every day. It's about the choice to show up and be real. The choice to be honest. The choice to let our true selves be seen."

~*Brené Brown, Ph.D. LMSW, author of The Gifts of Imperfection*~

A WORD FROM LORI

(the person who is a lot like you)

AS A CUSTODY evaluator, I make a concerted effort not to lecture or tell parents what to do. Rather, I endeavor to provide a roadmap by which families can find their own path and choose their own best outcome. I walk alongside the whole family system as a temporary teammate while reminding parents that they are indeed still a team—still a family, their child's family forevermore. They are simply organizing differently now.

This effective approach was developed over many years because I *know* life is ridiculously complicated. I am a wife, a mom, and a volunteer at school. I attend every game/event/ conference, and I plan extravagant birthday parties, the turkey dinners, and visits from Santa, The Easter Bunny, the Naughty Leprechaun, and St. Valentine. I am the chef, housecleaner, chauffer, as well as the daughter of aging parents, a sister, a friend to people in every corner of the country, and a business owner who juggles more responsibilities than can fit into the finite hours of a day. And, like most of you reading this, I also know what it's like to suffer a major disruption in my own family system and to stare down the looming possibility of divorce.

I'm going to let you in on a little secret: Characters in books do not just appear out of thin air. They are the voices of the authors' hidden archetypes—parts of ourselves that we mask and hide from the world to maintain the public images we deem important. It takes a beat for a first-time author to realize this. For quite a while, I really thought I was creating characters representing the most common attributes of the thousands of clients I've served. But Vanessa, in particular, in all of her bumbling, bleach-loving, cannot-quite-get-my-shit-together-but-damnit-if-I-am-not going-to-persevere-gloriously... She's my girl! Luke is, of course, a conglomeration of all the important men who have influenced my life, and Teo and Rea both have many attributes of my own children.

Fortunately for me, I have been doing this work long enough—and have extensive book and real-world knowledge and training—that when my own family system flipped upside-down, I was able to avoid the terrible mistakes you saw Vanessa (and Luke) make. However, the essence of the woman who is Vanessa— undone by the crisis and potential dissolution of her marriage, terrified about the total impact on her children—she is indeed a voice that is a part of me, of who I am, and how I might act if I did not know better. It took me three full years of writing and sessions with a therapist who sees therapists to sort through all of this and realize the depth of healing and repair that was possible for me, and my family, through the authoring of this book and the choices that emerged before me as I continued to write.

There are essentially six choices offered in this book, but at the core of every possible next step is the choice to put your children's well-being at the center of every decision and behavior.

I know you are tired and exhausted by the many roles you play, especially as parents "fighting" for their children within the financially—and emotionally-draining process of litigation. I know that right under your exhaustion are deep reservoirs of hurt, fear, disappointment, rejection, grief, sadness, and even rage. I know how difficult it is to not throw the person you feel is responsible for this pain and suffering in front of a bus, let alone *under* the proverbial bus when you want to talk negatively about them around or directly to your children. I know it seems impossible sometimes to hold your tongue, but I urge you to bite down on that sucker until you taste blood in those moments. I also urge you to believe that you have the power to preserve and even improve your children's and your own well-being through this process. This journey is rich with opportunities for healing, clarity, growth, and repair; and all family members can emerge on the other side... better.

Fifty years navigating life's unpredictable circumstances was anchored for me while I was listening to a powerful message delivered by Rev. Gregory J. Boyles, S.J. (Homeboy Industries). His affirming words caused me to rest firmly in knowing that, "Only the soul who ventilates the world with tenderness has any real chance of changing it." Amen Reverend, Amen.

And so, I do, even when I don't want to. And there are plenty of those days. But with resolute intention, I rest firmly and choose to show up with tenderness and lead with compassion in all arenas of my life, both personal and professional. In my life's darkest moments, I learned the all-important lesson that courage is *not* a feeling; courage is a choice, available to everyone, right now, right where we are, regardless of whatever's staring us down and whatever demons we need to face. I know now more than ever, through the experience of authoring this book, that it takes gallons of courage and a wholehearted commitment to show up as the best, truest, most vulnerable version of ourselves. And I also know that in doing so, the best of ourselves becomes accessible to everyone else, including our children; and we all grow better, together.

Quite a few people have asked me how the idea for *You Don't Have to Crush Your Ex* came about. The truth is, the idea of writing a book had called to me since age seven, when I submitted a short story to a contest at the local summertime fair. In that moment, forty-two years ago, a conscious decision was made to author a book one day. What book was never clear. Not the topic or purpose or the impact I'd wanted my message to make on any particular audience. I simply wanted to write a book, put my name on the front cover, and have a tangible legacy that would collect dust on bookstore shelves, mostly to satisfy my ego and say, "I did it."

Fast forward to today, and I'm steeped in pride to know that I did it—I created a book that will do a lot more than just collect dust. My ego is satisfied, and I'm confident that my message leads with a tenderness, kindness, and compassion for parents and for children, hopefully inspiring the awareness that we really are all just walking each other home. (Thank you, Ram Dass.) I am beyond grateful for the privilege of being a trusted child advocate in my community, and for the opportunity to minister as a professional who cares deeply about preserving the fabric of the entire family system. I sit here today, settled and at peace with the best version of me that I have become to date (knowing there's always more work to do!) as a result of laboring through my own story in the process of getting this message onto the page for you. It was a wild ride, and I know it was my foundational values that kept me grounded and connected to all the right allies of support through the messy middle. The same opportunity is available to you.

I think of divorce in this symbolic way: family law litigation is like a big old running race—a marathon, really. You know the banner of the finish line waves magnificently up ahead someplace; but there is a lot of congestion and a lot of unknowns between you and it, especially if you are anything like me and your pace group is at the way back with the strollers and the dogs and the street-sweepers close on my heels. So, you hunker down and find a comfortable rhythm, smile at the people around you, and make a couple of new friends. You keep moving forward, one foot in front of the other, pushing through the layers of pain as you round each next corner, but feeling steady in your running shoes (i.e., your foundational values)—the one reliable measure in your absolute control that keeps you upright. Even when people step on your toes, callously bump you, stomp on your foot, or make a snarky comment about your (outfit, hair, pace, first gen iPod) while running their own race, your values will sustain you. I urge you to remember, in those exceedingly frustrating (and sometimes rage-filled) moments, that the people behaving this way do not have the right shoes and have not yet gained the knowledge being delivered to you right now. In those intense moments, when you become emotionally flooded, take a beat, breathe, and center so you can respond instead of react.

Foundational values are the secret sauce that will keep you moving toward the finish line—to keep you from reversing course and choosing a path backward toward an unfavorable destination that leads to a dead end... or worse. You and your family, especially your children, are now moving toward the beginning of many new adventures—new life experiences just on the other side of that finish line banner. Two gifts of divorce, if you are open to receiving them, are growth and time. Embracing both will aid in your quest to figure out what foundational values you want to rest firmly on—the ones you will choose to define the person you are now, and are free to become, absent whatever chaos brought you to the decision of divorce.

> If you want support in declaring what your foundational values are right now, so you can consistently act the like person you want to be and become. Check out the Resources on page 473.

Each of us gets to decide who we are right now, today, and every new day after. Once we show up consistently as the person we choose to be, life becomes a whole lot easier. No one else gets to make that decision for, or take that decision away from, you. Choose wisely because…

The choices we make, really do make us!

Time is fleeting. Your children are getting older—and watching and growing and learning from your example. You have the power and agency to choose wisely on all fronts.

The words *Battle, Fight, Conflict,* and *Win* are contraindicated to a child's *best interest*; and, if you or your attorney are using them in the same sentence, stop, consider, and think with a clearer mind. The Hints, Hacks, and Hell-No's in this book are the keys to prevailing in an evaluation, and they are so simple; but simple is not always easy. Choosing to lead with the foundational values that define the best version of you will ensure that you finish the race in good standing, regardless of how the participants around you run theirs.

In understanding that another person's behavior has more to do with their own struggle than with you, grace is truly understood.

My hope is that you find your authentic (badass, glorious, vulnerable, worth celebrating) self along this beautiful journey and that each and every one of you loves what you find. It helps to understand that there are no "ends" in life, except for our universal final curtain call—just places we arrive, which are starting lines, choices, and magical opportunities for taking the next best step toward a better tomorrow in which you and your children will thrive.

Cheers to child-focused choices, sprinkles on Fro-Yo, and everything good that awaits!

—*Lori*

P.S. You are invited to read my personal story about the magical way life unfolded during the three years of authoring *You Don't Have to Crush Your Ex*. My story is captured in one chapter of a collaborative book with other authors who similarly transformed their own lives while delivering powerful messages intended for the benefit of others. The book is titled *You Cannot Make This St*ry Up*.

VANESSA'S HINTS, HACKS & HELL-NO'S

Vanessa | Setup | How the Heck Did We End Up Here?

Hint   Hack   Hell-No

Learn how to breathe consciously.

You are the only one who can "save" your kids. Hold onto your power as their parent. Your attorney works for you. You are the boss, and they are your guide through the process.

Do NOT rely on internet reviews of evaluators. (They are universally terrible.) Instead, ask around in the legal community and call the evaluator's professional licensing board.

Vanessa | Choice 1 | Prove He's an Idiot

Your child needs a sober advocate during this process, not an inebriated grizzly bear out for the blood of her mate.

Do NOT try to make your co-parent pay for any of their misdeeds. Making them pay is not your responsibility; and inevitably, your children will suffer the cost.

An evaluation report is a legal document. Legal documents should never be shared with children.

Do NOT diagnose your co-parent. Stop using diagnostic language altogether unless a professional, who your co-parent has seen, has provided the diagnosis. Even then, remember that people are not their diagnosis; they are people and, in this case, your child's other parent.

Focus on winning the war that matters—the long-term health, safety, welfare, and best interest of your child. That war cannot be won through destroying their other parent.

You *can* figure out the technology! Using a Dropbox account is super simple, and you need to get over this hump and create one before the evaluation begins.

Do NOT bring heaps and heaps of "proof" to your custody evaluation in hopes of making your co-parent look terrible. Preparing in this way says far more to the evaluator about *you* than your co-parent.

Do NOT coach your child on what to say (and not say) during the evaluation. It is harmful to them, and the evaluator will know. This will hurt your case, and children, BIG TIME because coaching is in the category of psychological abuse.

- Your evaluator will NOT be excited to see your heaps and heaps of unnecessary documentation.

- You and your co-parent are the only two people who hold the cards to your child's future.

- Conflict harms children. Reducing or eliminating conflict on your end is the best bubble-wrap you can encase your child in during this wild ride.

- Prepare a timeline of significant family events prior your first evaluation meeting.

- Know in advance of your first meeting what information the evaluator wants and will accept, and by what means of delivery is preferable. It's likely a Dropbox and never ever a suitcase.

- Listen to your gut. Always, always, always listen to your gut and make adjustments.

- Don't play the blame game. When you point a finger at someone else, there are three pointed back at you!

- Blame is the way that we redistribute our own anger and pain. Secure a counselor and get to work on yourself. It's the only way to "win" anything in this life.

- Install parental control software—Covenant Eyes, Circle Home Plus, Qustodio, Kaspersky Safe Kids, Locategy.

- Consistently showing up as your best self, and apologizing when you make a mistake is how you get into (and stay) in your child's good-graces.

- Always get sprinkles!

- Non-verbal language and unspoken attitudes speak louder than words.

- Do not disparage, talk negatively about, or in any way diminish the love and affection your child has for their other parent. This always hurts children and *will* backfire on you.

- When the floodgates on your child's mouth open, listen. You have two ears and one mouth—use them proportionately.

- Do not take the bait. If you defend yourself with "Mom said" or "Dad said," your child is cemented in the middle, which is detrimental to their psychological well-being.

- Journaling is useful IF you include a balance of your actions, reactions, and errors, too.

Be prepared to explain why your proposed parenting schedule is best for your child, not for you or because it's what you want. Explain why it is best for them.

An angry, shutdown, increasingly defiant teenager is a red flag. Get professional help sooner than later.

Do NOT interrogate your child after their evaluation meeting. This kind of psychological warfare is abusive and does nothing to foster trust with your child.

Time is a gift of divorce. Use it wisely and take care of yourself.

Children share things between homes when they feel safe. If they are shut down, they do not feel safe...with you.

We alone are responsible for the thinking, conduct, and behavior that drive and demonstrate our choices.

The best way to take your power back is to fix yourself—the parts that are wounded and bleeding. Heal the wounds before they fester. Only you can do that for yourself, and getting therapeutic support is a really good idea.

Do NOT monitor or restrict your child's conversations with their other parent.

Who your co-parent is to you, is not the same as who your child's other parent is to them. It is essential to separate your experience (your hurts) from those of your child.

Truth, in this experience, is subjective. Children will develop their own version of it.

If you have an attitude of "fighting a battle," your child has already lost.

You are the bus!

Listen to the judge and follow all of their orders.

Do NOT ignore the judge's orders and continue on a destructive path.

Vanessa | Choice 2 | Get Happy Again

Decisions made under the influence of any intoxicant are rarely, if ever, good decisions.

Get a good night sleep the night before your evaluation meetings. This is not the time to blow off steam with the substance of your choosing.

Neighbors will always see someone falling out a window at 5:00 a.m.

Mouth wash, gum, mints, and any amount of cologne/perfume will not cover the smell of alcohol or THC. The evaluator will make note immediately. This is a deal-breaker.

It's okay to cry here and there during your session, even if your attorney told you not to. It shows you are human. Crying the entire session, however, and not being able to keep some composure during the session suggests to the evaluator there may be something more clinical or pathological going on. Get help for symptoms of depression and anxiety prior the evaluation.

Parents who understand their child's basic need for a connected and ongoing relationship with their other parent (not the enemy) come out on top!

Do NOT use substances to calm your nerves or numb your pain. An evaluator will know when you are pharmaceutically-influenced.

Do NOT start a new relationship until you end the one you are in (with a dissolution judgment). Never, ever, ever start a new relationship while approaching a custody evaluation.

- Children almost always know more than you think (even if they are very young), and understand what is going on long before you tell them so.

- It is never too early to start a *developmentally-appropriate* discussion about the dangers of alcohol, drugs, cigarettes/vape, and porn.

- School must remain a safe haven for children during their parents' divorce. Protecting this space for your child is some of the best bubble wrap you can offer.

- School attendance and on-time arrival are very important in your custody evaluation—because they are *very* important to the welfare and success of your child (and all the other children yours attends class with, too).

- Never, never, never start a sentence with "your mother..." or "your father..." It lands as accusatory, hateful, and shaming to your child.

- Do NOT leave anything related to your legal case laying around or in any way accessible to your child, including electronic files on your device. Lock it all up.

- If you think you might have a substance dependance problem, or if someone who loves you has suggested you might, voluntarily

participate in a substance dependance
evaluation prior the evaluation. You'll likely be
sent to one anyway; and having that information
beforehand and getting started on the path
to recovery prior the evaluation will put
huge brownie points in your column for the
evaluation and the best interest of your child.

A DUII, especially if a child is in the car, is a total
and complete deal-breaker during an evaluation.
(It happens more than you might think.)

Well-adjusted children who thrive following
their parents' divorce feel like they have
two homes. They do not feel like "visitors"
with either of their parents or in either of
their homes.

Introducing children to a new partner before
you have a dissolution judgment is a mistake.
Wait to introduce any one new for at least
one year post-judgment, and not until you are
certain about the possibility of a long-term
commitment from that person. Vet new partners
carefully and run a background check (your
attorney can help). Absolutely no sex offenders
(regardless of how innocent their story seems),
no felons, and no one that is still married.

Children are not nearly as interested in your new relationships as you are. Dating with children has far greater consequences than dating as a single person. Use extreme caution.

If a kinetic family drawing is offered, allow and encourage your child to include members of their whole family on both sides with everyone, including parents/grandparents/other family members. Do the same in real life, too!

It takes two to tango. Taking responsibility for your part is key to winning your child custody evaluation. Admit your mistakes before the other parent points them out.

"Scared straight" is not a protective practice for your child during this process.

Do NOT dig, interrogate, interview, coerce, or otherwise railroad your child for information they are not willing and comfortable sharing with you.

When your child stops sharing, it is most likely an indication that they do not feel safe to do so...... with *you*.

Children are brutally honest and will tell the evaluator like it is, even if you told them not to. They will rat you out *and* will also show the evaluator every closet in your home with all the skeletons (stashes of booze and personal items) kept in there, too.

Always give your child the space they request to speak privately with the evaluator.

Do NOT give your dog (cat, bird, rodent, snake, fish) beer! *No animals were harmed in the telling of this story.*

Evaluators love animals, and how you treat them matters. Animal abuse in the home is highly-correlated with child abuse in the home.

Do NOT introduce a new partner until your dissolution judgment is signed. Your children will feel rejected and abandoned if you discard their pain for your own pleasure. You must remain the disciplinarian of your child, not allowing a new partner to assume this role before there is a bonded and mutual trusting relationship, which takes years and years to develop.

Read the evaluation, react, and then rest. Read it again. Discuss it with your legal representative. Read it again. Cry/scream/externalize (not in front of your children). Read it again. Cycle through the process of grief (denial, guilt, bargaining, sadness, acceptance). Read it again. Respond by taking responsibility first.

Do NOT lie—never, ever, ever, for any reason—to your attorney, an evaluator, a law enforcement officer, a child protection caseworker, or a judge. This will backfire and be "Game Over."

Truth, in this experience, is subjective. Children will develop their own version of it.

Eliminate the words "my child" from your vocabulary. Do not say or write these words anyplace during an evaluation or while testifying in court. Children are not possessions and they do not "belong" to you or the other parent.

Listen to the judge and follow all of their orders.

Do NOT ignore the judge's orders and continue on a destructive path.

Vanessa | Choice 3 | Be the Better Parent

Always check out the evaluator's webpage and prepare as they suggest (if it's available). If your evaluator does not have a webpage or preparation suggestions, consult your attorney and visit childfocused.net for some ideas about how to get started.

You are powerful and have exactly what your child needs to come through this in good shape and ready to thrive on the other side.

You are going to be alright. Believing this takes practice. Keep telling yourself so.

The "friendly parent statute" is one on which evaluators place a lot of value. Which parent has the capacity to facilitate and encourage a close and continuing relationship between the other parent and the child? Conflict harms children and sheltering children from conflict by facilitating and encouraging a close and continuing relationship with their other parent is a gold star parent quality.

In the darkest valleys, all things of majesty are born. Through suffering, we have opportunities to grow by seeing things through a new lens or in a new light.

- Read these books: *Joint Custody with a Jerk, People Can't Drive You Crazy If You Don't Give Them the Keys,* and *Loving Your Children More Than You Hate Each Other.*

- It will serve you well to bite your tongue.

- Wear your "advocate" hat. The very best way to take care of your child through this process is to: identify their needs, express your concern with examples of how or why that need is not being met by their other parent, and present solutions.

- Research the evaluators in your area and find the best fit for your family. Ask around, talk to your attorney, call their licensing board, and get familiar with their webpage.

- Evaluators hear and assess the concerns of both parents, understand the complexities of the family system, and offer recommendations to best fit the child's needs within the strengths and limitations of each parent. Evaluators make recommendations, which are not binding.

- Your child needs you to take care of their parents. Hold onto all the good qualities that first drew you to the other parent. You cannot fake "good" in the eyes of your child, and you cannot love your child completely if you hold contempt for their other parent.

- While your story with the other parent is important, the focus of the evaluation is your child. Make sure they are at the center of every concern you express. For example, instead of calling your co-parent an ass, identify the areas of the child's life where your co-parent's ass-like behavior impacts the welfare and well-being of your child. Connect the dots!

- Be ready to offer positive attributes of the other parent. Then leave the words alone. Do not immediately qualify them with "but that's a double edge sword" or "but then he/she does this other thing to negate that good thing."

- Children need one safe parent to thrive. Commit to being that parent.

- Tell your child you love them all the time. Children instinctively blame themselves. They cannot hear enough times that both parents love them, and that neither mom or dad is going anyplace. I personally tell my kids they are "stuck" with me, forevermore—that I will follow and stalk them until death parts us.

- Monitor and educate the people who are around your child about the impact of their words, opinions, and beliefs, so they can be a support to your child and not accidently inflict harm because they do not know better.

Establish traditions and transition routines. Transitions are *never* times for adult discussions. Children make thousands of transitions between homes post-dissolution, and handling these times sensitively is critical.

Misery does not only love company, it demands it. Steer clear of the that mess.

If the evaluator suggests a meeting time that interrupts a child's routine with school, activities, or a birthday party, *ask for a different meeting option.* You'll get big brownie points for putting your child's needs and interests first. Meeting with a child when they want to be someplace else is not helpful to the process anyway.

Children sharing freely about both parents, while with both parents, is the biggest indicator of their proper adjustment between homes *and* their parents' capacity to shelter them from negative opinions and harmful badmouthing. Aim for this gold star standard.

It is not "my time" and "your time." All time belongs to the child. While impromptu changes to the schedule are discouraged, agreeing in the moment is exerting your power to protect your child from conflict. Allow the ice cream and discuss the problem later.

- Children are the best detectives and spies. It's like having the CIA living in your home. Make double-dog sure all discussions about them and anything related to your divorce occur in private.

- Little things a child wants to make and offer the evaluator are treasures (cards, a picture, an art project, a hug) the evaluator will embrace. Nothing beyond this simple gesture is needed. No extravagant meals or presents, please. These are unethical for the evaluator to accept and cause unnecessary weirdness. A simple thank you goes a long way!

- Settle in for the long-haul. This process will always take longer than is comfortable and longer than you anticipated.

- Find a good therapist. Divorcing well and becoming your best self means navigating lots of grief work, disassembling the past, and creating something new. A seasoned and well-trained therapist can help you move more fluidly through that painful process.

- Assemble a community of support. It will be your lifeline through this process.

Avoid sharing anything with your child about the long-term parenting time plan they will follow until it is finalized in a judgment. Doing so beforehand sets children on a scary and unnecessary rollercoaster of what-ifs and maybes and more uncertainty.

Happy looks good on everyone!

Take the kids off the table with the pots and pans and rest of the family assets. They are too valuable to be mixed in with everything else; and parents know what is best for their children, far more than an evaluator, attorney, or judge.

Mediation before litigation is always the best practice for family matters.

Justice for children is the result of good choices made by their parents—the people charged with their daily care, health, safety, and well-being. You hold the cards to your child's future. Their ability to thrive depends on the choices you make and the life you create during the time they will spend in each of your homes and under your charge.

You're going to make mistakes—lots of them. We all do. You are going to do things that make each other mad, and even furious, at times. Do not let the emotions you feel for each other contaminate the emotions your child feels for their mom and dad. They need permission to love and be loved by everyone. Period. They need to move between you without carrying the heavy, ugly baggage of your marriage. They need to know that you still care for each other. The absolute best way you can take care of your child is to take care of their parents.

The best gift you can give your child is a childhood free from conflict—a childhood from which they do not need to heal. Keep doing the work you need to do to move forward peacefully. Learn the best strategies to co-parent. Do divorce better than you did marriage. Your child is worth the effort.

Show up for your child. Games and recitals will one day be replaced with weddings and grandchildren's birthday parties. If you want to be a joyful part of their future, be a joyful part of their now.

LUKE'S HINTS, HACKS & HELL-NO'S

Luke | Setup | How the Heck Did We End Up Here?

Hint   Hack   Hell-No

Do NOT take the family pet or your kids' stuff from the family home.

Do NOT drain the joint bank accounts—they are joint, not yours.

Research the best-fit attorney for you—one who cares about your child's well-being.

Live in the same community with your co-parent; the morning commute to school matters.

Children do not like change, and consistency is key to their proper adjustment.

Parenting time is the right of children, not of their parents. All time belongs to your child.

Do NOT be an ass. (It's the sagest hint/hack/hell-no in this book and a gender-neutral term!)

Luke | Choice 1 | Prove She's Insane

- Read all the fine print and get everything in writing.

- If it sounds/feels like a bad idea, listen to your gut and look for a better choice.

- Know this is going to take WAY longer than you think it should. Lace up your Nikes for the marathon.

- An adult's perception of everything (especially in crisis) is different than a child's. Get into your child's headspace and assess their best interest through their lens, not yours.

- The system is not perfect, but it's what we have and where you have to function. Ultimately, you made some of the choices that contributed to the problems; and you are responsible for some of the solutions.

- Marriage is grand. Divorce is $50 grand!

- You are responsible for educating and protecting your child from the harmful effects of badmouthing by other relatives (and anyone else your children are exposed to) while in your charge.

- The courts are very good at dividing assets; that is a simple math problem. And while finances are an emotional hot-button, they will be sorted out with or without the suffering you bring upon yourself with more poor choices.

- Children cannot un-see or forget traumatic events. Lifelong consequences are rendered in the split-second decisions we make.

- When your child does not mention or ask about the other parent, it is often a signal that they do not feel safe to do so with *YOU*.

- If your choices have left no option except for an evaluator and/or judge to intervene, then yes, the choice for a total stranger to make choices for your child is the only path forward.

- Be aware of the snowball effect of negative thinking. What we think becomes our truth; and in our truth, our language and behavior are birthed.

- Refer to Yoda's words.

- Prepare a timeline of important family events for your first meeting.

Be honest, especially about your bad choices and behavior. Get your version of events out before the evaluator asks you about them and take responsibility for your part.

Share developmentally-appropriate information with your child.

Your child's other parent is not the enemy. He/She is your child's other parent who your child loves and needs, and you are stuck with him/her for the long-haul.

Do NOT buy a guinea pig, puppy, or any other animal to win your child's favor during this major disruption in their life. Just don't do it!

Children have many characteristics and mannerisms of both of their parents. You cannot fully, completely, unconditionally love your child if you hate their other parent. It will not work; you cannot fake "good" in the eyes of a child.

The fewer changes for a child, the better. If the family home can be kept, it's best for the children. However, this is not always possible.

You can send your child to college or your attorney's child to college, but you cannot afford to send both.

The best revenge is a life well-lived!

Refer to your child's other parent as "my child's other parent" or "my co-parent." Children do not have an ex-mom or an ex-dad.

Listen to the judge and follow all of their orders.

Do NOT ignore the judge's orders and continue on a destructive path.

Luke | Choice 2 | Be Awesome

Organically ease your way into new roles. Showing up in new ways in all areas of your child's life will feel foreign and uncomfortable for them.

Do NOT use unflattering names, pictures, sounds, symbols, memes. Children may laugh (to appease you), but that means double the damage to their well-being.

Do NOT introduce anyone new to your child before one year following the dissolution, and not until you are certain it is a lasting relationship. Children need time to adjust.

Therapy records are sacred and your children need and deserve a confidential space.

- Develop a working relationship with the therapist and be open to their feedback.

- Set up online portal access with all of your children's providers, unless a court order or other policy prohibits it.

- No surprise visits.

- Be respectful and communicate your intent to participate, in advance.

- Exposure to conflict cannot be unseen or undone and has lasting consequences for your child.

- School must remain a sacred and safe environment for children.

- Be on your best behavior at your child's school and when speaking to their teachers.

- Sports and activities must remain a sacred and safe environment for children.

- Be on your best behavior at your child's sports and activities.

- Buying your children's affection is temporary, and expensive!

Our choices determine how protected or "stuck in the middle" children become in a divorce.

Children will always find out what you're up to. They are like little CIA agents living in your home.

A custody evaluation is often the path to establishing a stipulated agreement—a way for families to avoid the financial and emotional hardship of a courtroom trial, which often costs each party $10,000–$20,000 or more.

If the evaluator suggests anything to you while the two of you are working together, do it.

Discipline and punishment are very different things. Punishment is punitive, and makes children feel small and insignificant. The root word of discipline is "disciple" and that word means "to teach." Discipline empowers children to know more and do better.

Do NOT lie or deceive or withhold information from an evaluator.

Do NOT coach or encourage your child to express any particular opinion to the evaluator.

It is important that children have neutral and emotionally-safe people in their lives. Evaluators are listening for these people when interviewing your references.

- Be honest during your evaluation. The truth always shows itself through someone else if not through you.

- Disneyland Dad and Mastercard Mom leave children empty, and often angry and resentful. Children value your time the most.

- Ask permission before bringing a pet into the evaluator's office.

- Evaluators are very attuned to non-verbal communication (yours and your child's). They want to see and know the children are safe to talk about and love both parents freely. If your feelings are in the way of this, seek counseling before you engage in the evaluation. Your attitude speaks volumes through the process of evaluation. Make sure to align it with your foundational values.

- All time belongs to your child. It is not *your* time or the *other parent's* time.

- Be certain to have all paperwork completed in the timeframe the evaluator requests. This is important for the process, but it is also a test to see how well you follow directions.

Nothing will ever move as fast as you want it to in this process. Knowing this will save you some anxiety.

Your child will rat you out, especially if you've been behaving like an ass.

Until the moment you cross the threshold of a courtroom, there is always a path to settling the issues for your child. It's uncomfortable and requires give from both parties, but there is always a path to choose.

The courtroom and litigation are a lot like a game of chess. It becomes a contest of out-maneuvering each other, presenting the "best case," which at times has absolutely nothing to do with your child and the best next step for them.

Evaluators keep children's needs front and center, amidst the flurry of illusion created by attorneys who are paid to represent *your* best interest, not your child's.

Listen to the judge and follow all of their orders.

Do NOT ignore the judge's orders and continue on a destructive path.

Luke | Choice 3 | Get a New Lawyer

Selecting a lawyer who shares your foundational values is critical to your sanity, and the outcome for your child.

Your attorney works for you, you are the boss. If things are not working out to your satisfaction, especially if you are receiving guidance that feels wrong for yourself and your family, cut ties and find a better fit. Choose wisely!

At a speed manageable for your child, begin to involve yourself more actively in their daily life. Respectfully notify the other parent with enough time for her/him to digest that you now plan to attend school events, teacher conferences, and extracurricular activities. Be cautious with the other parent, as she/he is likely to feel suspicious of your motives at first. It is your burden to show her/him and your child that you are genuine in your desire to be more actively involved. You need to help your former spouse and children feel safe, to rebuild trust.

Respect your co-parent's boundaries. Schedule separate times for conferences if she/he requests that you do so and sit a distance away from her/him at sports and activities. Schedule private consultations with the children's pediatrician and counselor to introduce yourself and sign up for all online medical, dental, and mental health portals so you have direct access to information in these areas. It will take time and consistency to establish collaborative relationships with professionals who know your children. Be present, be positive, be polite, be respectful, and always mindful of how your new-established presence in these areas impacts your child. Everyone's sense of safety is paramount. This cannot be stressed enough. Unless everyone first feels safe, this will not work.

 Do NOT engage in adult conversation with the other parent at any time during which your child is present, especially during transitions and at their sports and activities. Actively minimize all opportunity for conflict with the other parent. A child's exposure to verbal (yelling and name calling) and non-verbal (anger, tension, hand gestures, and body language) is detrimental to them and erodes their sense of self-worth. Do not attempt to discuss any sensitive topic with the other parent (the parenting time schedule, grades, medication or health, etc.) when your child is present, even if they are 200 feet away from you on the soccer field. They'll know. They'll be distracted. They'll feel anxious and embarrassed and angry. Each time this happens, they will pull further away from you which leaves them vulnerable and at risk.

Do NOT compete with the other parent to win your child's favor at special times of the year, like their birthdays or major holidays, by giving them extraordinary gifts or once-in-a-lifetime experiences such as a brand-new car for their sweet-sixteen or a trip to Disneyland with their entire class from school. The same is true for pets. It is unwise to buy your child a puppy (as a bribe for them to spend time with you), or any kind of animal, until you are settled in a permanent residence and the child has had time to properly adjust.

Create new traditions and celebrations with your child now that they have a separate home with you. Some parents agree to have one birthday party for their child and one Christmas morning, all together, after the divorce. This can be especially challenging after parents re-partner, but it can be done. When children sense a bridge between their two homes (by seeing and experiencing healthy and cooperative adult relationships), they receive unspoken permission to ebb and flow between their two homes in an emotionally comfortable way. This is essential to a child's overall health and sense of well-being.

- Most importantly, demonstrate *flexibility* in general, and especially with holidays and celebrations, so that special times of the year do not become a source of tension and upset for your child. Emotional anniversaries (the yearly experience of emotional trauma) can result when tension, conflict, and upset erupt at otherwise joyful times in a child's life. How parents behave post-dissolution not only impacts their child, but future generations in the family bloodline. What you say and do, and how you behave now, will have an impact on your grand and great-grandchildren in positive or negative ways. Whether it is a positive or negative impact is up to you and the choices you make daily.

- Mediate; Don't Litigate. Get into mediation as soon as possible with the other parent and co-create a parenting time schedule that is best for your child. "Best for your child" may not equate to exactly 50% of their time. It is best that a child's post-dissolution life closely resembles his/her pre-dissolution life. Continuity of care allows a child to properly adjust after this significant disruption in the family system. Quality of time, not quantity, is most vital to the child's comfort, psychological health, and greater sense of well-being. All time belongs to the children—parenting time is the legal right of a child, not his/her parents.

- Be nice to your mother-in-law because the kids love their grandma regardless of how nutty she is and how poorly and unfairly she treats you.

- Take advantage of all of the resources offered to you: books to read, parenting classes to attend, support groups, communication platforms, and coaches.

- To crush your ex, you must "reliably demonstrate child-focused thinking and behavior."

- Kill 'em with kindness.

- When we know better, we do better.

- Settling matters for your child outside a courtroom trial saves time and money and is most likely to result in a plan that is unique to your family and the needs of your child. When both parents have a say in the plan, it decreases the likelihood of repeat litigation down the road.

- Who you choose to represent you makes a gargantuan difference—in your experience, your pocketbook, and the outcome for your child.

Children want your time more than anything else. They want to feel connected and engaged with you doing everyday normal stuff, absent conflict and anger.

The best child therapists know that both parents need to be involved for them to understand the child's complete family system.

Choose a new home as close to the family home as possible. Children quickly grow resentful around being separated from their familiar community and having to make long drives in the car (especially to and from school).

Own your mistakes. Sometimes you need to apologize 1,000,001 times when rebuilding trust with a little person.

Wait to introduce anyone new for at least one year post-judgment, and not until you are certain about the possibility of a long-term commitment from that person. Vet new partners carefully and run a background check (your attorney can help). Absolutely no sex offenders (regardless of how innocent their story seems), no felons, and no one that is still married.

All evaluators have negative reviews. Talk to real people about their experience. Rely on your attorney for their expertise in this area. Check with the evaluator's licensing board.

Respect and kindness will get you a long way in this process—with all of the professionals who support you, with your children, with your co-parent, and in all areas of your life!

Agree to disagree when needed and move forward. You do not have to like someone to work effectively with that person. Most of us have worked with a colleague or boss at some point who we did not like, but we still got our job done.

With every choice, you declare who you are; and with each new day, you will get closer to the person you want to become.

The same family structure, organized differently = success for children!

When your child knows they are loved unconditionally, and that you are solid, committed, and never ever going anywhere, you have earned your Gold Star Parent status!

RESOURCES

Our Family Wizard (OFW) is the world's largest co-parenting platform with a mission to help families living separately thrive. OFW provides both families and the professionals who serve them with the tools necessary for more seamless and successful co-parenting. Nearly one million users have leveraged OFW to share calendars, messages, journals, files, expenses and important information like health and school records. By keeping families in sync, OFW helps improve outcomes for children and parents.

With 55,000 custody cases that involve alcohol each year, parents, attorneys, and judges need a reasonable, trusted, and court-validated way to monitor alcohol consumption in real-time. In 2011, Soberlink revolutionized the way people can provide proof of sobriety without compromising child safety. Today, 10,000+ Family Law Professionals across all 50 states have adopted the system. With key features such as real-time results, facial recognition, tamper detection, reporting with AI, comprehensive monitoring agreements, and expert support, Soberlink remains the gold standard in remote alcohol monitoring.

For more information:

Hotlines

If you or your children are unsafe, consider reaching out to **The National Domestic Violence Hotline:** 800-799-SAFE(7233).

If you believe a child is physically, emotionally, or sexually unsafe, please call the **National Child Abuse Hotline** – Childhelp: 1-800-422-4453

If your child is experiencing any type of crisis they can text the **Crisis Text Line** HOME to 741741. A live trained crisis counselor is available 24/7 – *please program this critical information into your child's phone!*

If you or someone you love is experiencing a major mental health crisis, consider **The National Alliance on Mental Health:** 800-950-NAMI(6264) or text NAMI to 741741.

If you or someone you love is struggling with a substance dependence disorder **SAMHSA's National Helpline** is available 24 hours a day: 1-800-662-HELP(4357)

If you are having thoughts of hurting yourself, please call the **National Suicide Prevention Lifeline:** 1-800-273-8255.

If you are a **United States Military Veteran**, thank you! There is a crisis line dedicated to you and your family: 888-457-4838 or text: MIL 1 to 839863.

Foundational Values

The following is a list of personal values that will help guide your life. Reflect on the values that resonate with your truest intention, and those that will assist in becoming your best self.

Accountability	Cooperation	Excitement
Accuracy	Correctness	Expertise
Achievement	Courtesy	Exploration
Adventure	Creativity	Expressiveness
Advocacy	Curiosity	Fairness
Altruism	Decisiveness	Faith
Ambition	Dependability	Family
Assertiveness	Determination	Fidelity
Balance	Devotion	Fitness
Being the Best	Diligence	Fluency
Belonging	Discipline	Focus
Boldness	Discretion	Freedom
Calmness	Diversity	Fun
Challenge	Dynamism	Generosity
Cheer	Economy	Goodness
Commitment	Effectiveness	Grace
Community	Efficiency	Growth
Compassion	Elegance	Happiness
Competition	Empathy	Hard Work
Consistency	Enjoyment	Health
Contentment	Enthusiasm	Helping
Contribution	Equality	Holiness
Control	Excellence	Honesty

Honor

Humility

Independence

Ingenuity

Inner Harmony

Inquisitiveness

Insight

Intelligence

Intellectualism

Intuition

Joy

Justice

Leadership

Legacy

Love

Loyalty

Mastery

Merit

Mindfulness

Obedience

Openness

Order

Originality

Patriotism

Perfection

Piety

Positivity

Practicality

Preparedness

Professionalism

Prudence

Quality

Reliability

Resourcefulness

Restraint

Results

Rigor

Security

Self-actualization

Self-control

Selflessness

Self-reliance

Sensitivity

Serenity

Service

Shrewdness

Simplicity

Soundness

Speed

Spontaneity

Stability

Strategy

Strength

Structure

Success

Support

Teamwork

Temperance

Thankfulness

Thoroughness

Thoughtfulness

Timeliness

Tolerance

Tradition

Trustworthiness

Truth-seeking

Understanding

Uniqueness

Unity

Usefulness

Vision

Vitality

A SPECIAL INVITATION FROM LORI

If you've made it this far, and you feel like you need a little more support as you navigate the journey through your high-conflict divorce and your custody evaluation, I have three possibilities for you:

"Best Next Step" FREE Starter Video

In this video presentation, we will talk about WHY putting your child first is the right approach. You will learn exactly what it means to do this, what happens to children whose parents fail to do it, and the most common mistakes that lead to poor outcomes for children.

Make Better Choices with the "Child-Focused Divorce" Course!

This pre-recorded training will help you **customize your plan** for putting your child's well-being at the center of your dissolution process. You will be guided through the process of clarifying, redefining, and developing a plan for:

- **Roles and Responsibilities of Everyone Involved:** We will cover the basic roles and responsibilities for You, Your Child's Other Parent, Your Child, The System, and Your Child's Social Capital.

- **Meeting Your Child's Universal and Unique Needs and Desires:** Together, we will dig deeper into your current experience and find specific new choices for words, expressions, and behaviors that will nurture your child's well-being.

- **Your Mindful Approach:** You will discover more about YOU and the true guiding principles that will create a solid foundation for all of your future choices, create stability for yourself and your children, and impress the heck out of your evaluator and judge.

Use the coupon code (BESTNEXTSTEP) and get 20% off.
https://childfocused.net/resources/#course

Consultations

If you know you need personalized coaching around your particular situation, book a virtual session to consult with me personally.

www.ChildFocused.net/Consultations

ABOUT LORI BONNEVIER, MSW, LCSW

Court-Appointed Evaluator, Best Interest Consultant, and Custody Evaluation Coach

LORI BONNEVIER is a licensed clinical social worker in the State of Oregon. She graduated from Portland State University in 2000 with a master's degree in social work and holds undergraduate degrees in the disciplines of psychology and human services and an associate's degree in child development.

Since 2002, Lori has practiced primarily as a child custody evaluator and regularly provides testimony as an expert witness. In these roles, she also serves as a therapist, mediator, parent coordinator, coach, and consultant. As an evaluator, Lori's mission is to provide a competent, thorough, and unbiased assessment of all family members with the goal of developing a comprehensive plan that allows children the opportunity to maintain safe, healthy, and ongoing relationships with both parents and other significant people following a change in the family system.

Having expanded her practice to include consulting, coaching, and speaking, Lori is able to share her message of Child-Focused Choices with a larger audience.

Lori lives in Portland, Oregon. Her co-parent is a lieutenant firefighter and paramedic. They share a love for music, nature, humor, sports, cooking delicious food, the divine spirit, their two dogs and two fabulous children, Cooper and Finley. Their children are conscientious students and good friends to all, have both earned their black-belts, are accomplished athletes in basketball and softball, and play the guitar and piano. They are two of the best humans Lori knows and her grandest pride and joy.

GIVING BACK

Ten percent of all book sales will be donated to The Commons Law Center in Portland, Oregon. As a long-time member of this community, it is a pleasure and a privilege to collaborate with a nonprofit organization striving to best serve the legal needs of Oregonians, one family at a time.

The Commons
Law Center

The Commons Law Center is a nonprofit law firm where every day Oregonians can find affordable legal services.

Sliding scale and flat fee services help
expand access to legal tools and support.

Getting Divorced in Oregon
Making Child Custody and Parenting Time Decisions
Modifying Child Support
Enforcing Parenting Time Orders
Creating Safety-Focused Parenting Plans
And more!

Ready to Talk to Someone About Your Legal Questions?

503.850.0811
www.TheCommonsLawCenter.org

Visit the site below for more legal resources:

SCAN ME

ADDITIONAL COMMENTS ABOUT *YOU DON'T HAVE TO CRUSH YOUR EX*

"I have worked with Lori for more than fifteen years and seen firsthand how, for her, the children always come first. Her recommendations consistently advocate for the best interest of children. *You Don't Have to Crush Your Ex* condenses Lori's decades of experience into a very fun, easy-to-read book that every parent in a custody conflict should refer to while making choices for their children."

Jan Prunk, SS, SFF, Lori's Office Mom

"For forty years, as both a police executive and a military officer in the USAF, I have seen the negative impact of high-conflict divorce situations and child custody battles on families, especially the children. *You Don't Have to Crush Your Ex* will help parents in those situations make better choices and foster better outcomes for their children."

Bruce Prunk, Portland Police (retired)
USAF (retired)

"Brilliantly delivered and comically written, Lori Bonnevier illustrates the ever-dynamic chaos of what has evolved from one of the most prevalent cultural pandemics of our time to an entirely new normal. The heart-wrenching accuracy and transparency with which she writes pierces to the truth at the core of divorce and its inevitable rippling effects on the lives of all involved. In addition to acting as a complete navigation guide, *You Don't Have to Crush Your Ex* reveals the hope and opportunity to be found at every intersection of choice along what can often feel like a tragic journey through the unknown."

Alyssa Noelle Coelho, Bestselling Author of *CHOSEN*
Founder, Lionheart Creations Foundation
Sociocultural Anthropology Analyst

"My clients often want to know how to prepare for a custody evaluation. Until *You Don't Have to Crush Your Ex,* I was left to hand them dry and complicated reference material. Decades of experience have gone into the authoring of this unique book in which Lori infuses humor and valuable information in a choose-your-own-path styled book that is sure to help anyone who is faced with a high-conflict divorce and best-interest decisions about the welfare of their child."

Lonny Webb, MSW, LCSW, Founder and Primary Clinician, NeuroBehavioral Concepts and Evaluation

"I have worked with families as a clinical social worker for over twenty years. Divorce happens. I tell my clients that divorce is not the worst thing that happens to children; ongoing conflict and being put in the position of having to choose between their parents is. Having a resource that is supportive, non-judgmental, and truly practical is invaluable. Lori has created a gem of a book that provides tools for parents to help them navigate this life event with the most grace and the least conflict possible, allowing their children to weather this storm feeling safe and loved. I can't wait to offer *You Don't Have to Crush Your Ex* to my private practice clients as well as my Parent Coordination clients."

Tracey Biebel, LCSW, TraceyBiebel.com
Therapist, Parent Coordinator, Parent Coach

"*You Don't Have to Crush Your Ex* is simply superb. Lori tells a real story with true-to-life detail, visceral emotion, and a much-needed drop of humor. As a domestic relations mediator, I wish everyone I work with would read this book and take to heart the lessons in it. Everyone involved in a divorce claims to be doing what they do for the sake of the kids, but this book shows parents how to actually do it and what happens when they don't."

Alex Tillson, MS, Mediator/Court-Appointed
Evaluator, Mediate PDX

"I first met Lori Bonnevier many years ago when she served as a custody evaluator in a case that was going nowhere. My adverse counsel and I picked Lori from a group of evaluators we knew, and she did a very good job. In practicing law for nearly forty years, I came to know many evaluators. One of my professional sidelights was publishing a *Resource Guide for Divorce Lawyers,* now in its 200-page, 10th edition, with 290 professionals sub-divided in 16 categories that professional divorce lawyers need to prepare and try their cases. Lori is in the book! Recently, Lori shared with me a draft of her book *You Don't Have to Crush Your Ex*, and I recommend it highly."

John W. "Jack" Lundeen, Esq.,
Retired Family Law Attorney

"*You Don't Have to Crush Your Ex* is an insightful and well-written book that is a must read for parents going through a contentious divorce with children. The book provides a framework to assist parents in navigating the complicated emotional process of divorce and how to focus on the emotional health and well-being of your children while doing so. I highly recommend this book."

Mark Harwood, MS, CADC
Court-Appointed Evaluator

"My observations about Ms. Bonnevier are founded on perspective from forty-four years working in law on issues pertaining to child abuse, safety, child development and their intersection with Juvenile, Criminal, Family and State Agency Law. I've observed Ms. Bonnevier's work for about a quarter century. She merits recognition as one of the few top-level custody and parenting time evaluators in the Portland Metropolitan Area. She brings an excellent blend of intelligence, knowledge, perspective, and common sense to her work. Ms. Bonnevier is, in all respects, a very helpful source of knowledge about the custody and parenting time dispute process."

Rich Cohen, Esq. – Attorney, trial lawyer on abuse and neglect and high conflict parenting matters, author of chapters in *Oregon Legal Handbooks in Juvenile, Family and Criminal Law* pertaining to child abuse investigation and high conflict matters involving children.

"*You Don't Have to Crush Your Ex* takes an excellent approach, providing various scenarios in child-custody situations and thus having a better chance to fit each readers' individual situation."

Arthur B Knauss, Esq., Director of Legal Services – The Commons Law Center

"With her characteristic intelligence, compassion, and wit, Ms. Bonnevier has tackled the thorny issues surrounding child custody battles in a totally unique manner. *You Don't Have to Crush Your Ex* should be a must-read for all divorcing couples gearing up for a battle and for their friends, relatives, and in-laws as well. She has created different narratives that will allow the reader to truly envision the potential benefits, consequences, and outcomes of the choices they plan to make. She writes with a generosity of spirit along with a strong desire to help families, backed up by years of experience in the field of child custody evaluations. This book is accessible and easy-to-read, and is written in a way that will truly help families put their children's needs first. I cannot recommend it more highly."

Pat Bowman, MSW,
Child Welfare Branch Manager (retired)

"As a stepmom who walked through this arduous journey of court battles and co-parenting, I can say with full transparency that Lori's book would have dramatically shifted my family's experience with child custody. Her tactful and professional approach is well-balanced with humor, truth, and the necessary need-to-knows. I so wish I had her book 10 years ago!"

Ciara Gutierrez, Stepmom

"Lori Bonnevier has taken a painful and thorny subject and created an easy way to understand the challenges and pitfalls related to the transition from nuclear family to bi-nuclear family. Perhaps the hardest part of this transition is the felt experience of feeling trapped or having no choices. By introducing us to Vanessa and Luke (and their children, Teo and Rae), we learn that there are *many* things we can make choices about that will positively impact us and our children for years to come. Education about these choices is an invaluable service for families dealing with the stress of change. In addition to many valuable insights about change and transformation, Lori provides helpful resources and tools to support people on this often-painful path. Her Triskelion format creates an engaging and informative book that makes difficult topics easy to understand. Her three pillars of Advancement, Wisdom, and Choice provide each reader with the opportunity to commit to a process that is both healthy and functional. Three cheers for Lori and her wealth of experience in helping people to heal and grow."

Tamara Ellis, PhD., AFCC trained expert
in family transitions

"YAY for this important book—a beautiful juxtaposition of emotion and logic. Choice and Power are two words Lori uses immediately in the introduction. These simple words invoke Hope in the stressed reader. Reading *You Don't Have to Crush Your Ex* will help *all* readers to 'know more and do better.' Lori is simply terrific! As a nurse practitioner working in women's health, I am pleased (and relieved) to be able to recommend this book to anyone who is going through the challenges of separation/divorce."

Shanta L Schriever, WHCNP, Nurse Practitioner

"I worked with Lori as a fellow custody evaluator almost twenty years ago. I have watched Lori approach her work with families grounded in an abundance of professional knowledge and experience. We are lucky Lori is sharing with us some important lessons from her many years working with divorcing and separating families. In *You Don't Have to Crush Your Ex*, we get to step into the world of tough choices that parents make and consider our first reactions and—then look at other possibilities. Our children win, and we can too, when we consider the big picture."

Hillary Hyde, MSW, Assistant Professor of Practice, Child, Youth and Family Studies Program, Portland State University

"Having to watch my grandchildren experience a high-conflict divorce, I have observed firsthand the effects this ordeal has had on these little ones. *You Don't Have to Crush Your Ex* has given me a roadmap I can clearly understand that offers insight and knowledge to help my son navigate this sometimes-treacherous path. Using the wisdom offered on these pages, I had the ability to help him maneuver around the pitfalls and obstacles that are inevitable, thereby creating an environment where the kids feel safe, loved, and encouraged. Thank you, Lori, for courageously writing this book and giving us all this much-needed resource. Your great love and concern for children flows across the pages and awakens our awareness of the effects our actions and reactions have on them."

Lori Giesey, CEO of Magnificent Moments and
Award-winning author of *A Moment in Time*

"As a practicing attorney for more than forty years, I've seen the impact of high-conflict divorces on children. *You Don't Have to Crush Your Ex* is an excellent tool for parents to use as they navigate the rough road of divorce. This book enables parents to take the high road while preserving the best interests of their children and protecting their emotional well-being throughout the process."

Deborah Le Meitour, Esq.

"The most wasted day in life
is the day in which one
has not laughed."

~Charlie Chaplin~

ACKNOWLEDGMENTS

Writing a book is fucking hard!

(Yes, Please and Thank You, Amy Poehler — your timing was impeccable!)

NO ONE WRITES a book alone and I'm going to take a beat to acknowledge the many folks who influenced and cheered me on while I completed this marathon. None of the typical fluff. I promise to keep it real.

To My Family

To my children, Cooper and Finley, who make each step of the journey every bit worthwhile. You are the reason I wake (often in a panic at 3:00 a.m.!) and my last thought before sleep. The two of you have taught me more than would ever be possible in reverse. Thank you for choosing me to be your mom and for your special visits while in the other realm—how fortunate and blessed I am 💚.

To my very own Mr. Disappointment, you are more than enough. Thank you for accompanying me to the highest peaks and to the darkest valleys, where all things of power and majesty are born—where we can truly begin again. Without our breakfast at the Screen Door, this book would not be a book. And you slayed the EX!

To my parents, for providing all the things a little girl needs to dream, and all the resources to make her dreams come true. And for Uncle Ron, because having a bonus parent makes a difference.

To my sister, for putting up with my humor, for "letting" me wear your clothes, for being a good sport about the chickenpox I gave you that Christmas, and for always being there. I love you.

To the members of my extended family, for endless holidays filled with love and joy and laughter (and a few dicey moments ☺). Thank you for always showing up, acknowledging my successes with cash tucked inside cards, and celebrating each of my accomplishments along the way.

To Mike and Julie, for helping create some of my best-of-life memories, for seeing me through the worst of it, for standing loyal, and for your enduring friendships. I am me, because of you.

To Grandpa Joe, for all of our time together in the coop, for letting me use the sledgehammer, for cold beer in teacups, and for teaching me how to tie my shoe, to whistle (loud!), and blow a bubble with my gum. Thank you for the lake, and the worms, and taking all the slimy fish off my hook. For rubbing my stinky little girl feet during the late-night Benny Hill show. Thank you for a lifetime of unconditional love and for waiting until me, and then Jim arrived, before your final curtain call after ninety-six years. Because of you, I believe in something bigger and so much more than what my eyes can see.

To my Coaches, Teachers, Mentors, Colleagues, and Clients

To all of my early grade school and junior high and high school teachers who put up with all of my talking and class clowning! (I had to no idea how important my sense of humor would be for my work and sanity, and for this book!) For my softball and gymnastic and dance coaches who encouraged and believed in me and shaped my character through sport. For encouraging a competitive spirit, compassionate sportsmanship, and drilling home that there is "no I in team." You taught me to swing for the fence, that injuries will heal, and tomorrow is another day.

To my undergraduate and graduate school teachers who led by example who inspired with bold vulnerability, who told me I was someone special and convinced me I could make a difference—that I was indeed a change agent. To Astrid Schlaps, for making the first (scary) day of graduate school memorable and facilitating so many wonder-filled days thereafter. I wish I could have offered you the same comfort and hugged you a final goodbye.

For Pat Bowman who was willing to reach down the list and bring me on board. I remember the day you called and said you were coming for me—that I was the one you wanted on your team. You kept the office exciting and real, set an example for all of us, and showed me the way. For all of my colleagues at DHS, to Steve, and to Bruce and LaDonna Lofland, I especially thank you.

For Trish Cox without whom this book and my career would not exist. Thank God I submitted a resume. Thank God you found Margarita Murphy's hilarious. Thank God you took a risk and offered up your big coattails for a smooth ride in. I'm indebted to your teaching and guidance, kind heart, and generosity. You'll always be Gram-Trish to Coop and Finn, and are the best ever Greba to your own.

To the Oregon legal community, for trusting me to wade through the muck and find and polish the golden nuggets where, at first glance, there often appear to be none. For your friendship, late night calls, and emails before trial. For the exhausting cross-examinations (ha!). For both of the Paul's on speed-dial, thank you for fielding my Chicken Little moments and saving my bacon more than once. For Scott SJ and the inspiring conversations that you always made time for. Thank you for recognizing that I have not worked all these tireless hours to only help parents do better, but so that all of us can do better... together. We miss you!

To Judge Miller, you are the most grace-filled professional I know and the definition of a good human. Thank you for all of your help with the book and for crafting the Foreword. To the Oregon Bench, and in particular The Honorable Judge Grove, who has witnessed the full spectrum of my career. I'm so proud to be a part of a system that gets it, and cares so deeply about the best interest of children.

To my fellow mental health colleagues, who lock-arms and make me laugh, who meet me for food and drink, who sit by me and pass silly notes (and share your chocolate) at stale professional conferences, who relate to the struggles that accompany this work, who keep the same ridiculous hours and pour all of yourself into creating a better tomorrow where children are safe and families are thriving. Your superpowers are vast and impressive, and you are the real-world heroes. You are my heroes.

To my clients (parents, grandparents, aunts, uncles, and so many kiddos), thank you for allowing me the privilege of serving in a helping role for your family. It is a genuine honor to come along side, help focus the lens, and bring more peace than you had before. Thank you for doing your best to partner and collaborate in strength-based and solution-focused ways that put children's needs first. Thank you for the feedback—good and bad. I've read it all and have learned from every circumstance along the way. Family Law is not a perfect system, but it's the system we have; and I hope by me being a part of your experience, you felt a measure of safe shelter from the storm.

To My Badass Tribe

To Regina, for holding space over beer and pizza where I declared it was finally time to write this book and for our random parking lot meetings at just the right moments. I cannot wait to shop HomeGoods as little old ladies and decorate our senior condos with too many tchotchkes, and drink margaritas during the day and eat nachos until we're full. Cheesy potatoes, you say?

To Kristine, for being my reliable go-to and a steady voice of reason, and for the bazillion memories of raising our kids together. Your friendship and family mean the world to me.

To Tami, for being my discount partner and for paying attention and telling me I had to look. For all the yummy food, hours of talking, and sweet laughter. You saved my life. I am forever grateful.

To Tina, Jen, Melissa, and Tracy, for having my back, for showing up every time that it matters, for buckets of memories and bonds that surpasses time. You are my people, until death parts us.

To Jan, there really are no words. Some people are in fact irreplaceable. I love you, and I miss you already. Thank you... for all of it. I would never have made it this far without you.

To the women who gathered on Mount Hood, who made it safe for me to share a painful secret, for helping me heal wounds I didn't even know were bleeding, and for helping me to see and feel and become whole again. For being you. I am beyond comforted knowing we get to share time in this life.

For the best friends I never knew I had. *Steel Magnolias* make everything so much easier. I love New York. I love all ten of you. And may God ever bless and lay his gentle hand on all the Pop-Tarts®.

To My Professional Team
(It sounds so grown up!)

To Wayne and Laurie, to Kathy and Jake—you are truly Therapists of the Year! Each of you kept me sane through the chaos and showed me how to be a witness to my story, instead of trudging along as an actor in it. (Thank you, Ram Dass.) The four of you are serious game-changers.

To Alex and Lonny, for finding me at just the right times. Let the next epic chapters begin!

To Erika, for capturing the most precious moments of my life and for your friendship, wicked intelligence, and appreciable whit. I have mad respect for the images that birth from your lens.

To Dan Mulhern and his patient crew of artists who created the original cover, for entertaining my many, many, many emails asking for this, that, and something else. You've got the patience of a saint.

To Alyssa and CiCi, for bringing it home, in short order, at a cabin retreat far-far away. Espresso, tequila, chocolate donuts, and repeat. For bringing laughter and joy to help me across that stupid terrifying toll bridge. For hours of group "word masturbation" until we got it just right (so much LOL!). I have oodles of love for both of you and cannot wait to see each of you soar even higher.

To Aaron and your youthful up-to-date tech skills, you're beyond imperturbable to entertain an old and confused lady like me. Thank you for ushering my practice into the 21st Century.

To Dawn Teagarden, for doing a phenomenal job with the interior design of this book. I never do anything the easy way. Thank you for untangling the mess.

To all of the readers who previewed this book, thank you for your time and your invaluable feedback. This book would never have made it to print without every one of your insights, thoughts, and ideas. And to all who endorsed the manuscript, your words convinced me that it is finally time.

And to my writing coach, Amanda Johnson. We have indeed achieved a "raucous friendship" in this lifetime, too. What a wow-infused ride! Thank you for inviting me to the party, for seeing me, for holding space where I could grow enough to see, for your ridiculous slice-and-dice talents, and for protecting Iggy from the cut-room floor. For teaching me how to breathe with my conscious self and providing a community where every piece of me belongs. YCMTSU—the great co-author's truth—and because of you, it is now my truth, too. I cannot wait to turn the page and see what unfolds next.

Humbled by your collective kindness, collaboration, mutual respect, and grace,

XOXOXOXOXOXOX

Lori

P.S. In the highly-unlikely-though-seriously-amazeballs event you actually made it this far in the acknowledgments (I personally never read this crap) and sit where you are, astounded and unable to believe that I missed naming YOU—please know that I didn't, that you matter to me. It is with an acute knowing that I am influenced and changed by every person with whom I've rubbed shoulders and shared space, and I thank you for the extraordinary ways in which you've helped me to become myself.

FINGERPRINTS

All we have are choices,
Fingerprints at points of intersection
In directions with no road maps,
Or caution tape,
Or flashing red lights
Begging us to stop
And breathe,
And wake up
To realize that these choices
Are power,
Harnessed in motion,
Navigating a matrix
That is constantly shifting trajectories
And every single
One of them
Matters.

~ Alyssa Noelle Coelho

Made in the USA
Las Vegas, NV
02 October 2024

96225012R00282